Robert
Obredo .

Heaven, My Home

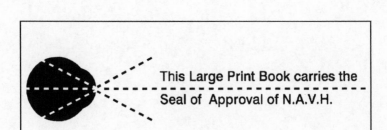

This Large Print Book carries the
Seal of Approval of N.A.V.H.

HEAVEN, MY HOME

ATTICA LOCKE

THORNDIKE PRESS
A part of Gale, a Cengage Company

Farmington Hills, Mich • San Francisco • New York • Waterville, Maine
Meriden, Conn • Mason, Ohio • Chicago

LIBRARY OF CONGRESS CIP DATA ON FILE.
CATALOGUING IN PUBLICATION FOR THIS BOOK
IS AVAILABLE FROM THE LIBRARY OF CONGRESS

ISBN-13: 978-1-4328-7221-2 (hardcover alk. paper)

Published in 2019 by arrangement with Little, Brown and Company

Printed in Mexico
1 2 3 4 5 6 7 23 22 21 20 19

For Nigton

Like a tree planted by the water,
I shall not be moved.
— *when Jessie Mae Hemphill sang it*

MARION COUNTY

TEXAS, 2016

Dana would have his tail if he didn't make it back across the lake by sundown. She'd said as much when she put him out on the steps of their trailer — which she did the second Rory Pitkin rolled up on his Indian Scout with the engine off, the toes of his motorcycle boots dragging in the dirt. She'd given Levi the key to their granddaddy's boathouse and a few dollars from the bottom of her purse and told him he had to be home before Ma and Gil got back or she'd burn all his Pokémon cards and make him watch. Lord, but his sister could be a bitch, he thought, enjoying the knifelike feel of the word so much he said it out loud, a secret between him and the cypress trees. The rust-red light pouring through the Spanish moss told him he'd never make it home by dark, which meant he'd broken two of his mama's rules: missing curfew and going boating alone on the lake. Levi was not al-

11

lowed to take his pappy's old twelve-foot V-bottomed skiff into the open waters of Caddo Lake, which was so vast that, if you had the time, inclination, and a day's worth of smoked oysters and clean water, you could ride it all the way into Louisiana. Gil said it wasn't nothing like it nowhere else in the country, the only lake to cross two counties and a state line. But Gil said a lot of things that weren't true — that he loved Ma, for one. He sure as shit didn't act like it. Levi's real daddy, he used to come up on her frying bologna on the stove and kiss her neck, make her titter and smile, kiss him back. But anytime Gil walked in a room, Ma was just as likely to cuss him as go stone still with terror, as if she could camouflage herself against the brown corduroy couch, where Gil had left a dozen cigarette burns since he'd moved in. Levi didn't trust Gil any more than he would a smile on a gator. But the water, Levi thought, now that he was traveling it on his own, well, ol' Gil might have been right about that. Caddo Lake was a monster, a body of water that could swallow a boy like him whole. In most places it resembled a weed-choked swamp more than it did a proper lake, a cypress forest that had flooded and been abandoned eons ago, and Levi could admit he was scared out here alone. Through the open sound south of Goat Island, it was a straight shot to Hopetown, the small community of trailers and shacks on the northeastern shore where Levi lived with his mother and sister and Gil. He blew away a lick of blond hair that had slipped over his eyes and gunned the boat's motor. He yanked the tiller left, chancing a shortcut.

In just the past few minutes, the light had melted from the color of plum brandy to the bluish gray of coming nightfall, and a December breeze curled up under the thin fabric of his windbreaker, a blue and white karnack high school indians jacket he stole from his sister's half of the closet. He got a sudden image of her and Rory Pitkin rolling around naked in the room he and Dana shared and felt a quiver go through his body that embarrassed him. He wasn't stupid. He knew what they were doing. *Fucking,* CT called it.

This was his fault, CT's, he decided. Levi had been playing football on CT's Xbox and lost track of time. He wanted to get a fantasy team in place because Ma had said there might be an Xbox under the tree this year if Gil came through on this deal he was running out of Jefferson. But in all the time Gil had been around, almost none of his plans ever amounted to anything that made Levi's life easier. They still didn't have milk in the fridge half the time.

Put out of the trailer for the afternoon, Levi had motored the small boat seven miles along the lake's coast to CT's family's cabin, way on the other side of the lake in Harrison County, had lost himself playing the video game, enjoying something he knew, deep down, he'd never have. He'd been so jealous of his friend that he'd stolen one of the game's controllers on the way out, slipping it into the pocket of his windbreaker. He hated when he did stuff like that, but neither could he stop himself. Something just came over him sometimes. It's like his brain just went black with *want* — for the stuff other kids had, be it an Xbox or a daddy living at home — so he lashed out blindly. He felt the corner of the controller pressing through the nylon jacket, poking him in his bony side. Out here on the water with only God as a witness, he felt hot with shame.

It was way past five o'clock now, the sky told him.

He didn't have time to go home the way he'd come, hugging the north shore of the lake, sailing along a thin canal of relative safety, porch lights on boathouses and craggy lake cabins twinkling hints of civilization. That would take nearly an hour. It would be full-on dark by then, and Levi hadn't brought a flashlight. He'd set out in a thin jacket with nothing on board but Pappy's old radio and a single oar pitted with rot that his grandfather had used to pull himself ashore. The radio kept cutting in and out. The antenna was bent halfway down, and in the pockets of silence, a deeper kind of fear took hold. He'd heard the lake went silent come nightfall, Spanish moss on the cypress trees dampening all sound, so that you could feel in this primeval lake on the edge of the state, this swamp at the edge of time, that you were the last man alive.

Not that he'd ever been on the water this late, not even when his granddaddy was still alive. Pappy believed in supper at five o'clock sharp. The *Swamp Loon* would have been drying in the boathouse by now, Pappy on his third or fourth beer in front of the TV. The old man steered clear of the lake after dark, always warning Levi how easy it was for a man to get turned around once night fell if he was moving solely by the light of a weak headlamp or a shy moon. The lake was big and complex — the many bayous, tributaries, and inlets like a tangle of snakes on the Texas side, at least the part that sat in Marion County — a wetland maze that had mystified outsiders for hundreds of years. If you didn't know the lake well, you could easily mistake one cypress tree for another, take the wrong bayou pass, and never find your way out, not in near black-out conditions. The thought made Levi's heart race. The radio shot back on, startling him, Patsy Cline cutting through a burst of static. It was a station out of Shreveport that switched from zydeco to country near suppertime — another sign he was late.

I go out walkin' after midnight . . .

Midnight.

The word felt like a warning. His granddaddy used to call it "spending a night at the Caddo Motel." *Now, don't you ever fart around and end up alone out here at night, son. 'Cause ain't a soul gon' save you.* Pappy was old enough to remember *his* granddaddy's tales of moonshiners and murderers hiding on the lake's many large islands. *Injuns and spooks alike, boy, thieves and Yankees too.* Pappy had grown up with gruesome tales of shootouts and knifings, not to mention ghost stories about souls roaming the waters, haints hiding in the trees. According to Pappy, wasn't no telling how

16

many souls had disappeared out on this water.

Levi tried to nose the dinghy around a thick stand of cypress, but pulled the tiller right when he'd meant to maneuver it left, his damp palms slipping across the gear. When he tried to correct his course, he ended up knocking the back of the boat against the roots of a cypress tree. He heard a few clicks in the engine, like a small pebble bouncing down a flight of stairs. He snapped off the radio and listened for any further sign of engine trouble. But the clicking soon stopped, and the engine hummed sweetly again. He wiped his palms against the front of his dirty jeans, then pointed the boat toward home. Levi was not as skilled on the water as Pappy was, having been allowed to work the skiff only a handful of times before his granddaddy died in September, ending their boating lessons for good — just weeks before he was supposed to make his skipper's debut in the Christmas boat parade in Karnack, helming the *Swamp Loon.* He'd saved up eleven dollars to buy every strand of colored lights he could get his hands on at the Dollar General in town. But now, riding out here alone, the sun about to leave him, he got a sudden image of this boat floating empty in the parade,

Pappy gone and Levi *missing*. He didn't know where the thought came from, but it felt real to him in a way that iced his bones, that made him admit he was terrified. A pair of crow's wings chopped the air above, and Levi, startled, came out of his seat. The boat tipped slightly, taking on a few cupfuls of the dull brown water and soaking the toes of his sneakers. He guessed he had less than a mile to go, and suddenly he wanted more than anything to be home, to be fussing with Dana over her leaving her crap on his side of the bed; even listening to Gil fart and cuss every ding-dang minute sounded good right about now. The fading sunlight had blackened the lake, as if dark wool had been laid across the surface, God tucking Caddo in for the night. Levi made a bargain with the Man himself: Get him out of here and quick and he would confess everything. He'd tell Ma he went out without her say-so and take his whipping like a man. He'd start acting right all around, even quit messing with Mr. Page and his Indians.

He just wanted to be home.

He heard the clicking again. And then the engine died a death quicker than any he'd imagined possible. No gurgling last breaths, like the gunshot victims he saw on TV, none of the babbling nonsense of Pappy's last

18

days — rambling sorries and sorrows over his friend Leroy — just a silence so stark he felt it in his chest. He realized he was holding his breath, waiting on the engine to hum again. But it was dead and cooling by the minute. Between here and home, he saw no other boats; the fishermen, pleasure cruisers, tourists with their kayaks, they were all gone. *Help.* It could have been a whisper or a scream, and it wouldn't have mattered. He was out here alone, and he knew it. If he kept due west, he would eventually reach the shores of home. But all he had for forward motion was the rotted oar, and he didn't trust he wouldn't turn himself in circles and end up drifting halfway to Louisiana. No, he should stay right where he was till morning. In a few hours, surely Ma or Dana would borrow someone's boat and come looking for him. He could make it that long, couldn't he, if he didn't lean so much as a fingernail over the side of the boat, where even now he could feel the wildlife that was burbling beneath the water? He felt something bump into the back of the boat. *Gator,* he thought, and flat-out panicked, jerking upright, standing even, as if he thought he could outrun it. The boat tipped again, taking on even more water, and now it was nearly up to his

19

ankles. Up ahead, he saw something.

It was a black shadow floating toward him.

He thought he heard the low hum of an engine.

But couldn't be sure he hadn't imagined it, that he wasn't just a little bit losing his mind out here. *A night in the Caddo Motel.* His every thought was bent away from this coming reality. A light clicked on and shone in his eyes as the shadow neared. Levi remained standing, waving his hands over his head, tilting the narrow boat this way and that. It rocked so much that it threatened to tip over for good. But Levi was desperate now, willing to risk capsizing if it meant being saved. "Here," he called, the sound like a single drop of water on cotton as the Spanish moss ate the words out of his mouth whole, needing the cries of lost souls as sure as it needed the blood of the bald cypress to survive in the swamp.

PART ONE

PART ONE

1.

The night Darren Mathews broke into his mother's trailer, he hadn't had a drink in over a month. Well, nothing more than a beer or two once or twice a week — and always in front of his wife, holding her gaze a few seconds before taking a sip, giving her a chance to speak or hold her peace, and grateful every time for her silence on the matter. In this new, highly precarious phase of their marriage, she had made her concessions, and he had made his. Their home life had stabilized, anchored against the rough waters since their separation and his time in Lark, Texas, by the simple pleasure of good sex, by its power to pluck out the best memories of a marriage for display and make you forget the ugly ones, the damaged plums hiding at the bottom of the bin. He'd forgotten how good it felt to fuck his wife, frankly, the ease with which the act braided together two souls. He'd forgotten how safe he felt with Lisa, how much his sense of himself rose and fell on the waves of her love and attention. And being wanted by Lisa — her near-constant reach across the sheets these days — had shifted the balance of power between them in ways that were new to Darren, who'd spent their entire courtship and marriage feeling like he was always chasing, convincing, winning over. Now it was Lisa who daily did what she could to please him, to be worthy.

She knew he almost hadn't come back to her, knew a life alone at his homestead in Camilla was an option for him, knew some part of his soul could live the rest of his days and die on the land of his ancestors; he preferred a night on the back porch in Camilla, spotting bucks nosing in the surrounding woods, to any convenience the city of Houston could offer. He was a country boy still.

He had his wife back, his life.

But it had cost him.

Several sessions with a couples counselor in downtown Houston — a heavyset white woman who wore way too much turquoise — had led to his decision to come off the road. At least, he thought it was his decision. It got hot in that room a lot, fairly musky with the work of excavating petty resentments only to bury them again — for good this time. And he admitted to zoning out once or twice. But they had ended their quartet of sessions — *I think you guys are going to make it* — with Darren agreeing to return to the Houston office of the Texas Rangers and work on the Aryan Brotherhood of Texas federal and state joint task force from his desk. Monday through Friday, he parked his Chevy in front of the office, took his lunch to his narrow cubicle, and spent hours and hours rooting through digital-surveillance data on the Aryan Brotherhood. Phone and bank records. Chat-room chatter. He was a desk jockey now, home most evenings by six, depending on traffic. That Lisa didn't make him do all of this stone-cold sober made him love her a little harder. Enough, he hoped, to cover the anger he felt over her demand that he stay off the road. Not that being home was the worst.

There was beer there.

And sex.

The thing with his mother nagged at him; sure it did.

But for a while he'd managed to convince himself that Bell's motives were not so much vindictive as desperate. She was a

25

woman on the cusp of sixty who lived alone in a rented trailer and whose only son was childless and spare in his affections, content to see his mother once a quarter, even less if he thought he could get away with it. Her boyfriend was both married *and* her boss, and he paid her less than minimum wage to clean toilets five days a week. She hadn't had a man to herself since she was in high school, and she bitterly resented the entire Mathews family for robbing her of the life she thought marrying Darren's father would have given her; she nursed her acrimony like a foundling pressed to her breast. The debt had now been laid at Darren's feet. He'd spent the past two months calling his mother daily, stopping by her place nearly every weekend. He cleared tufts of chickweed and bluegrass from around her trailer, swept the stairs, and cleaned the gutters without being asked, always leaving her a few hundred dollars and a case of beer on his way out.

It was a dance they were doing, this country waltz, each pretending that Darren was a son who had been waiting for just the right opportunity to take care of his aging mother, that he wasn't here now solely because she was blackmailing him. Although she never used such a crass word, and

26

neither did he. In fact, the one time he asked her directly about the gun, she'd taken it as his way of asking to spend more time with her, going so far as to invite herself to dinner at his home in Houston, which Darren recognized for the punishment it was. Starting with her ridiculous request for clams casino and Black Forest cake, the recipes for which she actually clipped from an ancient copy of the *Ladies' Home Journal* she'd had since she was in high school and mailed to Lisa.

She was drunk when she showed up to their loft in downtown Houston, asking even before her coat was off where the rest of the house was. Lisa hung Bell's balding rabbit fur in the hallway closet and made a point of squeezing Darren's hand in solidarity before escorting Bell to the dining-room table. Their windows looked out on Buffalo Bayou, but Bell wasn't impressed with that either. "We got dirty water in the country too," she said as Darren pulled out her chair. Lisa wasted no time setting their first course on the table, a chilled onion soup they ate by candlelight. Darren didn't touch a drop of alcohol all night, watching as Lisa and Bell raced each other to the bottom of a bottle of drugstore chardonnay, his mother's sole offering.

These past two months, his wife had asked very few questions.

She'd accepted his newfound interest in a relationship with his mother as a developmental fact of life, an inevitability she'd seen coming long before he had. She saw nothing nefarious in his announcing, out of nowhere, that he wanted to spend more time with her, look after her more if he could. Twice, she'd actually called it *sweet*. Tonight, her hair up in a thin ponytail, gold drop earrings swinging every time she laughed or nodded, she reveled in hearing Bell tell stories of Darren as a boy — how she put powdered red pepper on his hands while he slept to stop him from sucking his thumb (*Teeth woulda been bucked from here to Dallas if it weren't for me*); how she tied a string from her front door to Darren's first loose tooth to *yank the little sucker clean.* He didn't know why her stories were all teeth-related. But what did it matter? His mother hadn't raised him and didn't have the love or trust of the men who had, his uncles William and Clayton. It was, all of it, a fiction invented between the soup and the main course. Except one story she told about standing behind the chain-link fence outside the playground of his elementary school watching her son play red light, green

28

light and how she'd cried later when Clayton got wind of it and told the principal to bar her from the grounds. "Is that true?" Darren asked. When his mother mumbled, "Yes," he felt a warmth spread in his throat. His tongue grew useless, and he couldn't think of a single thing to say. By dessert, Lisa was quite tipsy. Skin damp and eyes bright and glassy, she looked at him and asked, "Darren, why am I just now getting to know your mother?"

Bell let out a tiny, bark-like laugh. "What a good question, Darren. Why *is* your wife just now getting to know me?" she said, using a tone that Lisa was too drunk to realize was openly mocking the way her words came out, individually wrapped, consonants and vowels sharply defined, every sound neatly in its place, unlike the slushy speech that poured out of Bell's mouth. She gave her son a little smile as she waited for him to explain himself to his wife. And when she was met with nothing but raw silence, she reached for the wine bottle on the other side of the table and poured the last thimbleful before rolling her grenade onto the elegantly dressed table, saying, apropos of nothing, what a shame it was that the San Jacinto County Sheriff's Department had never found the little .38 that killed Ronnie

Malvo — the reason Mack still wasn't cleared in that homicide — that the thing could be anywhere, but surely *someone* knew where it was. *Why, it would only take a phone call to Mr. Frank Vaughn to solve the crime.* She looked at Darren, making sure he understood she knew the name of the San Jacinto County district attorney, as she snapped her linen napkin across the lap of her Lee jeans. Darren gave her a shake of his head, a flaccid warning. He hadn't told anyone that his mother had found the suspected murder weapon on the Mathews property in Camilla, that she had it in her possession — that she had him by the balls.

"What?" Lisa said, pressing her finger against chocolate crumbs on her plate and licking them off. She had a tiny stain on her silk blouse — a drop of cherry juice from the Black Forest cake. She was glowing still, and Darren felt protective of her and the peace that had settled over their marriage. His mother would destroy it if he let her. It wasn't enough to threaten his career as a Texas Ranger; Bell Callis wanted his marriage hanging by a string too.

He hadn't slept that night.

But he'd gotten up the next morning and done it all over again.

Morning, Mama, you need anything? Just

thinking about you.

For weeks and weeks, he hadn't *stopped* thinking about her — which was all she really wanted, he told himself. The threat could be contained. He suspected the .38 lay somewhere inside the four-hundred-and-seventy-five-square-foot trailer she called home, and of course it had occurred to him to storm in one day and simply snatch it from her. But his mother had the speed and temperament of a feral cat. Any sudden moves, and she would attack. She'd make him pay for robbing her of the new authority she held. He knew her too well. He told himself he had it all under control, a lie that put him to bed at night. Until it didn't.

The Friday he finally broke began simply enough.

He had a get-together that night with some Ranger friends, and it was his turn to host. Roland Carroll had puked in their guest bathroom the last time, missing the toilet by a very messy three feet, and Lisa had said she'd just as soon not have his Ranger buddies over to their place anymore, so Darren had decided to move the party ninety miles up Highway 59 to his family's homestead in Camilla. Looking back on it, he could see he had already been starting to formulate a plan of action regarding his mother. Even before he heard the car turning up the dirt road to the farmhouse that afternoon. He had been watering the last of the banana pepper plants along the side of the porch, thinking he could have them pickled in time for Christmas dinner, when Frank Vaughn, district attorney for San Jacinto County, pulled into the driveway, the tires of his Ford sedan turning over clumps of damp red dirt. Darren hadn't laid eyes on the man since his grand jury testimony, when Rutherford "Mack" McMillan, long-time family friend, had escaped an indictment for the murder of Ronnie "Redrum" Malvo, a member of the Aryan Brotherhood of Texas and a grade-A asshole. At the time, Vaughn suspected Darren knew the location of the murder weapon — that he was covering for Mack — and in the end the grand jury had declined to prosecute. The degree to which Frank Vaughn put that on Darren was hard to say. But Darren knew this was not likely a casual visit. As Vaughn stepped out of his car, his stiff hair and the diamond chip in his A&M class ring caught the midday sun. "Afternoon," he said, squinting so that his face looked nearly masklike, dark slits for eyes. He was a few years older than Darren — maybe he'd even hit fifty — and was deep enough into a career that would have landed him in a big city a long time ago if he had had the talent or inclination. His district included several surrounding counties, all of them under his domain; the wheels of justice in this little part of East Texas turned on his say-so, and he liked it that way.

"I help you with something?" Darren said. He reached for the spigot along the side of the house. The lukewarm water slowed to a thin trickle as Vaughn arrived at the foot of the porch stairs.

"Thought I saw your truck in town." The DA's manner was grim but not at all un-friendly — neighborly, even, as if Vaughn had stopped by to warn him of a storm coming, of the need to batten down win-dows and prepare for hard rain. "Was hop-ing to catch you for a word."

"Well, you found me," Darren said, keep-ing his voice even, betraying none of the alarm he felt at the idea that the DA had been looking for him. Darren was all too aware that if authorities were to get wind of the .38 snub-nosed pistol that his mother had found on this very property last fall, he could be indicted on charges of obstruction or worse. He would not only lose his badge;

he'd face prison time.

Darren started coiling the water hose around a rusting hook that Mack — who worked for the Mathews family — had nailed to the lip of the wooden porch decades ago. It was cool outside, the air crisp and sharp, the sky like cut lapis, rain clouds having skipped town as quickly as if they owed somebody money. It was still a ways from a good December freeze. No need to wrap the onions and collards for another couple of weeks, Darren thought as he tucked away the hose. He worked with deliberation and patience in front of Vaughn, a show of steely calm.

"Well, you know we can't really let this thing go," the DA said, as if they were picking up a conversation recently interrupted. "A man dead and everything. Ronnie Malvo was a shit, wasn't no secret about it. But we can't have people just taking the law into their own hands. Not in my district, Ranger."

"Don't know what it's got to do with me. I said my piece in court."

"You did."

"And Mack was cleared."

"*He* was, yes," Vaughn said. "For now." He took a few steps forward so that he and Darren were face to face at the side of the house. "But if it's someone else involved in this thing, I'm gon' find out. You know that, Ranger. So consider this a courtesy call." He glanced down at the tips of his boots, tan ropers losing a good polish in the dirt on the Mathews property. When he looked up again, he had a hint of a smirk on his face as he told Darren point-blank, "I could have walked into the Rangers' office down to Houston, made a big deal about you not necessarily being cleared in this thing."

"Me?"

"I hope that's not the case, I really do," Vaughn said. And yet the smirk deepened, actually bent the lines around his narrow eyes as he added, "But if you insist on protecting Rutherford McMillan, you may find twelve men and women standing to weigh your fate. There *will* be another grand jury, mark my words, Ranger. You can testify in front of it or be the one sweating its ruling."

Darren visibly stiffened.

In the months since the Malvo homicide had been wreaking havoc on Darren's life and career, this was as close as the DA had come to a direct threat. He tried to soften it by putting a hand on Darren's shoulder to make him feel at ease, a gesture that was awkward because Darren was a good two inches taller than him, four in his boots, so that neither man seemed entirely comfortable with the balance of power here. "I'm hoping I can count on your cooperation in this deal," Vaughn said as he started toward his car. "My office will be circling back, going over everything again in detail. There'll be witnesses we'll revisit, new ones we'll want to talk to," he said, pausing to fish his car keys out of the pocket of his navy slacks and let this next bit land: "Your mother, for one."

Darren felt a bolt of panic.

He knew he needed to be careful, but still his voice rose in a way that embarrassed him. God help him, he sounded scared, stunned actually. "Bell Callis never met Ronnie Malvo, couldn't pick him out of a lineup but for the man's picture being in the paper. My mother doesn't know him from Adam."

"But she knows *you.*" Vaughn was eyeing Darren over the top of the driver's-side door. That smirk had unpacked its bags and settled in for a stay. Darren saw now the cocksure pleasure on his face, the look of a man who was up by a few hundred and holding a winning hand. "You've been spending a lot of time out to her place lately. Least, that's what deputies around here have been telling me."

"Can't imagine what you think that means," Darren said.

"Maybe it don't mean nothing . . . and maybe it do."

"Have you spoken to her?" Darren said, regretting the words as soon as they fell out of his mouth like loose teeth. He felt a loss of control that shamed and then terrified him. When he spoke again, it was with anger, righteous and mean. "My mother's not well," he said, because on some level it had to be true; it had to explain the whole of his life. "If I find out you've been harassing her —"

Vaughn raised his hand, not so much in a farewell as a dismissal, a signal they'd pick this up some other time. "We'll talk, Mathews," he said, sliding into the driver's side of his Ford Taurus. "We'll talk." A few seconds later, Darren heard the engine turn over. He stood still, as if the ground had shot up vines to strap his ankles in place. He couldn't move, even after there was nothing left of Frank Vaughn but a swirl of red dirt in the driveway. *Shit.* The jig was up. He was going to have to do something about Bell.

2.

He was expecting only five Rangers that Friday night — Roland from Company A, stationed in Houston with Darren; Buddy Watson, Company B, working out of the sheriff's station in Henderson County, south of Dallas; Ricky Nuñez, Company G, who'd driven all the way up from Corpus; Hector Martinez, Company E, Pecos County; and Patricia Nolan from Company F in Austin. Still, Darren knew things could get rowdy. In truth, he was counting on it; he needed cover for what he was planning. He'd brought eight pounds of barbecue and hot links up from the city, and, God bless him, he'd actually believed he wouldn't drink, forgoing liquor just to prove he could. But hell if he wasn't as grateful as a dog thrown a bone when Hector showed up with a bottle of Tennessee whiskey and Patricia with mescal and margarita mix. Both Buddy and Roland stocked his uncles' old Frigidaire Flair with beer, Shiner Bock and Miller High Life. They had each of them cleared forty-eight hours, had the night and the next day in front of them to cut loose, as it had been a hell of a month for everybody. When Darren left Houston that morning, Lisa had told him not to worry about rushing back — a first. She'd stood on her tiptoes to kiss him goodbye, stretching mind and body to offer her support. There had been more than fifty incidents of hate-tinged violence across the state in the four weeks since the election, and Lisa's feelings about the badge had softened. "Just come back safe," she said.

Darren set a Lightnin' Hopkins record on the turntable, a guitar-picking blues that made Buddy Watson roll his eyes and groan. But this was a rule they'd established early on: whoever hosted got to control the music and set the menu. Tonight was barbecue, but Ricky's wife had sent tamales anyway. Warming in the oven, they filled the house with a smoky sweetness as their corn husks browned and pork fat dripped and sizzled. Of the roughly one hundred and fifty Texas Rangers commissioned by the state, the six of them in no way represented *all* of the department's diversity, but they were the few willing to admit the job got a hell of a lot easier if you had like minds to shoot the shit with. Five men — three black, two Latino — and one white woman who had joined this unofficial fraternity out of solidarity. A second white woman, Vicki Brennan, one of the original members of their social club, had stopped answering their e-mails after the election.

As soon as the drinks were poured, the speculation began.

"What's gotten up her butt?" Patricia said.

"Scared, probably," Ricky said. He was wearing a black sweatshirt and matching Wranglers, and he'd downed two beers before he took a seat.

Roland made a face. "You really think she voted for him?"

"It shouldn't matter," Ricky said. "Not to this here."

He meant the people at the party, the friendships they'd forged. But Patricia huffed and shook her head. "Oh, it matters," she said. She was the youngest at twenty-six, having made Ranger just eight years out of the academy. A former ball player at Sam Houston State, she was nearly as tall as Darren, blond with a long face and strangely delicate features. She licked the salt off her glass.

"Vicki got her eye on headquarters, moving up the ranks," Roland said. "We're not liable to see her at one of these deals again." He pinched snuff from a tin he kept tucked in the front pocket of his shirt and balled it under his tongue.

Hector nodded his shaved head. "She's always been one of them," he said.

He didn't clarify who *them* was. But they all nodded their heads anyway.

"We all have to do what we can to get through," Ricky said, and the Rangers in the room agreed with the sentiment. One by one, they each acknowledged that something had shifted in the past four weeks, not just in the world at large but on the job too. They were dealing with things they'd never seen in their lifetimes, stories they'd only heard from the older men in the department: church burnings; the defacement of a mosque in Bryan; black and brown kids shoved in lunchrooms, spit on in gym class; a Mexican woman currently in critical condition after she was attacked in front of her husband and three kids in the parking lot of a Kroger in Fort Worth. Buddy spoke of a hotbed of trouble near Jefferson in Marion County. He might even have mentioned a missing kid out that way. But Darren might have remembered it wrong.

Things got a little fuzzy after that.

41

He managed to go an hour before switching from beer to whiskey, but the slide was fast. It made wax of his spine, the liquor did; made everything go soft at the edges, melting away all the departmental talk, all their tales from the field, of which Darren had none. He was landlocked at the Houston office these days, bored in a way he was scared to admit to himself, afraid the word hid a deeper truth as blue as the record that was playing: Darren was depressed, sick with a rage that was eating him from the inside. Daily, he marveled with befuddled anger at what a handful of scared white people could do to a nation. He never again wanted to hear them question the point of rioting in Ferguson or Baltimore, or Watts and Detroit for that matter, hear them wonder why black folks would torch their own neighborhoods, because in an act of blind fury, white voters had just lit a match to the very country they claimed to love — simply because they were being asked to share it. And that's the bit that stung, the hurt that cut bone-deep. After years of being lulled into believing that the universe bent toward justice, he saw how little friends and neighbors thought of his life, of his right to this country.

After Obama, it was forgiveness betrayed.

Before long, a third drink was poured, and Hector took a few beers and a pack of Marlboros out onto the back porch, and the party drifted out there. Patricia sat on one of the green metal lawn chairs and wrapped herself in a patchwork quilt that Darren's grandmother had made before he was born. The worn cotton smelled of the blocks of cedar with which it shared a hallway closet, and the sweet scent mixed with the tang of pine in the air. It was cool outside and pitch-black beyond the yellow haze of the porch light. Roland, who never slept a night outside the city limits if he didn't have to, flinched every time he heard a screech owl hooting. He was soon bumming smokes off Hector and daring any of them to say something about it. Buddy talked about the dispatcher in Corsicana he was putting it to three times a week: *Could suck the stone out of a peach.* Patricia called him a nasty bastard and threw a lime rind at his head. Ricky was already nodding off, his black gators hanging over the edge of the porch's love seat, a water-stained cushion folded under his head. They'd left the back door open, and the smell of tamales and barbecue crept into the night air. Darren sat closest to the warmth of the house, keeping an ear out for the oven timer.

He poured himself a fourth drink, marveling at his folly, that he'd actually thought there was a chance he wasn't going to end up knee-deep in brown water tonight. His skin flushed. He grew hot beneath the gray T-shirt he was wearing. He grew furious, actually, mad at himself. His brain loosened by drink, he could admit he'd stumbled badly with Frank Vaughn this afternoon. The man was bluffing, he told himself; he had to be. But if Vaughn had gone to the Mathews place solely on a fishing expedition, Darren had acted skittish enough to convince him to keep his line wet.

There was no way his mother would speak to the district attorney, right? It made no sense, not in the mind of Bell Callis, anyway. It would rob her of the very thing she'd always wanted, the attention of one of the Mathews men, her son at her feet. Without Darren, who would do her yard work and check on the plumbing line? If he went to prison, who would stock her fridge and pay her cable bill? Surely his mother wouldn't intentionally ruin her only son. *Right?*

Lightnin' had his own take on it.

You got love just like a hydrant . . . you know that turns it off and on.

The pick of his guitar was like a finger poking Darren's wounds.

Lisa didn't know about the money.

She didn't know the whole story; no one did.

Who could he tell, really? Heavy-lidded, he looked at the men sitting on the porch with him and Patricia in the lawn chair with her bare feet on the wooden railing, all of them deep in their cups. It would be so easy to say it right now, to halt the gossip and work talk with a confession: *Y'all, I'm in trouble.* But it seemed rude to burden them with the information, knowledge they'd have to reveal under oath if it ever came to that. Same with Greg Heglund, who was one of his best friends but also a federal agent. Darren's uncle Clayton, a former criminal defense attorney and a constitutional law professor, would understand the impulse to shelter Mack, an elderly black man who'd been accused of murdering a racist piece of shit, but he would insist that Darren get an attorney, and Darren didn't trust that that news wouldn't get back to his lieutenant in Houston. How many cops did Darren know who assumed a man was guilty as sin just because he lawyered up, a constitutional right made to sound dirty, like an act of deceit?

He suddenly realized how lonely he was with no one to talk to about the mess he'd made, the secret he'd been carrying around for months, the fact that he didn't know his mother well enough to predict what she might do in this situation. Lisa either, if he told her. They'd just gotten back to a good place. If she found out he'd put his freedom and their life together in jeopardy for Rutherford McMillan, would she understand or be through with him for good? He honestly didn't know. Both of the women in his life were ciphers. Loose with whiskey, his mind lazed to another soul completely. Randie Winston. The woman whose late husband's murder he'd solved in Lark back in October. He thought of the night they'd spent at that juke joint in Garrison, just over the county line from Lark, talking over bourbon and cheap vodka — his marriage, hers — how close he'd come to laying his whole life bare. He remembered Randie had almost taken his hand at the table. He still believed he could have confessed anything that night.

She'd reached out to him since then.

Just a message left on his voice mail a while back to say she'd taken his advice and buried her husband's remains in the East Texas town where he was born. *You were right.* It had moved him then, as it did now, to think of her journey from hating Texas to recognizing the part it had played in making the man she'd loved, realizing that it mattered to honor that for her husband, Michael, but also for herself. Drunk as he was, the whole thing made him misty. It was one of his proudest moments as a Ranger. He laughed at some story Buddy was telling even though he hadn't heard half of it. And then he told himself he knew what he had to do. *Tonight.*

He waited until they were passed out or sleeping, Patricia in Darren's childhood bedroom and the others sprawled across various pieces of furniture throughout the living room, their grease-soaked paper plates and beer bottles littering the hardwood floor. It was nearly two in the morning when he walked to his Chevy truck parked on the grass out front of the house. This late — or early, depending on which side of midnight you felt at home — the air was thin and chilly in Camilla, sweet with dew, and it cooled his heated state of mind to ride with the windows down. He was careful, going ten under the speed limit the whole way and cutting his headlights off as soon as he started down the twin tire ruts behind Bell's landlord's house that led to her trailer.

47

Though he'd been prepared for a confrontation if one was necessary, Bell's '92 Chevette was not in front of her home, nor were there any lights on in the trailer. A couple of nights a week, she and Fisher, her boyfriend, stayed in one of the empty cabins by Lake Livingston where she worked as a cleaner; he guessed he'd gotten lucky tonight. By the low light of a pocket Maglite, he searched every inch of the one-bedroom trailer, performing the task with the methodical care in which he'd been trained. He started in the kitchen and worked his way from one end of the tin-can house to the other. He went through every cabinet, every drawer, and every countertop canister; he searched the refrigerator and the freezer, taking the time to put a thick, grayish block of ice in the sink and run hot water over it. It was brisket, easily three years old.

The gun wasn't in the kitchen.

The living room either.

He took everything out of the TV cabinet, lifted every cushion on the bench couch attached to the back wall. The bathroom turned up nothing either. As he tore apart her bedroom, a certainty started to take hold. The .38 wasn't under the mattress. It wasn't in the bureau by the door, nor was it under the carpet Darren ripped from the floor with his bare hands, staples tearing at his skin. It wasn't in any of the battered shoeboxes she kept in her closet, though he did find pictures of his father he'd never seen before, faded photographs of Darren "Duke" Mathews when he was still in high school. He pocketed the Polaroids without thinking, his heart hammering away in his chest.

The gun was gone.

He remembered the space under the house and felt a shot of hope. She'd once hidden a case of toilet paper she'd stolen from her job beneath the floorboards. He should check behind the cheap latticework that ringed the underside of the trailer, the two and a half feet of crawl space between Bell's home and the cold hard ground. He turned for the front door just as the beams from a pair of headlights swung through the trailer's front window, throwing shadows against the back wall. He quickly leaped out of sight, pressing himself against the side of the wall and peering out of the window at an angle, expecting to see the boxy silhouette of his mother's car. But no; it was the outline of a police squad car.

Darren's first impulse was to make sure he didn't get shot.

He came out with his badge in his left

hand, his Maglite in his right, and his hands not so much up in the air as thrust out in front of him in total submission. He got all the way to the bottom of the steps before he could see the officer's face. He was a sheriff's deputy, one of the youngest Darren had ever seen, and though Darren's badge was clearly visible, the deputy's hand hovered over his service weapon. Darren stood firm in front of his mother's trailer and gave his name and title. The deputy, a white kid with spiky black hair, said, "I know who you are." And yet his hand was still inches from his pistol.

Darren played it calm, as if the two had bumped into each other at the post office instead of at the site of a potential B and E. "I know most of the men and women in the sheriff's department up here. My family's owned a place in Camilla for over a hundred years," he said, making clear his local pedigree. "Guess you must be new."

The kid didn't smile, and his hand didn't come off that gun either.

He was twitchy, a little unsure of himself in this situation he'd stumbled on in the dead of night. He told Darren to drop the flashlight.

Darren obliged, watching the Maglite fall in the dirt and roll a good two feet between the men.

"You here on official business, Ranger?" the kid said.

"I might ask you the same, Deputy."

"Got a call from the property owner up the way saying his tenant's son was out here fussing around when his mama wasn't home, said she wouldn't like it none." Darren had just enough whiskey sluicing through his veins to wonder if this was a lie, to entertain paranoid thoughts that Frank Vaughn had had him followed. "You have the tenant's permission to be on the property, sir?"

"I must have if she gave me a key."

The words were out before Darren could remember if he'd visibly damaged the front door when he'd jimmied the lock. He kept talking, tried to keep the deputy's eyes on his face and away from the door. He said the first thing that came to mind. "She asked me to feed her cat while she was out."

He was almost pleased with himself, with the simplicity of the lie.

"Cat?" The deputy's shoulders relaxed, and for the first time he took his hand away from his holster. It was dark out here, but Darren thought he saw the flicker of a smile finally. The kid was relieved. This would all be over soon. "And the cat's inside right

51

now?" he said, craning his head around to see the front door.

Darren blocked his view and said, "That's my exact problem. The thing got outside, and I can't find it."

"Did you look under the house? Let me give you a hand," the deputy said.

He started for his squad car; his belief that this all boiled down to a missing cat had so lifted his mood that there was a light bounce in his step, an eagerness now to do this Texas Ranger a favor. "Let me back up and aim my headlights under the trailer. You'll see anything that's hiding down there."

The back of Darren's neck went hot. He shook his head and told the deputy it was hardly necessary. "I've got my truck," he said, speaking more emphatically than was wise.

"Naw, that sits up too high. You not gon' see much of nothing that way."

The deputy slid into the front seat of his squad car and turned over the engine, then repositioned his bulky vehicle so that the underside of Bell's trailer was awash with light. The deputy shot one leg out of the car, preparing to stand, and asked Darren, "You want me to try to get up under there too?"

Darren shook his head, still thinking of a

way to stop this. But it would seem odd now, suspicious even, if Darren didn't try to look for the cat. *Cat.* He swallowed a bitter chuckle. What he was looking for under his mother's trailer would ruin him if it was discovered under the watchful eye of a cop, a member of the very law enforcement agency that would be investigating Darren should Frank Vaughn convene another grand jury to look into the murder of Ronnie Malvo. The deputy watching, Darren ripped back a large corner of the latticework beneath the trailer, got down on his hands and knees, and slithered in the dirt from one end of the structure to the other, clawing at the earth, picking through every mound of soil. He didn't know if it was relief he felt or a choking dread when he didn't find a damn thing. There was absolutely no telling what she'd done with it. That gun could be anywhere.

3.

Darren got called in to see his lieutenant
first thing Monday morning, a surprise
request that had him on edge soon as he
walked into the office. Fred Wilson had
been diagnosed with an ulcer two weeks
after the election despite the fact that he'd
voted for the incoming president, or so Darren presumed — though he was basing this
hunch on nothing more than the man's hat
and cowboy boots, an ostrich pair of which
were on Darren's own feet right now. Maybe
no man wore his heart on his sleeve — or in
his boots, for that matter. Judge not and all
that.

Wilson had a growing menagerie of home
remedies lined up on his desk sandwiched
between two towering stacks of files. Like
any good Texan, his wife of twenty-five years
claimed she was one-eighth Cherokee and
insisted that Fred supplement whatever his
HMO doctor prescribed with something

that grew up out of the ground. These days he was constantly nibbling on boiled cabbage or raw carrots or sipping watery concoctions his wife blended for him. On a good day, his belches smelled of coconut water and banana. Today, it was garlic. There wasn't a single window in the building that opened, and the air in Wilson's office smelled canned and sour.

Darren sat in the chair across from Wilson and rested his gray Stetson on his knee. He was in dark blue slacks, which he'd woken at dawn to iron, a white button-down, and a thin burgundy tie. He'd driven in from Camilla this morning, and he hoped the details of his run-in with the sheriff's department had stayed in San Jacinto County. Wilson had a file sitting on the desk in front of him, a folder thin enough for Darren's restless imagination to think it resembled his personnel file.

Wilson scratched at a patch of stubble he'd missed shaving this morning as he said that Darren had settled back in to work in the Houston office smoothly. After Darren's successful arrests in Lark in the fall, Wilson had been proud to welcome him back. He had found Darren a new place on the Texas Rangers joint task force, a partnership with the ATF, DEA, and FBI, that was working

55

to secure a massive indictment of key members of the Aryan Brotherhood of Texas on charges of drug running and illegal gun sales and various other felonious conspiracies. From behind his desk in Houston, Darren had been providing invaluable research support, Wilson said, by combing through thousands of pages of cell phone records and highlighting with a yellow marker anything the feds could use against the Brotherhood. That he'd almost gone cross-eyed from boredom, Darren kept to himself. Hands folded across his lap, he listened as Wilson told him, "Up to this point, I've been happy to have you back here in Houston."

Darren wasn't sure where this was headed, but it didn't sound good.

"How are things at home, Ranger?"

"Fine," Darren said, though the word caught a little in his throat.

"Heard you were out in San Jacinto County this weekend."

Here we go, Darren thought.

Wilson reached for a bottle of off-brand antacid. He shook a few into his left hand, which was the size and texture of a child's baseball mitt. "Look, I ain't one to get in a man's family business long as it don't affect what we're doing here."

56

"I can explain."

"No need. Whatever you was doing at your mama's house is between you and her. I'm asking more about why you were out in Camilla in the first place."

Then Wilson asked Darren point-blank about his marriage.

"You and Lisa in a good place again? I mean, you think she could let go of you for a few days? I know you said you wanted to stay put here in Houston and all. I wouldn't ask if the feds hadn't made a special request."

Darren ran his finger along the felt crown of his hat. He felt he'd missed something. "I'm sorry, sir, I don't know what you're talking about."

It was then that Wilson opened the file, though he never so much as glanced at it. He knew the contents by heart. "We got a missing kid up near Jefferson — Caddo Lake, really — in Marion County."

"That's Company B territory."

"I know it," Wilson said, sighing. He slapped the antacids into his mouth, and Darren watched him chew for a few moments of awkward silence. "But this deal needs special consideration. A lot of parts in this spell trouble."

"Like what?"

"The kid, Levi King —"

"How old?"

"Nine."

Darren got an image of himself at nine, teeth indeed bucked halfway to Dallas, no matter the tall tale his mother told about nursing his dental health, about having been a part of his upbringing in any meaningful way. When Darren was nine years old, the men who were raising him — his uncles William and Clayton Mathews — were his whole world.

Wilson nodded and let out a soft belch. He chased the chalky antacids with a swig of Coke, which was most certainly not on his wife's list of approved tonics. "Well, the thing is, the kid's connected. That's why the feds want a careful hand in this."

"Connected?"

"The kid's people are Brotherhood."

Darren made a face. He didn't even realize it till Wilson said, "Not the kid's fault."

"Of course not," Darren said quickly. He wasn't proud of the millisecond in which his disgust of the Aryan Brotherhood of Texas got out past his sympathies for the kid. But neither could he shake a lingering antipathy — or apathy, really — for the woes of a Brotherhood family. He covered it by pointing out the obvious mistake that had been made. "The feds asked for me?"

"They asked for a Ranger from the task force. I volunteered *you.*"

"Thank you," Darren said. It came out more like a question than a statement, and he hoped he didn't sound like he was making light of the situation or like he didn't appreciate being called to serve. Still, the timing wasn't right. There was no way around that. He couldn't go back into the field now. Not when things with Lisa were stable. And not when the situation with his mother had slipped out of his control. He hadn't talked to her since he'd discovered the gun was not in or underneath her trailer. She had not returned any of his calls. He'd spent a good five hours Sunday with his butt parked on the steps of her trailer, waiting for her to come home and explain herself; he had even driven by the Starfish Resort Cabins and RV Hookup looking for her Chevette or any sign of his mother in her fraying blue smock, swaying drunkenly as she walked between the cabins.

Darren shifted in his seat, his long legs as stiff as kindling.

Through the wall of Wilson's office, he heard the constant purr of phones ringing and Rangers talking in the hall, their boots tromping across the thin industrial carpet.

He had a stack of phone records sitting on his desk right now next to hundreds of pages of intercepted prison correspondence to and from members of the Brotherhood. He'd imagined he would spend the day looking for patterns and connections, cracking codes that ordered hits or sold kilos of meth or moved cash money through legit businesses selling everything from tires to beauty supplies to linoleum flooring in small towns all across the state. Since Darren's return to work, this had been his sole contribution to the task force that had been after the Aryan Brotherhood of Texas for years.

But now Darren was being called off the bench.

"The boy's father — Bill 'Big Kill' King — is an ABT captain doing a twenty-year bid at the Telford Unit up near Texarkana on a slew of drug-related charges. Sales, production, armed robbery, the works."

Never mind that he'd skated on assault charges in a separate case that had left a black man, a father of two, dead, Darren thought.

"And, lo and behold, in the time he's been paying his debt to society," Wilson went on, "his wife takes up with a low-level piece-of-shit hanger-on by the name of Gil Thomason who's done a few times inside himself, for running cons, mostly. Ponzi schemes and cheating little old ladies out of their bingo money. Word is, Bill King doesn't want his boy around the guy anymore."

"You think this is some kind of custody deal?"

"We don't know," Wilson said. "But the kid's been gone since Friday evening."

"That's coming on seventy-two hours," Darren said.

Wilson nodded, both of them knowing this didn't portend a happy ending. "The father, King," he said, "he swears he doesn't know where his kid is. In fact, reports from inside Telford say he's a mess over it. He's begging for the sheriff's office in Jefferson to do something, to not hold the father's crimes against the son. He even wrote a letter to the governor." Wilson looked down for the first time at the open file folder on his desk. Sitting on top was a handwritten letter intercepted by the Texas Department of Criminal Justice from Bill King, TDCJ no. 657372212, to the governor. King had addressed it simply to *Capitol Hill, Austin.* Wilson pushed it across his desk to Darren. The letter had never made it to the governor, and now it rested in his black hands. He didn't read it, not right away. He let it

61

sit on his lap so as not to smudge the pencil markings. He said, "Seems like a local matter."

"Officially, yes," Wilson said. "But I'd be lying if I told you we didn't see an opportunity here."

"Opportunity?"

Hearing the word back, Wilson grimaced. He set his hands down hard on his desk and interlaced his thick fingers. "Look," he said. "A little over a month from now we get a new man in the White House and a brand-new Justice Department, and who knows how the shit will shake out, if their priorities will line up with what we've been doing with the feds on this task force for six years. Six years, Ranger, we've been trying to take down this terrorist organization."

Terrorist organization.

He'd never heard his lieutenant describe the ABT that way. And he was vaguely aware that the term was for his benefit, that Wilson was selling something.

"Twelve captains and twenty other Brotherhood rank and file are potentially on the hook in this deal. It's a good case, Darren. Could be a game changer, the thing that dismantles the Aryan Brotherhood in this state once and for all."

"What do you need from me?" Darren said.

"What we need is an indictment, sooner rather than later. The feds want this in front of a grand jury before the change of power in Washington. Before a Trump Justice Department mistakes the Aryan Brotherhood for some sort of honor guard. The feds are close, they say, to having enough to make it happen."

This time, Wilson shoved the entire file across the desk. "Two members of the ABT caught in a pressure cooker of a domestic situation, each man pointing a finger at the other —"

"Is that what's happening?"

Wilson nodded at the handwritten letter in Darren's lap, instructing him to read it. "One of the men or the wife might start talking about Brotherhood goings-on they've previously been unwilling to discuss, information that could put the final touches on a bill of indictment. The FBI has not been able to attach Bill King to this larger Brotherhood case, mainly because he's been in lockup for years now and claims he's changed his ways. But if the wife and the new boyfriend get pissed enough, maybe —"

"You want to use the kid as leverage?"

63

Wilson winced at the implication. "We want to be delicate in the handling of the investigation, that's all, so that if any secrets should spill in the course of tracking down that kid's whereabouts, we might be able to use them."

"You think he's still alive?" Darren asked. He wasn't entirely sure where the question had come from. He hadn't read the file and knew next to nothing. It just seemed that if this was a domestic deal, the kid would have turned up by now.

The question shook Wilson; his face blanched to a pale gray. "I think it's been almost three days, and the sooner you get to the sheriff's office in Marion County, the better," he said.

"Why me?" Darren asked finally. "For obvious reasons."

"Not sure I follow," Wilson said.

Darren hated when white folks did that, when they acted like race was something they hadn't even considered until *you* brought it up. He guessed they'd been taught it was polite or something, like not mentioning you have a fleck of black pepper between your teeth. But Darren's only takeaway was the discomfiting realization that the person sitting across from him hadn't seen the real him for the past fifteen minutes. It was an invisibility that infuriated him. He thought he and Wilson were past all that. "Come on," he said to his lieutenant. "You sending me into a Brotherhood mess, least you can do is tell me why."

Wilson's face became pinched, like he was preparing to pass a particularly difficult kidney stone. He let out a little puff of air and conceded that, yes, there were reports of a lot of racial strife in the area where the kid was from, a small lakeside community called Hopetown, fifteen miles or so from Jefferson.

"I've never seen a Hopetown on any Texas map," Darren said.

"I don't think it's *been* on a map in twenty, maybe thirty years. It's a dying little town out there, and trouble's been stirred up by newcomers clashing with folks that's been living there for, hell, I don't even know how many years. Anybody wading in this thing's gon' need to talk to as many witnesses as he can, and they ain't all gon' look and talk like Brotherhood folk, if you get me."

"There are black folks in Hopetown," Darren said, cutting to it.

"A few, yes."

Darren agreed to do it before he knew how he would explain this to his wife.

65

"There'll be a Marion County deputy to escort you."

"Believe I can find my way around East Texas."

"It's for your own protection."

"I don't really think it's necessary —"

"It wasn't a suggestion," Wilson said, his final words on it.

"Anything in particular I should be looking for?" Darren asked.

"Any piece of paper or witness statement that can tie Bill King to Brotherhood operations, we'll take it," Wilson said. "It's Hail Mary time."

Darren stood up holding the file folder, Bill King's letter tucked safely inside, and slid his Stetson on his head. He was due for a haircut, but there would be no time for that now. He got all the way to the door before Wilson called for him to halt. "Oh, and, Mathews," he said, a knowing expression on his face. "No more break-ins, huh? I just got you back where I want you. Let's don't fuck it up."

Darren gave his lieutenant a tight smile.

Then he tipped his hat and left.

Only to walk back in two seconds later. "Speaking of the task force," he said, throwing it away like an afterthought, going for nonchalance. "You ever think to let San Jacinto County know that Ronnie Malvo was a snitch?"

Wilson knitted his brow. "And compromise a federal investigation?"

"Or get the DA out there to do what he should have done before Malvo was in the ground — consider other suspects."

It wasn't like Darren hadn't thought of it before. The Aryan Brotherhood of Texas didn't let snitches sing and live to tell about it. They'd just as soon cut out your tongue and make you eat it. In theory, anyone in their gang could have put a hit out on Malvo. Days Darren sat before pages and pages of Brotherhood misdeeds — ABT members suspected of everything from drug dealing to assault to straight-up murder — and he sometimes thought of how easy it would be to pluck out a name, like reaching into a bingo cage and coming out with a winning number. It scared him, how simple it would be to slap on Frank Vaughn's desk a mug shot of a tatted-up member of the Brotherhood and say it was Ronnie Malvo's killer, which would take the heat off Mack as the killer and off Darren as a potential accessory after the fact. He felt the disapproval of his late uncle William, who'd been a Texas Ranger too, a man Darren revered for his integrity, for the blind faith

67

he held in the rule of law. But Darren wasn't sure anymore that the law could withstand blindness. He'd protected Mack out of instinct, because his own read of history told him a black man should have a right to his own fear. Otherwise, he would forever be dying because of someone else's. *It's us or them, isn't it?* The belief felt like a heavy brick in his chest, chipping away at the bones in his rib cage each time he took a breath, breaking him from the inside out. But did that make it any less true? Had anything in the weeks since the election proved his cynicism wrong? Maybe the rules *had* to be different. Maybe justice was no more a fixed concept than love was, and poets and bluesmen knew the rules better than we did. He remembered an old Lightnin' Hopkins record, a song his uncle William never cared for but that William's twin brother, Clayton, would hum with a wry smile. *Yeah, I'm black and I'm evil, but this black man did not make hisself.* To Clayton, justice was always relative.

Wilson gave him a funny look, then said, "My understanding is that Frank Vaughn lost a pretty solid circumstantial case in a hang-'em-high county —" Something about the image he'd painted for Darren made Wilson go red, as if he'd unexpectedly passed gas in an elevator. He cleared his throat and continued. "Vaughn had his day, he had his grand jury, and he couldn't get an indictment. That ought to make him think twice about trying again anytime soon."

"Or it might make him try harder."

Wilson seemed to contemplate this for a second, then repeated his earlier directive: "Don't fuck this up, Mathews. I'm serious. Mack ain't your problem. That murder case ain't your problem." Darren couldn't tell Wilson that he was dead wrong — not without opening up the whole sordid story of the gun and his double-dealing mama. And no way he was doing that. He simply nodded dutifully when his lieutenant told him to get to Jefferson as fast as he could.

4.

He called Lisa from the road, left two messages for her, in fact, before he reached the freeway. Her secretary promised Lisa would call back as he nosed his Chevy through the last trickle of morning rush hour, making his way through the concrete city to Highway 59, the road that would take him out of Houston and into the heart of East Texas. He drove north, toward Jefferson, a town of a little over two thousand near the Louisiana border. The case file lay open on the passenger seat of the Chevy's cab, while the letter from Bill King rested against the steering wheel as he drove. He read it in snatches, pulling his eyes from the road for only a few seconds at a time. After he got past the town of Humble and George Bush's airport, the task grew easier, as the buildings and strip malls, tractor dealerships and fireworks stands gave way to naked countryside — thick groves of pine trees on both sides of the highway — and the traffic thinned.

Bill King opened by quoting Deuteronomy.

He knew God wanted him to be strong and courageous, to not give in to fear, because the Lord would not forsake him. He knew this. But he reckoned God had soldiers of grace on earth, and he needed someone to find his boy. He begged the governor, addressing him by his first name, to press the sheriff of Marion County to take seriously reports of his son Levi being missing.

Darren looked up, slowing as he realized he'd inched too close to the back of the semi in front of him. He wondered just how these reports of Levi being missing had found their way to Bill King in lockup. The letter had been written Sunday — or at least, that's when it had been put in the mail system at Telford Unit, where Bill King had served six years of a twenty-year sentence. In the letter, he admitted to being a less than Christian influence on the world and admitted to being a shitty father. The word *shitty* had then been scratched out and replaced with *bad.* But as the governor knew by now, Bill wrote — again in an odd, overly familiar tone — he was paying his debt to society and was in the process of surrendering his life to God and his faith. It would kill him to think that the government — in the form of local law enforcement — would punish his child for something Bill was already making restitution for. He hoped to leave prison *soon* — a word he underlined — to start a new life with his son, who was a victim not only of Bill's bad choices but also of the man his ex-wife had living in her house, a *low-life* who he feared had harmed Levi either directly or through utter neglect. His ex, Marnie, and the boyfriend, Gil, had some bad dudes hanging around their house. He should know. *I used to be one of those bad dudes.* He went on to urge the governor to warn the sheriff against taking anything he heard out of his ex-wife's mouth at face value, the lies she would tell on him and his family. He believed his son was in danger and that every second counted. *I'm begging you, sir. Find my boy.*

Darren folded the letter and set it inside the case file next to him.

It sat like a stone in his gut, the letter did.

He didn't have kids, maybe never would at this rate. He and Lisa had talked about it a lot in the beginning, that first year when they were trying to decide whether to buy a ranch house sitting on a few acres of former prairie land in a sparsely populated subdivision northwest of the city, which Darren had wanted, or a loft in a newly revitalized downtown Houston, close to Lisa's office and countless bars and restaurants, concert halls and art galleries, and a yoga studio she loved but rarely had time for. Lisa won, and Darren guessed it was fine they didn't have a scratch of grass to call their own — no place for a kid to learn to ride a bike, let alone a gelding, of which Darren had two, though they resided with Mack — because after Lisa won her first big tort litigation case, talk of having a kid faded away. Darren was not a father, no, but he'd been a nine-year-old boy once, and like Levi King, it had been during a time of significant domestic strife.

That was the year he'd lost his uncle William for the first time, the year his uncle finally married Naomi — after a painfully long engagement — and started a family of his own, the year William and his twin brother, Clayton, stopped speaking to each other. The men had raised Darren after his father died in Vietnam and his mother proved to be less than equipped to look after anything small and needy, and Darren was confused and wrenched to pieces over the

73

brothers' breakup. Clayton, who'd been in love with Naomi for years, banned his brother from the family home in Camilla, and Darren didn't see his uncle William for almost a year. It was the first time he'd ever truly felt like a bastard, like a boy without a family, at least not the kind of families he'd seen in movies and picture books: a mom and a dad and a couple of kids. It was just Darren and Clayton all of a sudden, and the house, his entire childhood, actually, felt empty without his beloved uncle William — the man who'd taught him how to fish, how to shoot a twelve-gauge, and how to grow tomatoes as firm and sweet as apples. Darren had always resented Clayton for sending William away, for robbing him of the other father figure in his life. It would be years before he understood the particulars of the love triangle that had destroyed his family, the lack of innocence on the part of both Naomi *and* William. The facts couldn't be plainer: William had stolen Clayton's girl right out from under him.

Clayton was a senior at Prairie View A&M when he'd first seen Naomi, a freshman in pedal pushers and a sweater set, her hair freshly pressed and curled. She was so pretty, dark brown hair and smoky, almond-shaped eyes, he would have tripped on his

74

loose shoelace if she hadn't slowed on the quad to point it out to him. Their eyes met, and Clayton was done for. Prairie View was the premier college for colored folks in Texas, but he almost hadn't gone there, had almost broken Mathews tradition and enrolled in Wiley College in Marshall for the chance *not* to be known as William Mathews's twin brother — for a few years, at least. But the moment he laid eyes on Naomi Cortland, he knew he would be grateful for the rest of his life that he'd chosen to be a PV man. William was an ROTC student at the same school, majoring in math and history, and seemed wholly indifferent to Naomi when he first met her, even calling her "scrawny" in private. He was caught up at the time with an education major from Lufkin. A few months into his courtship of Naomi, Clayton was already thinking marriage, but he didn't want to buy a ring until he'd paid for law school. During Clayton's third year at Texas Southern's law school in Houston, William completed his first voluntary tour in Vietnam and returned to PV to finish his degree. William and Naomi got to talking, more than just a few passing words in the hallway of Clayton's dormitory. There were long conversations about the war and why William had gone. He suffered from a patriotism that pulled him along by the navel, he said; it was a feeling he was always trying to catch up to, was always scratching at the heels of a love for the country he wanted America to be. He was willing to fight for the ideal, believed that duty and service could get him there. At the time, Naomi wanted to be a nurse and she understood a life of service, understood wading through blood and shit on the hope that you could fix what was broken. *It's the fight,* William often said. *The nobility is in the fight.* Clayton, head in a law book somewhere all the way down to Houston, seemed distant to both of them, and at the dinner following Clayton's graduation ceremony, William and Naomi sat him down in a quiet corner to tell him they were engaged. Clayton called William a cheat and Naomi a fool; she'd be a war widow by Christmas, he said, William taking a bullet for a country that would never love him back. They were words he never did take back, not even as he stood at his twin brother's graveside after William was killed in the line of duty as a Texas Ranger.

Darren sometimes wondered if the brothers' deep differences, the divide between the two sides of the law they represented — William, the Texas Ranger, and Clayton, the former criminal defense attorney — was colored as much by matters of the heart as by a true ideological disagreement. Later in life now, Darren could see how trying to straddle the line between the two men's belief systems — the impulse to police crimes against black life and to protect black life from police — had gotten him into all this trouble with Mack and the Malvo murder.

As for his uncles' breakup, William was dead now, and Clayton had finally rekindled what he'd lost all those years ago. He and Naomi were living together in Austin, where he taught classes at the University of Texas School of Law. They hadn't married yet, but Darren was sure it was coming. It was a mess of a situation that gave him a headache if he spent too much time thinking about it. He was never sure if he was supposed to be aggrieved for William or happy for Clayton. And Brotherhood or no Brotherhood, he felt for Levi King or any kid whose home life was dictated by the messy romantic lives of the adults charged with his care.

He called his mother about an hour outside of Marshall, less than ninety miles from Jefferson, the county seat of Marion County, on the cell phone he'd bought her last month. She answered right away. There was music in the background and a whip of wind. She was outdoors somewhere, radio propped on her janitorial cart, Darren pictured, as she listened to Betty Wright and the rhythm and blues of the put-upon. She was curt with him, vexed at being interrupted and checked up on by her son. "What you want?" she said without turning down the music, and soon Darren heard voices in the background and tinkling sounds too heavy for wind chimes. Beer bottles, he thought. Bell wasn't at work. She was partying somewhere with a crew of folks. No need to punch a clock with Darren slipping her a grip of money on the regular. He cut right to it.

"Where is it?" he said.

"Where is what, boy? Told you I'm busy."

"The gun, Mama. Where in the hell did you put that gun?"

"Hold on, let me take you off speaker-phone."

"Mama —"

"What? They not gon' say nothing," she said. "It's Fisher and some of his people out to Lake Charles. They ain't thinking about no small-town mess."

"You're in Louisiana? What about work?"

"I'm with my boss, so I ain't in no kind of

trouble," she said. "I don't know why you care so much, haven't been around to see me no way."

"I saw you Thursday," he said. "I mowed your lawn."

Her guilt routine was on autopilot, and when she was caught out and corrected, she merely sucked her teeth and said, "What do you want, Darren?"

"Where is it?"

"Safe."

"Where?"

"It's probably best if you don't know, don't you think? Plausible something or other," she said, rooting around in her brain for the word. "Deniability, that's it. I saw that on Investigation Discovery." On the cable box that Darren was also paying for. "I don't want my baby to have to lie."

"I'd only have to lie if someone was asking about the gun," he said. "Which no one will if you don't say a word about what you found."

"I've kept your secret so far."

"It's not just me. It's Mack's life on the line too. They could try to put either one of us in jail for the murder or the cover-up."

"Mack ain't kin to me, so that's not my concern." She put her hand over the phone and asked someone in Lake Charles to pass

79

her a crawdad and some corn, then took her hand away and made Darren a promise: "It's you I'm gon' protect. I'm your mama, not gon' let no one come for you."

He heard something in her voice that made him want to believe her. It was, strangely, one of the most warmly maternal moments he'd ever felt with her. He allowed himself the fanciful thought that he'd read this situation wrong from the beginning. Maybe the reason his mother had removed the murder weapon from the property where he'd been living really *was* to protect her son. Maybe all the times he'd been by her house these two months, all the meals they'd shared, had truly been her way of trying to get closer to him. She'd taken his money simply because he'd offered it. But had she ever outright blackmailed him over the .38 pistol? He had to admit the answer was no. Maybe he was wrong to judge his mother by her past misdeeds, many though they were. "So you haven't talked to the DA?"

Bell let out a rough, throat-clearing laugh. "Do you want me to?"

"No."

"Then stop worrying, son."

"Where is it, Mama?" he said, laying bare his desperation. "I'd just feel better if I knew

80

where it was, if I could get hold of it and secure it some —"

"And get your fingerprints all over it? That's the last thing you need." He heard the top popped off a bottle. Bell took a sip and let out a tiny exhale followed by a soft, ladylike belch. "I told you, son, I got you. We got each other."

"Thank you," he said, feeling momentarily confused, unmoored by the affection he felt from his mother. *I love you, Mama.* He tried it in his head before he said it out loud. It felt right for once. He wasn't sure she'd heard him. The music, the beer bottles, a man and woman laughing in the background, Bell asking for a light for her cigarette. He heard the paper burn as her lungs filled, heard her blow out a stream of air as she might have done to cool the sting of alcohol on a cut when he was young if she'd raised him, been present for any of his pain.

"That's right," she said, soothing him further. "Mama's got you."

Another drag on the smoke, and then: "Speaking of which, Puck is asking about rent again. He saw the cable company come through, that flat-screen you bought me, and he's saying three fifty ain't gon' cut it no more. He wants five hundred a month from now on." Her voice ended in the lilt of inquiry.

"And you want me to pay it?"

"What the hell have we been talking about for the last ten minutes, Darren?" She sounded exasperated, but no more than he felt on the other end of the phone line. Something between them, some hope he'd allowed himself to touch, had been broken, and Darren felt wronged anew. It seemed every time he was ready to lay down their history and start over, to build on the love that was in there somewhere, every time he reached out to forgive her everything, he got his hand slapped. She made her demand. "You think you could run by and pay him for me? Fisher and I gon' be here at least through the weekend," she said.

"I'm working, Mama, heading north to Jefferson right now."

"Well, get that little pretty girl of yours to run it up the highway to my place. We family now, whether she understands it or not —"

"I told you, Mama, she likes you."

She clucked her tongue, her mood souring every second she wasn't getting what she wanted. "Well, family helps family. Don't make me have to do anything to remind you of that fact, Darren. That little pistol of Mack's can stay where I want it . . . or *not.*" Then a word or two to Fisher or whoever in hell she was with, none of it that Darren could follow. His head was spinning; he was dizzy from this emotional round-about. Forty-plus years on this road with her, and he was right back where he'd started. "Love you, son," Bell said. *Love you too, Mama.*

■ ■ ■ ■

PART TWO

■ ■ ■ ■

5.

Deputy Bryan Briggs met Darren near the courthouse, or, rather, he stood at the corner of Polk and Austin waving his arms like a rodeo clown, as if he thought Darren might miss the county courthouse right in front of him, as if Darren were a foreigner who couldn't read street signs. Briggs looked to be in his twenties, though his belly had leaped forward a few decades. He had the paunch and posture of an older man, despite his boyish face, the plain eagerness in his features. He was white, which for law enforcement in Marion County, Texas, nearly went without saying. He watched, hands on his hips, as Darren parked his Chevy truck in a spot along Polk Street downtown, next to a mural of an ancient steamboat called the *Mittie Stephens*. They were only a block from Big Cypress Bayou, once the main source of travel and trade in and out of Jefferson — a town named after the nation's third president and at one time one of the largest cities in the state. The bayou was a broad waterway that fed into Caddo Lake, about eighteen miles to the east, which itself was an old trade route across the border to Louisiana. In the old days, steamboats from Shreveport and New Orleans came through the lake and into the then port city of Jefferson. It's part of what gave the town its peculiar culture, heavily influenced by French settlers from Louisiana. Its town square looked like a shrunken-down French Quarter — colonial and Queen Anne buildings with second-story galleries bordered in intricate wrought iron — but without its sense of humor or even the tiniest hint of debauchery; the city square was like a courtesan who'd found Jesus. There was something pinched about Jefferson, not so much buttoned up as hemmed in, a sense of propriety in its genteel appearance — the quaint red-brick streets downtown and the perfectly manicured residential gardens — that made the city look like it was trying too hard, like it had something to hide.

It was a town that time had passed by.

Once bustling, it was now little more than a sleepy tourist spot, its streets filled with antiques shops and storefronts where you could buy tickets for tours of historic colonial homes in town or for Jefferson's famous ghost walks. You could also buy books about Jefferson's antebellum history, the period of its heyday, before Shreveport overtook Jefferson as a center of bustling river trade; when the rail barons of the Texas and Pacific Railway Company bypassed Jefferson for nearby Marshall, the town was done for good. Darren had been here only once before, when he was twelve, to visit Clayton's freshman-year roommate from Prairie View. Marcus Aldrich had been living in Jefferson for years then, having met and married a white woman who ran one of the two dozen bed-and-breakfasts in town. The marriage had ended, and Clayton had driven north to give his friend a hand moving out of the Dogwood Inn. Though Darren suspected he'd made the two-and-a-half-hour drive to relish an I-told-you-so and to encourage his buddy to finally do something with his PhD in history besides handing out brochures for plantation tours at the inn. Apparently, Darren's life choices weren't the only ones his uncle Clayton had something to say about.

Darren stepped out of his truck, which he'd parked on Polk Street. Deputy Briggs was waiting for him, his fleshy hip leaned against an antique gas street lamp wrapped in Christmas tinsel and tiny bells that tinkled lightly in the faint bayou-scented breeze. They were close enough to Caddo Lake and Louisiana on the other side to catch the peaty scent of swamp water, the musk of oyster shells, and the sweet smell of Spanish moss. It perfumed the streets of Jefferson as much as the smell of fried catfish and gator coming out of the restaurants at lunchtime.

"I'll pull my cruiser around from behind the courthouse," Briggs said. "You can follow me out to the highway. It's a couple of twists and turns to get us there, but you stay close, and I'll make sure you don't get too turned around."

"No need," Darren said, smiling to make clear he appreciated all the fuss, that he meant no discourtesy. "You give me directions, I'm sure I can find it."

"Well, you might and you might not. Hopetown's tucked deep in the woods along Caddo Lake. I drove clear past it the first time I was out there," Briggs said, pulling out his car keys. " 'Sides, I got orders from the sheriff." Who'd gotten his orders from Wilson, Darren knew. This was the deal he'd agreed to. He nodded his assent, then climbed back in his truck to wait for Briggs's escort.

When Darren parked his truck behind Deputy Briggs's white cruiser in the tiny hamlet of Hopetown, Marnie King and Gil Thomason were sitting out front of their trailer, which was painted a weepy blue with white trim, one end propped up on bricks. Nearly seventy-two hours after they'd reported Levi King missing, they were still refusing to let anyone in law enforcement inside without a warrant. Gil Thomason knew his rights, he said, and was listing them loudly when Darren climbed out of his truck. "I mean, goddamn, if the boy was in the house, we wouldn't have called y'all in the first place," he said. Gil looked at his girlfriend, the boy's mother, wanting another person to bear witness to this insanity. But Marnie was staring into the distance, looking at neither Gil nor the sheriff's men gathered in a front yard that was littered with rusted boat parts and strewn trash. She rolled an unlit cigarette between her palms like a worry stone. Finally, she reached into the waistband of her leggings and pulled out a lighter. She lit the cigarette and told Gil to shut the fuck up. Her voice was husky, like aged molasses that had crystallized and developed sharp edges. And she was tiny, her feet the size of a child's. She was wearing a pale pink tank top, and Darren could see the outline of her ribs through the fabric.

Everything in Hopetown looked as mean and underfed as Marnie King.

Her and Gil's trailer was situated in the middle row of a grid of dirt lanes, each populated by mobile housing of some kind: trailers, a couple of vans, and one houseboat that had been dragged off the water and made over for cabin living. Someone had affixed a satellite to its roof, had built a grand walkway to its front door using crushed oyster shells. There were two black lawn jockeys flanking the entrance. Someone with a warped sense of history — and humor — had placed tiny confederate flags in their painted black hands. Darren found himself scanning for signs of the Aryan Brotherhood of Texas, which included checking Gil Thomason's skin for ABT tattoos. Marnie King's boyfriend was wearing a long-sleeved BIG PINES LODGE T-shirt, and the only thing visible from where Darren was standing was the look of indignation on his face. "The fuck is he doing here?" Gil barked.

He was nodding at the black man with

the badge and the hat.

Steve Quinn, sheriff of Marion County, turned to see Darren for the first time. He was in his late thirties, young for his position, with dark hair and white skin that was pockmarked by acne scars. Still, he was handsome, solid-looking. Standing next to a squad car parked in front of the trailer, he gave Darren a good, long once-over, voiced no objection to what he saw, and said, "Ranger Mathews is here to help us find your son."

"*My* son," Marnie said, making it clear. "You talk to his grandmother yet?"

"Again, ma'am, every protocol I got says we got to start here, got to rule out any trouble at home, even the possibility that your son may have run away, that he might be hiding out at a friend's house right —"

"I know exactly where he is," Marnie said. "This is Rosemary's doing."

"Well, if I could take a look at his room, ma'am, I could rule out —"

"What, and give this SOB a chance to snoop through my shit?" Gil said. "I don't give a shit 'bout the star on his chest, not letting a nigger in my house."

Sheriff Quinn sighed with an expression that looked exasperated and vaguely embarrassed. Darren felt a jolt of rage; it made his

93

heart race, made the tips of his fingers tingle. He wanted to slap somebody, Gil Thomason, for one, but also his lieutenant for making him drive two-hundred-plus miles to be insulted to his face. He willed his brain to cool, tried to remember that this was about a nine-year-old kid, tried, as ever, to be the better man. He sighed from the weight of it. He lifted his Stetson from his head and knelt before Marnie King sitting on the steps to her trailer. She smelled of baby powder and cigarettes, her breath fermented and soured by whatever she'd been drinking before the cops showed up. "Ma'am," he said. Gil tried to step between them, prepared to protect Marnie from the strange black man, pressing his knees damn near in Darren's face. The Ranger shook his head sharply and said, "You gon' need to back up by about two feet, son." That *son,* cousin to *boy,* set Gil off.

"Nigger, I will —"

"What?" Darren said, hand on his Colt before Gil could make a move.

Gil backed up, but only by a few inches, and Sheriff Quinn said, "Now, now, let's don't have that." It was unclear if he was talking to Gil or Darren.

To Marnie, Darren spoke with a kindness that did not hide his distaste for her life choices, any one of which could account for the disappearance of her child. "How long has he been gone?" He searched for something in her eyes, which were a muddy green, the same swampy color as the water on Caddo Lake.

"He ain't come home Friday afternoon," she said, bony chin jutting forward. Darren glanced at his wristwatch, as if it had only just occurred to him that it was Monday. "Well, ma'am," he said, "the odds of finding a missing child who's been gone longer than forty-eight hours are very slim. We want to help you find your boy."

It wasn't his real mission here, but they didn't need to know that.

And anyway, locating the missing kid would make him feel better about the plan that had hatched in his brain when he was about a hundred miles shy of Marion County: if he could find any evidence — real or manufactured — to connect Bill King to the murder of Ronnie Malvo, both he and Mack would be off the hook with San Jacinto County and DA Frank Vaughn, and Wilson would have what he needed to nail Bill "Big Kill" King. Ordering a hit on a criminal informant would make for a sweet indictment to add to the federal case against the Aryan Brotherhood of Texas.

95

Darren had already worked out a twisted quid pro quo in his mind, had had a debate with his uncle William on the drive up. Bill would get his kid back in exchange for the rest of his life in prison, which was where he belonged. William, because he was dead, hadn't said a word, and yet Darren could feel his disapproval, cold as haint's breath on his neck. He'd turned up the radio and rolled down the windows in his truck — anything to drown out his fear of falling off the cliff of his own morality. The music was Lightnin' Hopkins and Jessie Mae Hemphill, single-string, sharecropping blues from a time when there was no sense of right and wrong when it came to dealing with white folks. There was only survival.

"He's not *missing*," Marnie insisted. "His grandmother's got him."

Softly, Darren said, "And if she doesn't?"

And that's when he saw the fear, saw that beneath her repeated insistence that the boy's grandmother had taken him, Marnie King wasn't so sure, that it was merely a theory she was clinging to because the alternative, when it flashed across her mind just now, made her shudder. Darren could feel her struggling to hold on to her outrage; he saw a quiver of terror in her knitted brow. It was radiating off her body. She glanced up at her boyfriend, Gil, standing next to the stairs, and clamped it down quick. "This was Rosemary's doing," she said.

Gil nodded, scratching at his hairline, the thick tufts of loose curls just starting to go gray. He had on a loose pair of black Wranglers that were hanging on by a belt with a brick-size buckle that, if it were real silver, could have put a new paint job on the trailer, got it a new set of wheels. He was barefoot in the rocks and dirt around his home, as if he were afraid to go inside for his boots for fear the sheriff would scuttle in behind him. Whatever was in that trailer, for Gil Thomason, it was worth burning time that Levi King didn't have. Darren looked up and saw a teenage girl standing in the front window. She had milky-white skin and eyes ringed in black, and she was wearing a leather jacket two sizes too big. She was staring at the whole scene, Gil and Marnie in front of the trailer door, the sheriff and the deputies, and Darren. They locked eyes, the girl and the Texas Ranger, and now he saw quite clearly that she was crying, had been for some time.

"This is some shit Rosemary King cooked up, trust me," Gil said with the authority of a man who knows his way around a scam. "Take the boy, get the sheriff involved, and

97

then get that judge she put on the bench to cook up some reason to poke around here, some reason to say we ain't fit, and lickety-split, Marnie loses custody, and Rosemary don't gotta pay no more child support."

Sheriff Quinn shook his head. "Y'all the ones called about a missing boy."

"He's *not* missing," Marnie said, her voice shrill and ice cold. "You go talk to that old bitch in Jefferson, and you bring me back my son." Her voice cracked on the last word, cracked something in her wide open. Marnie started to cry, fat drops falling on the pink tank top, darkening the fabric to a deep blood red.

Briggs had been right: Hopetown was hard to find.

It was an unincorporated sliver of land tucked at the end of a one-lane dirt road so choked with vegetation — pines and pin oak shrubs, chickweed growing every which way — that anyone who didn't know what was back here would give up and turn around within the first few yards. The only other way to access the tiny village was by boat, across the northern part of Caddo Lake. But the nearby lakeshore was lined with ancient bald cypress trees draped in Spanish moss the color of an old man's whiskers, the trees' knobby roots standing up out of the water like a line of troops keeping outsiders away. There were people living out here completely hidden from sight by both land and water. The air smelled of peat moss and dead fish and the damp, boggy soil at the shoreline.

And horseshit. Which was odd, because the only four-legged creature in sight was a mangy dog nosing through a Hostess cherry-pie wrapper in the grass.

Darren, Sheriff Quinn, and Deputy Briggs had moved their vehicles to a spot near a row of boathouses a few yards from the shore, so the men could speak freely. Quinn was walking Darren through the boy's last day. "The mom and the boyfriend were running errands out to Jefferson and Marshall, which, knowing Gil Thomason, could mean anything from stopping at Kroger for hair cream and toilet paper to selling credit card numbers under a bridge somewhere. Guy's a total piece of shit. Fake IDs, credit card numbers, and drugs, of course. He's a real jack-of-all-trades lowlife. That's why he don't want us inside."

"Surprised the judge hasn't signed off on a warrant yet."

"I think everybody's hoping there's a simple answer to this deal, that the boy took off or maybe the grandmother *is* involved some way. There've been no shortage of domestic problems coming out of that household," Quinn said, nodding toward the blue and white trailer in the distance. Standing this close to the shoreline, Darren had a wider view of Hopetown. Behind the rows of trailers was a shallow dell, green and lush, verdant to the exact degree that the trailer park was dry and desolate. There was a house or two back there. Not mobile homes, but actual houses built on foundations more stable than bricks and wheels. There was a thatched hut of some sort too, round like a domed mushroom made of grass. Darren thought again of the smell of horses and wondered what was back there, in this other Hopetown. "The kid's had problems," Quinn said. "Skipping school, some petty vandalism. My deputies been out here more than once."

Darren made a face. "He's nine."

"And got a daddy in the pen and a mama shacking up with a criminal. Ain't nobody gon' say it out loud, but I will," the sheriff said. He glanced at the squad car parked behind them, where Briggs sat with his feet out the driver's-side door. He was texting on his phone. "But the Kings don't necessarily inspire a lot of sympathy in these parts. Except for Rosemary. She's a different story."

"Her son Bill King, he's a captain in the Brotherhood."

"Lot of folks willing to forget that. Rosemary King is big shit in Jefferson."

"What about Thomason? Is he ABT?"

"Wannabe," Quinn said. "But those are the worst ones."

Darren nodded. He liked Quinn, felt the guy was shooting straight with him, and the sheriff didn't appear at all resentful of Darren's presence in his county. "Bill King seems to put this on Gil," he said, "thinks Marnie's boyfriend might have done something to the boy or put Levi in danger in some way. Folks is all kinds of hot right now. Hell, I got two kids at home, and I'd have torn this county limb from limb looking for 'em if they were gone. There's something wrong about Thomason for sure, straight trouble. But so far there's no sign of any foul play, nothing like that. The boy just up and disappeared."

He'd left his house in the afternoon, Quinn said. His older sister — the girl in the trailer window — had let Levi take out their granddaddy's boat, even though they both knew Marnie wouldn't have allowed it. The boat hadn't been touched much since Marnie's father died sometime in the fall, and no one was taking any real care of it. But Dana King had a boyfriend over and wanted some privacy. She told Levi to stay gone for a few hours. The boy got himself all the way to Karnack on the other side of Caddo Lake — a body of water so big, Darren came to understand, that parts of it had names unto themselves, as did the handful of islands — some several miles long — that rose up among the water lilies and moss-draped cypress trees. Quinn, who kept a map of the lake in his cruiser, spread it over the hood of the car. He ran his hairy pointer finger across the inlet called Clinton Lake, past Goat Island, and through the bay of Carter Lake to the west, where Levi had spent most of the afternoon at a friend's house, playing video games. The boy, CT, was the first person Dana called when her brother wasn't home by dark. Darren took a closer look at the map. Even on paper, Caddo Lake was bigger than he'd imagined. It looked like a beast with a fire-breathing head to the north — the bayous and creeks shooting from its mouth resembling a forked tongue and flames — and a body so massive it claimed parts of Louisiana. It was a gnarled inland sea, wholly untamed. Darren looked out past the boathouses to Hopetown's craggy shore. Only a skilled sailor could navigate the fortress of bald cypress, the tree roots — or knees, as they were called — like billy clubs sticking out of the water. Caddo Lake was both majestic and macabre. "That's a long distance for a nine-year-old in a shoddy boat."

"It's a different world out here. I've seen seven-year-olds driving fifteen-foot bass boats. They put 'em in canoes out here soon as they can walk. Hell, the old-timers on Caddo like to talk about boating to school, trying to keep their homework dry. The water is just part of everything for folks on the lake."

"Still, something could have happened to him out there."

"Naw, we got an eyewitness says he got the boat home," Quinn said as he glanced back at Deputy Briggs in the other squad car. "Neighbor out that way," he said, pointing past the trailers and vans to that other Hopetown, the green valley and houses across the way. "He says he saw the boy locking up the boathouse. Didn't see the boat itself but assumed he was just coming in for the night. Marnie and Gil wouldn't let us inside that either, but you can see it's locked." He pointed toward an unpainted clapboard shed with a tin roof and a thick padlock looped through the handles on the door. Darren looked up. He saw no streetlights, no lamps affixed to any of the boathouses, no lighting of any kind. "He's sure it was Levi King?"

"You wanna ask him yourself?"

Darren smelled horses again, heard the clop of hooves in the dirt. He knew there were three of them before he turned his head to see the posse on horseback. The first man was black and easily in his late seventies; the other two were younger and astride twin mustangs with coats the color of charcoal. They were Native — Texas Indians — one in his late teens and the other nearing forty, his skin leathered and bronze, his hands on the horse's reins, communicating by tiny movements, gently holding his stallion in place. They were all armed, the men with a .45 revolver each and the teenager with a rifle hanging by a leather strap on his back. The black man looked at Darren and gave a nod and his name. "Leroy Page."

6

They were from that other Hopetown.

The original residents, it turned out.

"Some kind of freedmen's deal, black folks been living back there since after the Civil War," Quinn said as they sat on an ornate sofa in Rosemary King's sitting room, as the black maid had called it when she invited the sheriff and Darren to wait for Madame. They each had a cooling cup of tea in front of them, matching china cups on the gilded coffee table. Neither had touched the tea in the twenty minutes they'd been waiting to see Mrs. King.

Back in Hopetown, Mr. Page had confirmed his account of Friday evening. As the community's oldest resident, he'd taken it on himself to keep the peace in town. "It's been some problems with the new folks moving in," he said without getting specific. "So I make it a point to keep my eyes open." He'd been doing patrol on horseback, he said, "when I saw the boy locking the boathouse there." He gestured to the same rambling shed Quinn had pointed out. "I gave him a nod, but he ain't speak. The way they raised him, *you* know," he said, looking at Darren. Turned out, Leroy Page didn't like the boy much, didn't like his mama or the trash she'd been bringing around Hopetown.

Still, he and the men were offering to help. The older Native man, Donald Goodfellow, said he could get a search team together in less than an hour. Word had spread, and Donald would wish the same thing done if it were one of his kids. The teenager on the other horse was his son Ray. Sheriff Quinn said everybody was getting a little ahead of themselves.

"Heading to talk to the boy's grandmother right now," he said. "Probably get this straightened out before the sun sets." His manner was relaxed in a way that Darren couldn't understand or entirely abide. He asked the old man to describe what the boy was wearing, to be crystal clear about what time of night it was.

Leroy Page frowned, working to get the answer just right.

It was the watery look of the cataracts in his eyes that made Darren realize the man was probably in his eighties. When he'd come off the horse to give his account of Friday night, Darren had read the age in his bones, the slight droop in his posture. He was an elderly man with poor vision upon whose recollection of seeing Levi the sheriff had set a theory: Levi had made it home on Friday night and disappeared around here. Darren thought the sheriff was relying too heavily on unverified facts. He mentioned the water again, but Quinn waved it off. "It only looks deep," he said. "But Caddo ain't but about four feet in some parts. Ain't been nothing you could drown in since the steamboat days, when the water table was higher." Still sounded pretty deep for a nine-year-old.

Quinn took one of the butter cookies on a serving platter, made a face after one bite, and put it back. Whatever, Darren thought. It was Quinn's investigation. Darren was here to fish for what he could on the Brotherhood connection, to find intel for the task force. All he needed was to get in a room alone with Gil, Marnie, or Bill King, and he'd make his plan work. Not a one of them was worth the horseshit he'd had to scrape from the soles of his boots at Rosemary King's front door. That the woman in whose palatial Victorian colonial Darren now sat had raised a captain of the Aryan Brotherhood of Texas — a man who now sat in a Texas penitentiary — made about as much sense as a freedmen's community sharing real estate with Nazis. Meaning it didn't. Not one bit.

Darren had gotten two texts since they'd been waiting.

One odd — his old friend Greg asking, U where i think u are?

And one ominous — Mack texting, We need to talk.

Darren was sliding his phone away when Rosemary King entered her parlor followed by a rakish man slightly younger than her, in his late fifties. Rosemary was a broad-shouldered woman with a head of blondish-gray hair that was coming loose from a chignon. She was flushed. Her cheeks and sternum — peeking through a crisp white shirtwaist dress — were both pink with heat. The same could be said for her guest. The man was wearing a suit jacket — linen, even though it was December — and no tie. Darren had no knowledge of the layout of the house, but it sure appeared they'd just come from upstairs. The curved staircase was behind them, the banister wound with Christmas holly and white poinsettias.

Rosemary asked Mary, her maid, for two

glasses of water. "With ice," she said, sitting down and shooting a sidelong glance at the man beside her. There was something intimate and conspiratorial about the look that made Darren uncomfortable. What exactly had they walked in on, and why hadn't this woman been ready to receive the sheriff who was looking for her missing grandson? "Sheriff, can I have Mary fetch you anything else? Would you prefer a Coke or some coffee?"

"No, ma'am."

"Ranger?"

"I'm sure Mary's done enough," Darren said.

Rosemary turned her attention back to the local sheriff. "Steve, I told you when you called yesterday, I haven't seen the boy since before Thanksgiving. Marnie doesn't exactly make it easy for me to have a relationship with my grandson."

Darren leaned forward and said, "Perhaps this is something better discussed in private." He gave a courteous nod to the man sitting in the King Louis armchair across from him. The man smiled, tickled in some way.

"Oh, he can stay," Rosemary said, reaching for the glass of water Mary proffered before it even hit the coffee table. "Roger

Pressman's my lawyer."

Darren shot a look at Quinn, who nodded and said, "Roger."

"Steve."

The two men knew each other.

Roger Pressman drank his ice water in three gulps and then held out the glass for Mary to get another. The black woman, who'd made no direct eye contact with Darren, returned from whence she'd come without saying a word.

"Any reason why you felt the need to have your attorney present?"

Rosemary waved off the thought. "He just stopped by."

Again, that look between the two.

Roger smiled and said, "But as long as I'm here."

Rosemary fiddled with the pearl-drop necklace she was wearing. "Roger handles all personal and professional matters for the King family. This business with Levi is of concern to him as well. I'd feel more comfortable if he stayed."

Quinn nodded.

But Darren thought the whole thing had an air of cunning. He even wondered if the apparent interrupted afternoon liaison was a put-on. Hadn't she known Quinn and Darren were on their way? Deputy Briggs, who was sitting in his cruiser outside by the mansion's carriage house, had phoned ahead.

Darren looked into the older woman's eyes. They were a robin's-egg blue, nestled in the pale crepe of her skin. There was something probing there. She was watching Darren Mathews as closely as he was watching her. Twice, her gaze darted down to the badge on his chest. The fact of its presence, of Darren in her house, seemed to catch her unawares each time she looked at him, made her shift ever so slightly in the gilded chair she was sitting in. For that reason, maybe, she addressed Sheriff Quinn alone; Darren was as invisible as the black hands that brought her ice water. "I haven't seen him," she said to Quinn. "And I wouldn't put it past his mother to make up a story like this just to get my attention, to find some way to get more money out of me."

"I'm sorry," Darren said. "But how would your grandson going missing be a way for Marnie to get money from you?"

Rosemary directed her answer to Quinn. "Who's to say she doesn't have the boy holed up somewhere just to scare me and demand more money?"

Roger put a cautioning hand on her knee. "Let's not open ourselves up to a charge of

111

slander. We know how opportunistic Marnie and Gil can be." He had a ruby signet ring on his right hand and a diamond pinkie ring on his left, but no wedding band.

"She gets two hundred a month from me and still has her hand out."

"Two hundred is not that much money for two kids," Darren said.

"The older one is not my kin," Rosemary said. "Marnie is looser than a circus tent in a windstorm, as my mother used to say. Two hundred is what the judge ordered Bill to pay in the divorce. Child support for Levi. I'm just covering the cost until he gets out of jail." She shot a glance at Roger. "Soon, we hope."

"Your son wrote a letter to the governor," Darren said.

The mention of her son from Darren's mouth lit a match to Rosemary's already simmering dislike of him. She again refused to address him directly, telling Roger, "I don't want to talk about Bill."

"Bill has been writing to the governor for the past three years," Roger answered for her, a chivalrous act to keep her from having to talk to Darren, as if he'd gently escorted her by the elbow around a puddle in the road. It gave Darren an odd feeling of dislocation; for a second he actually didn't trust his visibility. He felt as if he'd wandered onto a movie set. He could see the actors, but Darren was reflected in none of the action around him. "Bill King has changed inside," Roger said. "He's gotten right with Christ. He's renounced his former ways, the ugly things he's done. We have every belief that the parole board and the governor himself will see fit to consider him for early release."

"It's time," Rosemary said brightly, with the confidence of a woman used to getting her way.

Quinn said, "Ranger Mathews is a part of a joint task force that's investigating the Aryan Brotherhood of Texas. Any information your son has that could help authorities might give him a leg up on early release."

"No," Roger said quickly. Again, he patted Rosemary on the knee, the gesture this time not so much one of caution but of reassurance, his hand lingering there. Rosemary pressed her coral-painted lips together till the skin around them reddened and then turned purple. Her jaw was clenched so tight, Darren could see the vein in her temple, serpentine and angry. "I've instructed my son to make a clean break with that trash," she said. "He will come home with no burdens. He will not spend the rest of his life looking over his shoulder for someone aiming to get even with him for telling tales out of church. He will serve his time. Then he will start over. I told him to forget he was ever involved with Nazis."

Oh, really?

Darren knew he had the power to wipe the smug surety off her face, and it thrilled and frightened him how good it felt. He couldn't believe he was actually entertaining the idea of fabricating evidence, didn't recognize himself at all in this moment. He had the terrifying thought that the feelings of invisibility and dislocation were coming from his own mind. "I'm afraid it's not that simple," he said. He felt a slow rage building inside of him at the idea that Bill "Big Kill" King could just forget that he'd been a member of a gang whose initiation rite was the obliterating of a black life. He had savagely killed a man and never done any time for it after a Marion County jury had let him walk; it was selling opioids and meth to whites that had crossed a line for the good folks out here. "You talk about the Aryan Brotherhood being trash. Well, some of that trash came out of your house."

"I did not raise a racist."

"Says the woman who's barely spoken to

me since I walked in."

"I have no problems with black people, Ranger Mathews. I have two of them in my home, Mary and Clyde, my driver. I just don't like strangers in my house, especially ones looking to use my son. Bill has changed. He wants nothing to do with the Aryan Brotherhood, and he won't say a word to you." Sensing how that hung in the air, she quickly added, "And not because you're black."

Despite himself, Darren smiled. "Now, see, I wasn't even thinking that."

Sheriff Quinn groaned as if he'd belched up something sour. "Whoo, boy."

Roger had his head down, having newly discovered a loose thread in his pants. But Darren did not suffer from the peculiar affliction that felled many a well-meaning white person — an allergic reaction to race talk, emotional hives breaking out and closing the throat completely — so he wasn't fazed by any of this. "Mrs. King, your son —"

"I'm not saying I've always been comfortable with black people," she said, rather softly, again playing with the white pearl at her throat. She'd grown pensive, thinking about what had happened to her son. "I don't socialize with them. It's just not like that around here; it's not how I was raised. My people came over from Louisiana right before the Civil War, and we just had our ways of doing things. Never meant blacks any harm — they're just not *my* people, if you know what I mean?" Frighteningly, Darren saw both Roger and Quinn, whom he'd come to like, nod their heads in understanding. Darren felt his limbs stiffen on the ridiculous sofa. "I didn't fuss when they integrated the high school," she said. "I had a colored girl in my home economics class. She made the best lemon Bundt cake I've ever tasted, and she smelled like lavender and honey," she added in a tone of mild surprise. "We both liked the same type of lip gloss. We even talked about boys. But I would never have brought her home. I don't believe I've ever had a black person in my home, not counting Mary and Clyde, of course . . . and you."

"Rosie," Roger said, a soft attempt to stop her from talking.

She shook her head, indignant, mad she'd been bullied into admitting any of this. Her neck grew tall, as did her sense of herself as a good person. "But listen," she said to Darren, "I have never discriminated against a black person in my life, Mexican neither. I've never kept them out of my hotel. I mean, not since it was illegal to do that sort of thing. We have always followed the law."

Rosemary King, it turned out, owned the Cardinal Hotel, where Darren would be staying in town. She wanted that point made and even said she'd call ahead to ensure that Ranger Mathews got one of their best rooms, a suite on the first floor with a view of the garden in back. The luxury hotel was one of the oldest in the state. Her people had built it the year they'd moved from New Orleans to Jefferson and turned it into the most exclusive palace for moneyed tradesmen and shipping barons during the nineteenth and early twentieth centuries; there were even rumors that President Benjamin Harrison had stayed at the Cardinal. But guest records had been lost in a devastating fire in 1910.

The hotel was her family legacy. And Bill's too, if she could get him to turn his life around. "He was a good kid," she said. "I didn't see the signs; what can I say? One day he's friends with everybody, then he gets into a fight with a black boy at school, and suddenly I hear the n-word a lot more, suddenly he starts socializing more with boys who don't like the blacks. Then the little things — egging houses in the black part of town, kid stuff, you know. Then refusing to let Mary cook his food. I saw all of it happening; I just didn't know it would lead where it did. It's like I looked up one day and my sweet son had tattoos on his arms and a mean streak a mile long. And then he stopped coming home altogether, started hanging with some real bad guys, some down the highway in Marshall, some right here in Jefferson."

Darren told her, "Gil Thomason might be one of those bad guys."

"Wannabe, at least," the sheriff said.

Rosemary spit out her assessment: "White trash."

"Your son seems to think Gil might have hurt Levi in some way."

She looked down at her hands, two fists in her lap. She unclenched them and then smoothed a few wrinkles in her dress. "I wouldn't doubt it."

Something shifted in that moment.

Quinn felt it too. He caught Darren's eye.

Things were looking bad for the kid.

Marnie and Gil Thomason had sworn he was with his grandmother while refusing to let the sheriff and his men search their trailer. And here was Rosemary saying she hadn't seen her grandson in weeks. "I know that must sound terribly cold to you," Rosemary said. "But the truth is, I never got to know Levi. Marnie rarely allows us to spend time together. I don't even know how well he remembers his father. He was just a pup when Bill got himself in trouble. The hope has always been that once Bill got out, the two of them could become father and son for real, and I could be a real grandmother. But maybe the State of Texas has got *its* way of punishing Bill for what he's done, and God's got other ideas." Darren saw her eyes water, but the tears, he felt, were for the loss of the dream she couldn't fulfill for her son rather than for the nine-year-old who was still missing. Wherever Levi King was, he was on his own.

7.

They searched the house anyway. Twenty rooms, including a library, a study, a sewing room, and a dining room large enough to double as a ballroom, as it did in the late 1800s when Rosemary King's people settled in Jefferson. After Rosemary's great-great-grandmother was widowed, she'd sold the family plantation in Louisiana, moved to Jefferson, and built the Cardinal, which became the centerpiece of the town's sense of itself as the cosmopolitan capital of East Texas in the steamboat era. She became a grand dame of Jefferson society but never remarried and raised a daughter in the house that Rosemary King had lived in since she was born. The dining room had once hosted governors and bankers and plantation owners from as far away as Denton and Dallas. The house on North Vale Street was the largest in Marion County, Quinn said, and was a regular feature on the circuit of tours of historic homes and gardens in Jefferson. Once a year, Rosemary allowed the mayor and aldermen to hold parts of the town's elaborate Civil War reenactments on her front lawn. She was, Quinn made it known, a very big deal around Jefferson.

She put no restrictions on the search, even silencing Roger when he'd tried to object. It was Mary who walked the sheriff and Darren through the house, as if they were regular guests whom it would be rude to leave wandering around the place looking for the facilities. Darren asked her if she'd ever met Mrs. King's grandson Levi. She said, "Once," speaking so softly that if Darren hadn't seen her lips move, he might have thought he'd imagined the entire exchange. Though Quinn had gotten an "Afternoon, sir," Mary avoided eye contact with Darren; he wondered if it pained her for him to see her in her maid's uniform, a collared, ill-fitting, double-breasted dress that must have been a hand-me-down from the previous girl or maybe the one before that. Rosemary had said she'd never had a black guest in her home, so until today, Mary's humiliation had been visible to white callers only and thus private in some way. Darren bearing witness to her servitude made it real, and she seemed to resent him for it.

There was no sign of the boy in the house, not even in the bedroom that had clearly been reserved for his visits, which Rosemary had said were few and far between. There was a twin bed covered with a red comforter dotted with pictures of quarter horses, saddles, and spurs. The walls were painted a pale blue. There was a desk in a corner with only a single book on its attached shelf — the King James Bible — and the only toys in the room were a plastic dump truck that would interest no child over the age of five and a stuffed cocker spaniel lying on its stomach. The room had the same desolate feel as the one that had been set up for Bill King's return home from prison, both of them waiting empty and untouched.

They searched the carriage house too.

Clyde, Rosemary's driver, smoked a cigarette along the side of the building that housed a copper '53 Mercedes and a silver late-model Cadillac, both shiny as freshly minted coins. He nodded to Darren but didn't speak either. There was nothing indicating that Levi had been in either vehicle. Still, Darren cringed watching the sheriff compromise potential evidence by running his ungloved hands inside both cars. They would need a clean sweep of the cars one day, wouldn't they? Darren wasn't sure where that thought had come from. Was he saying he thought the old woman was somehow connected to her grandson's disappearance? Not exactly, but she was being cagey about something. Why the hell else had her lawyer been present? As a former law student, he knew he was wrong for thinking like that. But he didn't like the woman. A second later, Quinn declared their work done. He neither dismissed Darren nor invited him to come along after he told Briggs he was heading back to the office. "I'll let you know if we hear something on that warrant," he said to Darren before turning and walking down the drive to his cruiser.

"Something's off," Darren told Wilson on the phone. He mentioned the odd dynamic between Marnie and her boyfriend, Gil, the way she cowered, and the fact that the boy's grandmother had a lawyer hanging around, plus there was the bizarre lack of urgency on the part of the county for a lost kid from a trailer park. He liked Quinn, he said, but nobody seemed all that hot to find this kid. "Except for Bill King," he said.

"I'm working with the state to get you in

123

to talk to him as soon as possible."

"Unless he's hiding the kid in his cell, I don't see what good that does."

"Bill King's potentially sitting on a shit-ton of evidence against the ABT."

"He won't talk," Darren said, remembering Rosemary's stridency and presenting it as fact here. Some part of him knew he was putting on a show, not wanting Wilson to think him too eager to get in a room alone with King.

"We'll see about that," Wilson said.

Darren remembered the sister all of a sudden, the image of her crying inside the trailer, and he mused aloud about finding a way to talk to her alone.

"Don't you dare. This is Sheriff Quinn's deal to run. Marion County didn't ask for an assist. Your presence there is a courtesy offered by the local sheriff. Act like it. Remember your mission out there. Just make sure you're in that trailer when the warrant comes through."

"Yes, sir."

"And hey, Mathews, you didn't mention anything to Frank Vaughn, the San Jacinto County DA, about Ronnie Malvo being an informant for the task force, did you?"

"Of course not," Darren said, feeling an irrational fear that Wilson could read his mind, the things he had planned to redirect that case. "Why?"

"He's been calling my office," Wilson said, sounding puzzled, and for a moment Darren pictured him hunched over a stack of those pink message slips his secretary still used. "Left word Friday and then again today. Mentioned your name both times. Want to be clear we're on the same page before I call back."

"Of course, sir," Darren affirmed dutifully, damn near clipping his words like a soldier's steps. Why was Frank Vaughn calling his boss?

"The good work you done down in Lark got you over the hump of people pointing the finger about you knowing more than you've let on about the Malvo deal. Steer clear of it now, hear? Keep your eyes on the prize out there in Jefferson, Mathews. We got a real shot at flushing the Brotherhood out of Texas."

"Copy," Darren said flatly before ending the call.

He resented the suggestion that he, of all people, didn't understand the danger of the Aryan Brotherhood, that he was somehow shirking his duty to fight this particular form of homegrown terrorism. It pissed him off, frankly, made his blood run hot. He understood the threat of the Brotherhood in a way that Wilson never would, and he privately derided his lieutenant's naivete, saw privilege in his earnest belief that the ABT was going anywhere. Darren thought he finally knew better, and it turned something heavy that had been sitting in his stomach for weeks now. It raised a sour taste in the back of his throat and put a name to what he'd been feeling: *despair.* Away from his daily office drudgery, the sterile combing of records that kept him off the road, he could finally admit that some part of him had merely been going through the motions these past weeks. In truth, he was the least optimistic he'd ever been that the Brotherhood and what it stood for would ever truly be eradicated. There were too many of them; in tattoos or neckties, they were out there. Everywhere. The country seemed to grow them in secret, like a nasty fungal disease that spread in the dark places you don't ever dare to look. The country was in more trouble than any task force could handle. Darren knew this better than Wilson, better than the entire department maybe, no matter how much it scared him to admit it. He thought of Levi King and reached for the boy like a twisted lifeline, a dull ray of hope. Darren couldn't stamp out hatred in a day, but what he *could* do was find a nine-year-old and give himself permission to nail the boy's father for Malvo's murder.

Bill King's freedom would be the price he paid for his son's life.

He was standing next to his Chevy truck parked a few feet from the Cardinal Hotel, a red-brick building that was a full city block long, with black shutters and a second-story balcony where four Lone Star flags flew. Briggs was out of his cruiser as soon as he saw Darren was off his phone. He hiked up the beige pants of his uniform and asked the Ranger if he was hunting for a place to eat. Briggs had a buddy who ran the kitchen at the Steamboat Palace, and he could probably get them a table. Darren looked around the nearly empty streets of downtown Jefferson and suppressed a chuckle. Even though it was only four o'clock in the afternoon, he told Briggs that unless he heard word about the search of Marnie and Gil's trailer, he was turning in for the night. Briggs offered to help get him settled in the room, keep an eye on things, as had been his orders.

Darren made that sound foolish. "Don't need someone to watch me sleep."

127

"But Sheriff said —"

"If I leave the hotel, I'll call, I promise. You'll be by my side," Darren said. Briggs nodded, liking the idea that he was needed. "But I'm good for now."

He grabbed the duffel he always kept in the cab of his truck. He tossed the strap over his shoulder and nodded to Briggs. The hotel's receptionist saw him through the window and had him checked in "on the house" by the time he approached the front desk in the lobby, which strongly resembled Rosemary King's gilded parlor, although the Cardinal Hotel showed its age in a way that both Rosemary and her home did not. Seen up close, the baseboards were scuffed, and there was dust on the red velvet curtains; the carpet in his suite was worn in the hallway to the bathroom, which had an ancient claw-foot tub, and one of the windows didn't open. Still, there was a weight to the place, a sense of history that was both regal and sad, a loss of glory in every ornate detail. Kind of like the town itself. Darren sat on the edge of the four-poster mahogany bed, heard its springs creak beneath him; the mattress emitted a smell of rose water and dust. He waited until he was sure Briggs had finally gone, and then he walked outside, climbed into his truck, and headed back to Hopetown.

Darren didn't even know what the kid looked like, had nothing to show Leroy Page to confirm or deny whether this was the boy he'd seen Friday night. Short of announcing his intentions to Sheriff Quinn, there was only one way to get his hands on a photograph of Levi King. He drove hunched over the steering wheel — ignoring a second call from Mack — so he could pay attention to every ditch-like rut off Farm Road 727, every weed-choked path, to be sure he didn't miss the narrow red-dirt road that led to Hopetown. His tires were coated with it by the time he pulled in front of Marnie and Gil's blue and white trailer. The sun had wandered below the tops of the cypress trees on Caddo Lake to the west, and a honeyed light poured through the Spanish moss, dotting the surface of the water with circles of gold. Inland, dozens of loblolly pines and hundred-year-old live oaks ringed their arms around the trailer park, giving the place a warm, homey feel it didn't deserve.

He had a hard heart for the folks out here. Two trailers down, some of Marnie and Gil's neighbors were doing a fish fry out of the back of a van that was covered in bumper stickers and had seashells glued to the doors, large rhinestones affixed to the luggage rack. There was a DON'T TREAD ON ME flag hanging in one of the windows, and a beach towel with the state of Texas crossed through with dixie stripes spread out inside the front windshield. Darren could hear the pop and hiss as cornmeal hit a vat of hot grease bubbling in an old oil drum. A white woman in her fifties stood next to a gas-station cooler full of cod or catfish, rolling another fillet across a plastic plate covered in meal and flour. Cigarette dangling from the corner of her red painted lips, she said with little fanfare, "Nigger Town's that way," the second Darren stepped from his truck. He kept a hand near the Colt .45 in his holster as a bearded man emerged from the van, tilting the whole thing to one side as he stepped out onto the dirt. He took one look at Darren and let out a whistle, two fingers in the corners of his mouth, then yelled out, "Gil!"

The door to the blue and white trailer opened suddenly, ricocheting off the side of the structure as Gil stepped out. He was still barefoot but now had a .38 tucked into the waist of his blue jeans. "The fuck?" he said. " 'Less you got a warrant, you need to get back in that truck and get gone."

130

The dude from the van started walking over, and in seconds it was two against one, and Darren remembered that he hadn't told a soul where he was. He could draw, but it went against every rule of de-escalation in his training. He kept one hand near the Colt and held the other out in front of him to show he needed cool heads all around. "I'm here about Marnie's kid," he said.

"You talked to Rosemary?"

"Searched her place and everything," Darren said. "He's not there."

A strange look flashed across Gil's face. Darren thought he caught a flicker of fear, followed by a prolonged and affected look of utter bafflement. He ran his fingers through his loose hair, shook his head as if Darren had just told him water wasn't wet. "Well, the little fucker sure as shit ain't here. Maybe he ran off somewhere. Marnie don't want to believe it, but he ain't no saint, that one."

"Need your help with something, Gil," Darren said. "In case this ain't a runaway type deal, in case that boy is out there somewhere in a lot of trouble."

"I don't have to tell you nothing."

"Who is it, Gil?" the bearded neighbor asked.

The woman with the painted lips said,

"Bo, you want your pistol, hon?"

"I'm a Texas Ranger, and you brandish a weapon, I'll arrest you on the spot. This here, ain't not a bit of this is any concern of yours. Go on, now."

To Gil, Darren softened his tone, reminding himself that this was all about a nine-year-old no one had laid eyes on for three days. "I don't need to come inside. I'm just hoping for a picture of the boy, something to show your neighbors, folks who live up that way," he said, pointing past the trailer park to the part of Hopetown the woman cooking fish had so matter-of-factly called Nigger Town. "Sheriff Quinn got reports that a man by the name of Leroy Page might have seen Levi on Friday evening. It's crucial that we confirm that as soon as possible. He's the best lead we have right now."

The bearded neighbor nodded to Gil. "You want me to get the others?"

Gil shook his head, smiling faintly now, wearing the look of a wolf having stumbled upon a wounded white-tailed deer. *This gon' be easy,* his expression said. He yelled over his shoulder into the open door of the trailer, "Dana!" It was Marnie who came out of the trailer first. She was unsteady on her feet, her face flushed from an afternoon of drinking. Darren would recognize that gait anywhere. Dana, the teenage girl he'd seen earlier, poked her head out next. Gil told her, "Get this man a picture of your brother. One from the school, not them your mama took. Get it now." Dana disappeared into the darkness of the trailer.

Marnie turned to Darren and started shaking her head. "What's he saying, Gil?" she said, her voice clotting with snot before a sob wrenched itself free of her control and she wept. "He ain't find my boy?"

Darren shook his head. "No, ma'am." He heard a television playing. *Jeopardy!* or *Wheel of Fortune,* one of those. The applause was too bright, too much, coming out of the tiny trailer. Dana returned with a wallet-size photograph, bent at the corners. She held Darren's gaze when she handed it to him. She had the same wide-set muddy-green eyes that stared back at Darren from the photo in his hand. Levi was blond, hair lighter than his mother's and his sister's, and he saw some of Rosemary in the boy's face, something vaguely patrician in his bearing that did not fit the world around him. There was something else too. You had to look closely to see it, but it was there behind the eyes, the tiny upturn of his mouth. *Rage.*

8

The original settlement of Hopetown now called to mind a ghost town, the rotting wood shells of an old church and a general store standing gray and skeletonized, empty houses dotting the landscape, weeds and wildflowers coming up through the porch boards, tree roots tilting the foundations. And yet there was life back here, in this other Hopetown; fruit trees and cornfields and lush vegetable gardens stretched out in front of the few houses that still stood tall and proud, painted in yellows and shell pinks, dusky blues — except Leroy Page's home, which was as white as the Christmas snow that occasionally fell on Caddo Lake. A strong smell of fresh paint lingered about the house when Darren climbed out of his truck in front of the cottage. It was one story with a large attic window, an unblinking eye on the world past Mr. Page's tidy front porch. He was growing collards and turnips, rainbow chard and cucumbers, had a pecan tree shading one side of his house. He was picking the last of its harvest off the ground beneath the tree, his back hunched as he scooped up the nuts and dropped them into a crinkled paper bag in his hand. His house sat on a quarter acre next to the stables and a conical grass hut that rested atop a hillock, a mound of compact earth. Donald Goodfellow and his son were seeing to the three horses.

Leroy Page pushed himself to standing and nodded at Darren. "You can tell the sheriff we ain't turned up nothing yet. Sun's setting soon. We'll be back at it tomorrow." He hollered for Ray, Donald's son, to run the pecans up to his grandmother. "Tell her I'll take a half dozen eggs for 'em." Ray, who'd come running as soon as the older man called his name, took the paper bag and started cutting across a field, heading for a yellow house twenty or so yards from Mr. Page's. There were no streets in this part of Hopetown, at least none that hadn't been overgrown by time and wild grass, so there was nothing separating neighbor from neighbor back here; it was as if they all shared the same plot of land, were all one big family. In fact, Ray's grandmother, a short, compact woman with a face bronzed and freckled with moles, came out on her front porch to receive the bag of pecans and hollered out to Mr. Page, "Eggs is gone, Leroy, Lou and her girls got 'em first, but I got a tray of red-corn pudding in the oven. We serving at six thirty if you want to eat with us tonight." Mr. Page nodded in a noncommittal way, the gesture likely impossible for the woman to decipher at a distance. To Darren, he shook his head. "Margaret knows I can't eat her corn pudding. The Pages, black folks in Hopetown, we took ours sweet. The red in her red-corn pudding is chopped habanero peppers, and I'll be up all night if I take even a bite of that." He shrugged. "I grow 'em but can't eat 'em no more."

Darren told Mr. Page that he needed to follow up on a few things, that he was here on official business. The old man nodded agreeably. "Come on in, then. I don't stay out here after dark no more, least not without my pistol."

They moved through the dim house, passing framed family photos on the walls, sepia prints in mahogany frames. Stacks of newspapers crowded the hallway, along with fishing equipment, paint supplies, and abandoned quilting projects, swatches stuffed in an oak secretary. In the kitchen, a radio sat atop the Frigidaire. A tinny Jessie Mae Hemphill blues was playing, the prayer of a country violin. *Like a tree planted by the water, I shall not be moved.*

"And you're sure, Mr. Page, that this is the boy you saw locking up the boat shed Friday evening?" Darren held out the school photo.

The old man hardly glanced at it. "I known that boy since he was a baby," he said, pulling a Miller High Life from the fridge. He popped the top with an opener he kept on his key ring. "It was the King boy, sure as I'm standing here."

"And what time was this?"

"Half past six, maybe a quarter to seven." He took a sip of the beer.

Darren ignored his own thirst and glanced at his watch. He took stock of the sky through the kitchen window, the view of Ray's grandmother's yellow house and the lake beyond. It wasn't quite dark, but it would be soon. It was only six fifteen. The old man guessed what Darren was getting at. "I had my light on me," he said, pointing to a homemade tool belt hooked on a nail on the wall from which hung a silver flashlight. "I was on patrol that night."

"Yeah — what is that?" Darren said,

remembering the horses and the guns, the feel of a posse on the hunt. "Some kind of neighborhood-watch thing?"

"It's legal, whatever it is," the old man said, eyeing Darren with mistrust.

Darren threw up his hands to show he meant no harm, that beneath the badge, he was still a black man. "With neighbors like you got," he said, coloring his tone so it was clear he meant the residents of the trailer park he had to pass through to get to Mr. Page's part of Hopetown, "I can't say that I blame you."

"They ain't neighbors," Mr. Page said, slamming the beer bottle on top of the shellacked wood of the kitchen table. "Them folks down there is trespassing."

"What's that, now?"

"They living on my land," he said, gesturing to the house, the yard and gardens beyond, the stables and buildings, his indignation reaching all the way to the turnoff from FM 727, the road that led to Hopetown. "All this is mine."

Leroy Page had been born in this house, his mama and his grandmama too, he said. His people had settled these parts as free blacks after the Civil War, had built a utopia on the shores of the great lake, tilled the soil with the values they held most dear —

138

not just liberty and self-sufficiency, but also forgiveness. *Forgiveness* was a word from the masters' Bible that they'd been forbidden to read. But grace came naturally to Leroy Page's ancestors, was built into their DNA, a native intelligence that told them that true freedom was letting white folks go. You could rage over what they done, or you could be free. It wasn't a twofer type of deal. "Black folks," Leroy said, "are the most forgiving people on earth."

Darren couldn't place the look on his face, didn't know if it was pride or shame he was witnessing. This was a point his uncles had often debated ferociously, whether forgiveness made black folks saints or stooges. The year Darren stopped going to church — claiming at twelve to be too old for Sunday school — William, back in the house in Camilla on some short errand his brother had allowed, sat Darren down at the kitchen table and said, "This family has flourished under the teachings of Christ, son; we have made a life based on fellowship and service and forgiveness." Clayton actually snickered at the kitchen sink, where he was rinsing turnips that he'd grown in the garden himself. That word was dangerous, Clayton said. It gave white folks the idea that impunity was theirs for the taking, for in a world where forgiveness was forever being served like an all-you-can-eat buffet at the Lunch Bucket in town, what was their incentive to pass fair laws, to police with integrity, to refrain from spitting on folks on the street?

"It's not 1966, Pop," Darren had said, just to show he could keep up.

"No, it's 1986, and you see that Alabama cracker that Reagan's trying to put on the federal bench?"

"Sessions will never be confirmed," William said, lighting one of the Lucky Strikes he smoked until his death. He had always kept a large box of matches on their kitchen table for this purpose, and it was the first time Darren noticed that Clayton had kept in place this reminder of his twin brother.

"The point is they have the gall to appoint a Klan-loving fool. Forgiving them for everything before the Voting Rights Act is what makes them think they have the right. We done we-shall-overcomed ourselves right into this mess."

"But you marched, Pop," Darren said. This conversation felt like a greater sacrilege than the talk of him skipping out on church. "What are you saying?"

"I'm saying you have to forever hold them to account. Look away at your own peril." He set the wet turnips on a washcloth.

140

"Forgiveness has a limit."

It was a luxury black folks couldn't afford, Clayton said.

William looked at his nephew. "Darren, maybe I need to head back to Sunday school with you since I don't remember where in the Bible it said that."

Clayton, he said, mistook his Christian faith for weakness. "I know who I am, who my people are. I know the power of our grace, of our faith. Real forgiveness has no limits," he said, before allowing that, yes, Clayton was right, that "it's only possible when the pain of the original offense has ceased."

"Well, good luck with that," Clayton said caustically as he filled a pot with tap water for boiling. "How long you and Naomi been married now?"

He meant it as a bitter joke, one he was man enough to laugh at. William chuckled too, but it sounded hollow and sad. Soon, the brothers went back to not speaking, Darren's home life again emptied of his uncle William's presence.

In Mr. Page's kitchen, the old man finished his beer and opened another. For decades, he said, Hopetown had been a self-contained community, with a church and a school, a decent drinking hole with live blues and zydeco on weekends, a general store, and a meeting hall where they held nativity plays and elections. Leroy's great-great-grandfather had been the town's first mayor. Every member of the Page family, going back generations, had served on the town council at one point or another, up until the town lost its incorporation back in the late 1970s when black folks started leaving, preferring life in Marshall, Longview, or Dallas — places that offered more for them than a literal backwater in Marion County. Even Jefferson wasn't enough of a draw; the town's top industry was tourism, the reselling of an antebellum glory that hadn't gone all that well for black folks the first time around. There were better jobs, better lives to be had far away from Hopetown. As black families left, one by one, Leroy bought up much of the abandoned land and vowed to stay in the place he considered his birthright, but time ate away at the plan like moths nibbling at boiled wool. To speak of it made his eyes cloud over, made his voice grow wistful and thick with longing. "I was gon' die here," he said. He nodded, admiring some picture of the place he held in his mind. "Yes, sir, this here, this little piece of heaven. I was gon' spend the rest of what God give me right

142

here — fishing, taking care of my horses, growing my collards and peppers."

"I grow peppers too," Darren said, the words shooting out with the eager delight of a man meeting a fellow countryman in a foreign place. He looked into the old man's eyes, which were dark as roasted chicory and set in a face that was long and weathered by time, and he thought he understood the man at once, his connection to the land, to the roots that had raised him up. Mr. Page, too, seemed to regard Darren anew, saw something in him that met his approval. "My people got land too," Darren said. "Down to San Jacinto County, twelve acres the Mathews family has held on to since not long after Hopetown was founded."

"So you understand what it took to build all this. Don't seem right to piss it away. But ain't nothing left for nobody else but me, I guess. I'm the last one. My girls stayed through high school, out to Jefferson, but they were done come college. Got one in Dallas, the other selling real estate up to Arkansas. She on me to sell all this, come live with her family in Little Rock. They got a pool, she said. What I'm gon' do with a pool growing up next to that my whole life?" He pointed to the majesty of Caddo Lake, just a few yards out the kitchen window. It was past dusk now, and it was hard to tell the cypress trees from their gnarled shadows, what was real and what wasn't. Again, Darren got a sudden image of Levi King out on that water, alone in a boat, just before sundown.

"What about the trailers, Mr. Page?" he said.

He remembered Gil Thomason's shit-eating grin when he'd mentioned the name Leroy Page, and it niggled at him, the sense that he made a misstep back there. "You've had some trouble with the boy's family out that way?"

"Ain't had no problem with the boy's grandfather. Lester Wayne. I rented him a few acres back in the eighties, when it was clear Hopetown was on the dying side of history. When it was just me and what's left of Margaret and her people, Donald and Ray, Margaret's sister and her kids. Some of her cousins."

"You rent to them too?"

"Don't charge nothing but a couple dollars a month, just to make the contract binding. My daughter Erika, she taught me that. But I won't take no real money from the Caddos living here. This was all theirs to begin with, even before you and me, son. The Indians was here before the French,

144

the Spanish, the English, *and* the Africans. You know what the Hasinai — that's kind of like a tribe within a tribe, you feel me, them's the Caddos what come from around here, north to Arkansas and down to Nacogdoches — anyway, you know what their word for 'ally' is? *Tayshas.* That's right. *Tayshas. Tejas.* Texas. The people in my family have always looked out for the Indians. Just like they always looked out for us. *Ally.* That's what we are. Friends. Family. I owe them my life."

"The trailers, sir," Darren said, wanting to control his first real interview on this case, feeling the town dynamics here might be at play when it came to Levi King's disappearance. "And your relationship with the boy's family?"

"Lester was the first trailer, the only one till this summer. He moved out here after his wife died down in Marshall, set up that little trailer and kept to himself. He was an old redneck, sure he was. Got drunk and fished most days of his life. But him being without his wife, I cut him a lot of slack. My girls and I lost their mother early, so I knowed him, kind of. Now, Lester could talk mean, about the loud, dirty colored folk in town, had a little ol' dixie flag on the antenna of his El Camino. But he treated me decent, always paid his rent on time, and on occasion me and him got to talking. He and I served in the army around the same time, come to find out. Neither of us saw combat and had feelings about what we might have missed, how guns and Europe might have changed us. Would we have come back home if we'd seen Paris or Rome? I was sure I would've. Lester wasn't. We learned we'd actually been stationed at the same base in Louisiana, me in the colored barracks and him with the white boys. I guess you could say we got to be something like friends, drinking together on my porch out there, listening to Karnack High School ball games on the radio. I liked him, I did. I was willing to forgive the stuff he'd said when we met, what I took as his ignorance, having spent no real time with black folks. I was willing to lay down all the history didn't neither one of us ask for and just meet him man to man. I reached out a hand to him and look what it done me."

"What about Marnie King?"

"That's when the trouble started. She moved in when her husband went away to prison. He's a skinhead, something like that, and I guess with him locked up, she ain't have no place to go, and her daddy took her in, her and them kids. Levi was still in diapers. Then she took up with the one staying out there now, and his cracker friends started coming around. Started calling me *nigger* on my own land. I told Lester I wouldn't have it, told him to get his girl under control. Lester seemed overwhelmed by the changes, five of them now living in that trailer, his daughter slinking from one crooked racist to another, and I don't know, but about three months ago, his heart give out. The old man wasn't buried a week before Gil started sub-renting out the acres I let to Lester. And before you know it, it's more trailers and folks living out of vans, more coming in week after week. Like a whole cancer of hate is spreading out across Hopetown, my home."

"Can't you just kick them out, get the sheriff to evict them?"

"Lease I gave to Lester got another year on it. And wasn't nothing in the papers said he or his people couldn't rent out part of what I rented out to them. It wasn't nothing I even thought about when I drew up the papers. Sheriff say they got rights too, the folks in the trailers. So I'm stuck. And it's been some trouble."

"Like what?"

"Mess they've been doing, trying to run us off," Mr. Page said.

Darren told him he would do what he could to get him some relief, some protection from the county. Maybe if he talked to Sheriff Quinn directly, he could get the man to understand something had to be done. That it wasn't right for a man to be harassed on his own property, especially when it was at least likely that Gil Thomason was engaging in illegal activity on the premises. "Maybe after we get through with that search of his trailer, it'll be easier to push him and others out."

"No matter," Mr. Page said with a sigh, the air seeming to burn his chest on release, to hurt his heart to say that it was all over now anyway. "I'm selling." He jammed his hands into the pockets of his blue jeans, which were rubbed through with grease in places, grass stains in others. His shoulders dipped, and then he let loose a hangdog smile, chuckling to himself. "Another few months and every one of them gon' be out of here whether they like it or not. Boy spray-painting *porch monkey* and *nigger* on my house and threatening me ain't gon' do a thing to stop it. Nor disrespecting Margaret's people and her house of worship. I'll be in my daughter's place in Little Rock when they come out to raze all of it."

"And Margaret and her family? What happens to the Caddos in Hopetown when you sell?"

Mr. Page gave a look as vague as his response to Margaret's dinner invitation. "It's all being worked out. They gon' be protected, I promise you that. I wasn't raised to leave good folks behind. We don't do people like that."

Mr. Page's mood had visibly soured at the mention of Margaret and her family.

"Not letting nobody run them off, no matter what else they try," the old man said, nodding his head toward the trailer-park squatters outside.

It set off a bottle rocket in Darren's brain. He remembered the sheriff's words: *the kid's had problems.* Vandalism, he'd said, along with the fact that his deputies had been out to the family's trailer more than once. Gil himself had said the kid wasn't a saint. "The boy, the spray paint," he said. "It was Levi?"

"Him and another little rat-faced punk that stay down there. I've caught them red-handed spray-painting my house. Took me and Margaret's boy half a day to put a fresh wash of paint over it. Told you I didn't like the boy none."

Darren nodded as if this were perfectly reasonable. But he felt something tickle the back of his neck. Keeping his voice calm,

149

his tone almost offhand, as he said, "Hey, Mr. Page, tell you what, long as I'm here, you don't mind if I search your property, do you, sir? Be a shame not to be thorough about this."

The air in the room got sucked out as if by a cyclone.

Mr. Page's eyes narrowed as he reconsidered Darren and his purpose here, his gaze lingering on the silver badge. Then he shot a quick and furtive glance at the tool belt hanging high up on the kitchen wall; the decorative paper behind it was salt and pepper shakers in orange and red. The belt held the flashlight but also a sheathed knife and a holster that cradled the .45 revolver he'd carried before.

Darren moved his left hand to his own pistol, rested it on the grip.

Mr. Page, now looking again at Darren, studying the gun and the badge, suddenly dropped all talk of peppers and collards and tales of black Texans going back a hundred years. He looked angry with himself, as if he'd left the back door open and a coyote had wandered into his home. "No, Ranger, I don't believe I *will* let you search my home nor none of this out here I still own. Not without a warrant. Sorry, but I been burned before." And then, smug in the protection of the law, he said, "You come back again, I want a lawyer present."

"You have a lawyer?"

"Come back, and I guess you'll find out." He motioned Darren to the hall that led to the front door. Darren nodded to show he understood he was being dismissed. "Just tell me one thing," he said. "Did you see anyone else out Friday night around the same time Levi was locking up the boat shed? Anybody out for a stroll, walking a dog, anything?"

"The only dogs around here is wild. Bite your hand off if you try to give 'em even a cold biscuit," Mr. Page said. "Like I said, I've been burned before." He walked Darren to the front door and promptly put him on the other side of it.

9.

He had a pair of headlights on his tail the whole way on the road out of Hopetown, like ghost eyes in his rearview, creeping out from behind the trees as he took one slight swerve in the road after another. He couldn't see even a silhouette behind the blast of white light from the car's front grille. He pictured the bearded man from the van, Gil Thomason's neighbor Bo, the man who'd offered to *get the others,* a phrase that called to mind a mob or the wrong kind of clan. But he couldn't be sure the driver of the car behind him wasn't Mr. Page in the '76 Buick Darren had seen parked along the side of his newly painted house, the old man wanting Darren and his questions to get the hell away from Hopetown. In any case, the message was being delivered with alarming speed. As Darren neared FM 727, the paved road back to the highway, the car behind him revved its engine and Darren saw the headlights approach. The other car was going fast enough that it stirred the air, lifting it into the open windows of his truck's cab; someone, he smelled, was burning cedar somewhere. The other car made a drastic pull to the right, spun its wheels, turned around, and flew back to Hopetown, dirt swirling in the red haze of its taillights. The vehicle tipped a little as it made the narrow turn, and only then did Darren recognize the overloaded van of Gil's neighbor. Darren slammed his brakes, then leaned out of the driver's-side window, his service weapon pointed back toward Hopetown, waiting in case the van returned, along with the posse Bo had at his disposal. He sat rock still, heart thumping in his chest.

His breathing didn't completely even out until he was back on Highway 59, coming into Jefferson from the west. To get to the Cardinal Hotel, he had to pass Rosemary King's place on North Vale. The house was lit up, the former ballroom's chandeliers twinkling in the front windows. There were people gathered around a dining-room table, Darren could see from the street. There was a Christmas tree done up in white lights and doves, and a line of cars in front of the house stretched a few blocks, nearly to the town square. Her grandson missing three days as of sundown tonight, and Rosemary King was having a dinner party. Darren couldn't make sense of it. When he parked his truck in front of the hotel, he looked through the bug-crusted windshield to the sky, dusted with stars weak above the town's lights, and wondered if they shone any brighter wherever Levi was, why he and this kid had crossed paths at all. There were probably tens of thousands of missing children in the country tonight; why'd he get the case of one who spray-painted the word *nigger* on an old man's house? He tried to remember the boy was nine, again pictured himself at that age, hair pilled between cuttings, buckteeth filmed in some sugary substance, the times he'd acted out at his elementary school — stealing cash and candy from a teacher's purse in the lounge, pulling fire alarms, calling his phys. ed. teacher a jackass — always asking the school principal to call his uncle William all the way in Huntsville, a whole county away, where he lived with Naomi and his real children (as Darren thought of his uncle's new family) instead of Clayton. Anything to get William's attention, to force the man to claim him again, to step in as the father figure he wanted most. Looking back, it was possible the worst thing he ever did as a kid was harden his heart to his uncle Clayton, the one who stayed behind, the one who never left him, the one who forgave him everything, even becoming a Texas Ranger like his estranged brother.

He knew he needed to call Mack but was dreading it and so first he called Clayton at his home in Austin. He held a tenured position at the law school at the University of Texas, teaching constitutional law and holding informal firesides with progressive students at the house he now shared with William's widow. Clayton was the only one Darren knew who hadn't been crushed by the election. He'd regarded the outcome with a kind of knowing amusement, nihilism as spectacle. Not a bit of the macabre circus surprised him. America was always going to end up with Donald Trump, he'd said, one way or another. He was in a good mood when Darren called; he thought he'd finally found the final ingredient in his grandmother's oxtail stew, he told his nephew. Attempting to re-create a recipe that had never been put down on paper was an occasional pastime of Clayton's. He'd spend days trying different versions, swapping out bay leaves for sage or corn starch for flour. It was an idle and ceaseless pursuit, for there was no way to know if he ever got it just right, if it had been a tomato base or beef broth. It was a childhood memory he was trying to bring to life, and his twin brother was no longer here to weigh in. Clayton was now the last person alive who'd ever tasted that bit of history.

"I need you to do me a favor, Pop," Darren said.

"Lisa said you're in Jefferson."

How the hell had his uncle spoken to his wife before Darren had? "Yeah, I got pulled in on a case out this way, which is why I'm stuck here for another day or two. I need you to handle an errand for me."

Clayton hollered for Naomi to lower the sound on the TV then took a sip of something that made him suck at his teeth as it went down. Darren could picture him in a loose cardigan, standing over the stove with a glass of whiskey. He hadn't had a drink since Friday night, but he sure as shit wished he'd had a few before he said, "Pop, I need you to run up to Camilla and pay Mama's rent."

"I will do no such thing."

"I'll pay you back, it's just I promised her —"

"What kind of trouble is that woman dragging you into?"

Other way around, Pop. "Just do this for me, and when I get done up here, I can explain everything. It's five hundred, and you don't even have to see Bell. You can just run it over to her landlord. He stays in the little clapboard house by her."

He hated how desperate he sounded, the lilt of begging in his voice. It made Clayton suspicious and that much more likely to say no, which he did, several more times. "Your mother is a country knave, a grifter, and a liar. She couldn't walk a straight line if you drew it in crayon in front of her. The sooner you let go of this romantic idea of maternal love and devotion, Darren, the sooner you'll be able to focus on what you have in front of you. Lisa. The job, if you still want it," he said. Clayton had begrudgingly accepted Darren's return to the Texas Rangers. What choice did he have, now that he'd lost his greatest ally in the push to get Darren to go back to law school? Lisa had backed off the fight completely. "Your mother in your life will be nothing but heartache for you, Darren." Clayton had never forgiven her for abandoning her son after the death of Darren's father, Duke, even though it was Clayton who'd fairly snatched Darren from

Bell's teenage arms when he was only a few days old. But there was no point in getting into that now. Clayton had made himself clear on the matter.

He made the call to Mack from his truck too, not wanting to chance anything being overheard through the walls of a hotel. The old man started talking fast as soon as he heard Darren's voice. "The district attorney been by here, once when I wasn't home. He talked to Breanna, Darren," he said, sounding breathless and afraid. Breanna was Mack's twenty-year-old granddaughter, his only family, with whom he shared an A-frame cabin on the western edge of San Jacinto County. She'd been present the night Ronnie Malvo rolled onto Mack's property; in fact, it was ugly talk from Ronnie about Breanna that had led in part to the armed standoff between the two men, Mack threatening to shoot Ronnie over the latter's harassment of his grandchild. "And then he was back by here today," Mack added, voice watery with worry. "Come up on me while I was pulling weeds, said he want to go over some more things."

"You didn't say anything, did you?"

Mack fell silent, and Darren felt a tightness in his chest.

He heard the blue note of a rusty hinge and then the screen door slamming. Mack had stepped out onto the front porch, not wanting to scare Breanna about any of this. "I told him I had a pot on the stove, how it wasn't a good time and all. That seemed to put him off, but what was he doing here?"

There was a commotion in Darren's side-view mirror; a man with thick grayish-blond hair pomaded into a wide curl that sat like a question mark on his head was pulling on the arm of a younger woman. She wasn't white or black but some dusky in-between that Darren couldn't ascertain at a distance. They were walking from the direction of Rosemary's mansion, the man with the booze-fueled swagger of a lothario who'd left a party with his prize. But she was pulling away from him, nearly stumbling as she tried to step onto the curb a few feet from the entrance to the hotel, her voice shrieking what Darren heard as a sharp *no.* Thinking the man was taking liberties or worse, Darren put his hand on the door handle, ready to rescue a woman who appeared to have been overserved, when suddenly she laughed and fell back into the man's arms, almost like a dance move. The older gentleman helped steady her on the concrete pavement in front of the hotel, then gently escorted her to the front doors. He looked at the truck as he passed, his and Darren's eyes meeting in the Chevy's side-view mirror. The man gave Darren a nod. "Evening, Ranger."

Later, Darren would curse himself for the two things he'd missed that night: first, the impossibility of the man being able to see his badge in the small side-view mirror, and second, the deft way the man turned the woman's body as they walked past the truck so Darren never saw the true expression on her face.

In the moment, he was too distracted by the mess with Mack.

"I thought they couldn't try me on this thing again," Mack said. "Double jeopardy or something like that. They can't make you stand on murder twice."

"That was just the grand jury, Mack. Vaughn can keep going for an indictment for the next twenty, thirty years if he feels like it."

"Aw, man, no," Mack said, as if he'd just been shown the fine print on this deal. "Naw, this ain't right, Darren. I was cleared. The jury said I didn't do it."

"The *grand* jury," Darren said, feeling suddenly tired. And thirsty. He didn't have anything in his truck, and there were no liquor stores in the town square, yet another way Jefferson played the redheaded stepchild to New Orleans, sitting sourly in family photographs, chafing beneath a rococo Victorian collar.

"Mack, listen to me, call that lawyer you had."

"I can't afford that kind of help 'less Clayton's willing to pay again."

"If he won't, I will," Darren said before considering how bad that would look. He was talking too fast, making mistake after mistake. Why the hell had he bothered Clayton tonight? "No, no, I can't do that, but listen to me, Mack, as long as you telling the same story, you're fine. They don't have anything new, you understand that, don't you?" he said, letting Mack know without saying it that he hadn't turned in the gun. "You just keep denying any involvement."

"Of course." And then Darren heard footsteps, Mack coming off the porch and walking away from the house; the background noise went from the hum of a television to the hum of tree frogs in the pines surrounding Mack's land. "But Darren, see, there's things in this that you don't know."

"Don't need to." The less he knew, the

161

better. Mack had never actually confessed. It was a gun on his property, that's all Darren really knew. And that's all he wanted to know. Any more, and to protect Mack, he'd have to perjure himself.

"That night, Darren, I had —"

"Don't," he said. "Stop. Just stop."

Mack fell silent on the other end of the phone. His voice came back soft and ashamed. "Don't mean you no harm."

"I'm sorry, Mack," Darren said, not wanting the old man to feel he'd been scolded. "It's just I'm on this job up here in Jefferson, a missing kid —"

"Aw, no," Mack said with a feel for the tragedy of it.

"I guess I'm just a little on edge."

"Understood."

"But, look, Mack, you do me a favor?" *Good Lord, am I really gon' do this?* "Any chance you could run five hundred dollars to Puck who stays up in front of my mama's house?"

"I don't have that kind of money on me."

"Run over what you can," Darren said. "I'll fill in the rest later." He hung up before he felt any more nauseated. He left his truck parked in front of the Cardinal's front doors and brought in the last of his luggage.

■ ■ ■ ■

Someone was in his hotel room. He knew it the second he walked in.

As soon as the door swished closed across the ruby-red carpet, he noticed the lit floor lamp, which he didn't remember leaving on. Other than this slim shaft of amber light, the room was completely dark, including the hallway that led to the king-size bed, the bathroom, and the walk-in closet. Somewhere in that darkness, a body was moving. Darren had no idea how they'd gotten in or how long they'd been waiting for him. He pulled his .45 from his holster and a penlight from his pocket. He started down the hallway, safety off, raising his gun as the door to the bathroom swung open and Greg Heglund stepped out, squinting against the laser-like white light shining in his eyes.

Darren aimed the gun away from his best friend and cursed his name.

Greg found this infinitely more amusing than Darren did. He chuckled as he flipped the switch for the hallway light. He reached out to embrace Darren, who rolled his eyes and ducked Greg's touch. "You didn't wash your hands."

"Did you know that urine is mostly sterile?"

"Mostly."

"Come on, man," Greg said, comically holding his arms out for a hug.

"How'd you get in here?"

Greg flashed his pocket badge. "And you add white on top of this, I can get in pretty much anywhere except Diddy's White Party. Ironic, right?"

Darren rolled his eyes. Greg was a white guy who'd had an affinity and an affection for black folks his whole life, and he often took certain liberties when it came to his sometimes questionable sense of humor. But he was a solid dude whose heart and politics had always been in the right place, even before he joined the Bureau. Darren was happy to see him, but he felt a little ambushed. "When you sent me that text, you didn't say anything about being in Jefferson."

"I thought I'd surprise you."

He was wearing a black suit and a black tie, and with his boyish good looks and bright, eager green eyes, Greg looked like a Mormon or a particularly cheerful funeral director. "And anyway, I was supposed to be gone by now."

Greg had parlayed his limited role in the

164

double homicide this October in Lark — namely, those four minutes on camera discussing hate crimes — into a spot on a task force that was documenting a rise in hate crimes since the election. He echoed the same fear as Lieutenant Wilson, that no one knew where the Justice Department's priorities would lie on the other side of Trump's swearing-in. And before the current administration turned off the lights on its way out, the feds wanted all of this written down. They wanted history to remember. Greg had been traveling through counties in East Texas, from Houston up to Dallas, documenting every church and mosque defacing, every black doll hung from a tree as a joke, and every real black body found the same way. There'd been two in Texas this winter, one out near Waco and the other up in Bowie County, where Bill King was currently incarcerated. Greg, it turned out, had even been to Hopetown. He'd met and talked to Mr. Page, to Margaret Goodfellow and her extended family. There were reports that intimidation and threats had been coming from the newer residents out there, the folks in the trailer park. And then, of course, there'd been the explicit vandalism. "The n-word," Darren said, nodding.

"Among other things."

"Page said something about a church."

"Not a church like you or I understand it, but a house of worship, yes," Greg said. "It's a hut, a round hutch-looking thing Margaret Goodfellow's people built."

"They're Indian, Caddos."

Greg nodded. "Some of the only ones left in this state. The rest settled in Oklahoma, forced out along with every other tribe under the sun."

There were rumors of Caddo in the Mathews bloodline, but Darren had never met a Caddo Indian until today and knew nothing about the tribe except what his seventh-grade Texas History teacher had seen fit to share, which was not much.

"What happened to the church?" he asked.

"Couple kids tried to burn it down. Levi King was a little shit."

Darren sighed from the weight of trying to mitigate. "He's nine."

"And then he's nineteen," Greg said. He sank onto the edge of the suite's living-room sofa. "Right now, he's just playing out what he sees around him on a level he can handle; he takes out his anger at the world on anybody different, repeats what he hears in his house. But ten years from now, I guarantee that boy's gon' be jumping into the

Brotherhood just like his daddy, and then he won't be just spray-painting the old man's house; he'll be killing Leroy Page."

"Sounds like some ISIS shit," Darren said. "Mix an unhappy home life with few *legal* economic opportunities, shake and stir, then let ferment —"

"And in a few years, you got a homegrown terrorist."

For a moment, Darren saw the whole thing play out as if it were a reel from a nightmare, saw how likely it was that, given time, Levi would be a racist as dangerous as his father, who'd choked a black man to death behind a gas station and lit his body on fire. Darren had a furtive, almost painful thought of putting down a sick puppy, of turning his back on Levi completely. He knew it was wrong. He had to allow for the possibility that none of this would happen — his badge required it. Levi was a nine-year-old whose future could not be divined from the leaves of his family tree. Plus saving Levi gave Darren moral cover for framing Bill King. He didn't have to like the fucking kid, but he still had to look for him, he said.

"Oh, that kid's dead." Greg said it so matter-of-factly, he very nearly followed it with a yawn. He glanced at his watch and looked up at Darren, who'd felt a jolt of something when Greg said the kid was dead, the whisper of truth in it and the press of responsibility. Greg wondered if Darren had eaten yet, said he'd not had a proper bowl of gumbo since he'd been here, and now that he was staying for a while, he might as well get some Creole food. Darren tensed, every muscle prepared for a blow, when he asked Greg why he was staying. Some part of him already knew the answer, knew the shit show that was coming. "We think this is a hate crime," Greg said. "The FBI wants me to stay."

PART THREE

PART THREE

10

Greg wanted to drive the twenty miles or so across the border for the real shit. But Darren didn't feel comfortable leaving the state, not while he was on a job. Nor did he want to chance running into his would-be minder Deputy Briggs, at the riverboat restaurant, so they ended up at a bar called Froggy's, the only place in downtown Jefferson where Darren could get a real drink in peace. The gumbo was a roux-less embarrassment — thin as soup, with bland sausage and hard pieces of okra floating in an oily red lake that had been peppered to death — but the liquor was top shelf. Darren ordered a Knob Creek neat and Greg lined up two beers on the bar top so they could talk uninterrupted for the next half hour. They cut quite a sight, the two of them. Darren had removed his badge and looked like a black cowboy who'd wandered into the wrong bar; Greg, with his tailored suit and wing-tip shoes, stood out like an Easter Bunny at a Santa Claus convention, an oddity that even his race couldn't close the gap on. The other white men in the bar were dressed in T-shirts, Wranglers, and work boots.

Greg liked Mr. Page for the homicide.

A homicide that Darren had to remind him hadn't been established.

"Three days, no one's seen or heard from the kid, and you said yourself the grandmother doesn't know where he is. But what we *do* know, by his own admission, is that Leroy Page was the last one to see the kid Friday night."

"A weird admission if you killed the kid."

"Or genius," Greg said. "Make himself seem honest and cooperative."

Darren remembered being brusquely escorted out of the old man's house this evening when he'd asked to search the place. *Cooperative* is not the word he would use to describe Leroy Page. "What's the motive?" Darren said, attempting but coming up short at making this all seem absurd. He shivered to think how casually he'd contemplated the kid's demise himself. He glanced at his face in the red-tinsel-framed mirror behind the bar. Either the mirror was warped or the bourbon was moving at light speed because the man he saw was grotesque to him: skin the color of tree bark on a dying oak, ashy and gray, and a hunch in his shoulders that had settled in he didn't know when. He hadn't been himself since the thing with Mack had fucked with his lens on the world, making him unsure when he was on the side of right and when he was dead wrong.

You're losing yourself, son, he heard his uncle William say. *Don't let anybody steal your grace.*

But why, he wanted to ask, *is the weight of grace always on us?*

"Do you know somebody left dog shit on Mr. Page's doorstep?"

"The kid?"

"It's bigger than Levi, that's what I'm trying to tell you. Do you know a man broke into Margaret Goodfellow's home, stood over her bed in the middle of the night, and threatened to rape her? An eighty-year-old woman? Do you know somebody shot through the stables? Lucky they didn't kill the old man's horses. They broke into his boathouse, stole a two-hundred-dollar motor."

"And all this started after the election?" It fit a pattern of racial violence that had emerged over the past few weeks, Darren thought, like a ghostly relative in a daguerreotype who had always been there but was now impossible to ignore.

"That's coincidental, not causal, in this case."

"Thought you don't believe in coincidence," Darren said. He nodded to the bartender for another drink, even though Greg wasn't through his first beer.

"This all jumped off when Page decided to sell the land."

"Who's he selling to?"

"Some developer out of Longview, man named Sandler Gaines."

"Developer?" Darren said. He grabbed a notepad from his front pocket and wrote it down. "What, he'll tear it all down and build lakefront condos?"

"Who knows?"

Darren thought about Margaret Goodfellow's and her family's homes on the lake. How did Leroy Page imagine they wouldn't be razed along with everything else? He thought of the friendly trade of eggs and pecans, greens out of the garden, the offers of daily meals and fellowship, and he felt rather acutely a loss of something that he didn't have a real claim to, hadn't known existed twenty-four hours ago. The sale of Hopetown, its utter demolishment, seemed a spiritual impossibility. Could Texas, which left standing monuments to its own defeats and embarrassments, really destroy the history of Hopetown, a community that had thrived against all odds, even the arrival of the ABT?

He asked the girl behind the bar if she'd ever heard of the place. "Slave settlement, out on the northeast shore of the lake?"

She was in her twenties with thick black hair and skin as pale as moonstone and as luminescent too. But that was makeup, probably. Her nails were painted and too long for this line of work, but she was on display here, her small-town stage. "That's just an old wives' tale," she said with a faint smirk as if she thought Darren was putting her on and she liked proving she wasn't a sucker. "My maw-maw used to talk about runaway slaves and ghosts on the water, but I never known one black person to live on the lake. They can't swim," she said, not so much missing who she was talking to as using him as proof. "*You* know."

Greg, disappointed, shook his head as she moved on to another customer, wiping the countertop with a rag as she went. "There go my plans for the night," he said, revealing he'd had designs on the girl, plans that had now soured. Of course, he took a

175

second look at the girl's cornbread-fed ass. "Maybe not."

"No shame," Darren said.

"Plumb out, I'm afraid."

"Marnie's boyfriend, Gil Thomason, was he involved in any of the harassment in Hopetown, the threats against Mr. Page and the Caddo Indians?"

"Of course. He's HCIC out there. Head cracker in charge."

"Jesus, Greg, keep your voice down."

But nobody could hear them over the George Strait that was thrumming through the overhead speakers. Didn't stop their stares, though. Darren kept his eyes on two white dudes sitting at a table by the door. One of the men — eyes black beneath the brim of a red ball cap whose white lettering Darren didn't need to read to catch its meaning — was watching Darren a little too closely. Slowly, Darren pulled his badge from his pants pocket, held it so it caught the amber light of the neon signs behind the bar, then set it on the oak-lined bar top. The guy with the red cap leaned across his table and whispered something to his drinking buddy, and Darren turned his body so that his back wasn't to the man and his holster was more clearly visible. Greg saw all this and gestured for the check. Darren told him to put his hand down and instead ordered another bourbon to show that he wasn't going anywhere.

Greg knew what he was doing. "Ain't worth it, D."

"I'm still thirsty." Darren shot a look of cold rebuke to the other table.

"Thought you quit anyway," Greg said, nodding at the third glass of bourbon that had found its way to Darren. He looked at Greg and made a face, somewhere between mild irritation and confusion. He and Greg had spoken only twice since they'd seen each other in Lark, and his drinking hadn't come up either time. Greg seemed to feel that he'd said something wrong, that he never should have opened his mouth. He ordered another beer to show he wasn't judging. Then, with a pinched look on his face, he said, "Lisa told me."

"When did you and Lisa talk?"

It wasn't unheard of. In fact, there was a time when the triangle of their friendship was equal on all three sides. In high school, Lisa and Greg were as close as Greg and Darren were. They were all part of a junior bar association that competed in mock trials with kids from across the state. And when all three were in law school, Darren knew that Lisa and Greg had stayed friendly while they were both at the University of Texas and Darren had flown the state for school in Chicago. But over the years Greg and Lisa's connection had thinned to nothing more than the slim filament of their mutual connection to Darren. To Greg, Lisa was his wife. To Lisa, Greg was his friend. They no longer socialized together. Darren couldn't remember when the pattern had cemented itself, but neither had he complained. He'd been happy to have each of them to himself. So it made him unexpectedly jealous to think of the two of them talking without him.

"We crossed paths at the federal courthouse in Houston."

"What were *you* doing there?"

It came out sounding like more of a dig than Darren had intended. It was no secret that Greg's career had lagged behind Darren's and Lisa's. As a civil litigator, she outearned them both. Her clients were local and national corporations who paid handsomely for the services of her firm. But success for both Darren and Greg was measured in winning cases, in the number of assholes sitting in prison cells somewhere cursing their names. Greg, at forty-two, had yet to land a big case, not even the first unsteady rung in the ladder of advancement within the Bureau. The arrests in Lark in the fall had finally gotten him involved in something he desperately wanted to be doing: investigating hate crimes, annihilating a racist Southern legacy. These things mattered to Greg; they were part of why he joined the FBI. But Darren wasn't blind. He knew as well as Greg did that charging an elderly black man with a hate crime would make a career; it was so odd as to guarantee national attention if he built an actual case, if he sent the last descendant of a freedmen's community to prison for killing a child with ties to the Aryan Brotherhood of Texas. It would bring *Dateline* and *20/20* and a salivating Fox News to Greg's front door. Darren could practically see the Netflix true-crime documentary they would make. And he thought he could smell the ambition on Greg, a rank cynicism that was practically seeping from the man's pores, so overheated was he with the possibility of a big case. Greg drummed his short fingernails on the bar top. "At the very least, he's a suspect, and you know it," he said when he saw the look of wariness on Darren's face. "Maybe the old man had had enough."

"But murder? A nine-year-old?"

"Who knows what happened out by the boathouse that night. Maybe the kid at-

179

tacked him, made some threat about what his mama's boyfriend would do —"

"Self-defense," Darren said. "Which is all Mr. Page and the Native folks out there have been doing, protecting themselves from bullies. Let me ask you this, has there been any evidence that Leroy Page has expressed racist views?"

Greg gave Darren a rueful smile, before he said, "HCIC, head cracker in charge, that's a direct quote from Mr. Page during our interview."

Darren shook his head. Greg was being grossly unfair.

"Look, I'm not any more happy about this than you, but —"

"*Cracker* and *nigger* are not the same, and you know it," Darren said.

"I do," Greg said with mild indignation that Darren didn't know him better. "But you know who does *not* have the capacity for that kind of nuance? Your next president," Greg said, his face screwed up with frustration. "This is the dilemma we're in. If we don't prosecute hate crimes against whites — *if* that's what this is," he said, just to get Darren to hear him out, "if we don't prosecute crimes against white lives to the degree that we do those against black lives —"

Darren laughed so hard the bourbon nearly choked him, burning at his throat. Greg put a hand on Darren's forearm and looked his friend in the eye, an expression of bafflement and pain on his face. "I'm serious, D. You see who's about to walk into the White House? You see where this country's at? We're in trouble, man. There's a point to what I'm trying to do. A case like this would make it easier for the new Justice Department to know that hate crimes aren't some kind of liberal hocus-pocus. They're real and deadly and unacceptable in American life. They need to see the FBI taking *every* hate crime seriously. The hope is that a case like this makes them more committed to prosecuting when the tables are turned, when it's a black man killed, that this could change the game."

"So this is the Jackie Robinson of federal hate-crime cases?" Darren was a little bit drunk; his tolerance over the past couple of months had dried up, a muscle atrophying when he needed it most. He would drink his weight in bourbon right now if he could, would do anything to avoid talk of Leroy Page killing a child, the nag of truth in what Greg was saying.

"No," he said, pushing back on this whole thing. "Page sold everything. He's moving

181

in a matter of weeks. It's over. And we're talking about a nine-year-old. He knew the boy's grandfather, for God's sake —"

"Yes, the man he blamed for turning a once idyllic black community into a haven for white supremacists and Brotherhood sympathizers."

Darren shook his head at the logic. "They were friends, the old men."

But Greg kept pressing his case.

He asked Darren to imagine he was the descendant of slaves, to which Darren rolled his eyes and said, "I'll try."

Imagine, Greg said, you come from hard-working people who literally built a town on hope, hope for what freedom in America might mean for them, who supported themselves and lived in prosperous peace for well over a hundred years. And then along come some white folks who ain't got shit and don't know shit, and they start tearing at what you built, creeping in on it. Worse, they hate you for what you were able to do with nothing. They leave shit at your doorstep. Literally. They threaten the people you hold dear. They make your life hell, your paradise a living hell. And then one night, you see this little one all alone. It's just the two of you. Nobody watching. And maybe he mouths off or something, calls you, a grown-

182

ass man, a nigger. And you lose it, can no longer hold back the rage, and it doesn't matter if it's a nine-year-old kid or a ninety-year-old woman, you are simply through. *Done.*

To Greg, this made emotional sense, but it also required vigorous prosecution. But Darren — chafing at a depiction of a violent impulse he didn't recognize within himself or in the men who'd raised him — wasn't buying any of it. He took pleasure in laying down a cultural trump card, speaking with an authority his friend couldn't touch. "Black folks ain't like that," he said. *Or all of y'all woulda been dead by now,* he wanted to say but didn't. Instead, he offered a different sentiment from Leroy Page: "Black folks are the most forgiving people on earth." But even as he said it, the memory of the man stating that he didn't like Levi tapped Darren on the shoulder, demanding his attention. He thought of the old man growing wary when Darren asked to search his place — squirrelly, actually — treating Darren as a traitor for asking questions about the death of a white boy, and he heard his uncle Clayton's words again: *Forgiveness has a limit.*

11.

The Bureau had Greg staying at a motel off Highway 59, so he drove Darren the block and a half back to the Cardinal Hotel in his Ford Taurus, then reached across the front seat when Darren opened the passenger-side door. In the shaft of light from the dome bulb inside the car, he went in for hug, which ended in an awkward mash of forearms, Darren going for a bro shake and Greg wanting more, some reassurance that their friendship remained intact despite the heavy conversation tonight and the tack Greg was clearly planning to take with his investigation. He said, "We're good, right?"

Darren didn't have an easy answer, but the question touched him. He knew Greg's heart even if he thought his ambition might be clouding his view of the situation out in Hopetown, just as Greg thought Darren's compulsive sense of familial duty to every black person he came across — and particularly those over the age of sixty-five — had blinded his judgment of Leroy Page. Even without knowing about Mack and the case hanging over Darren's head back in San Jacinto County, Greg could feel his friend's distress over even the possibility that Page was involved in whatever happened to Levi King. The two men knew each other like brothers. Could they still love each other through whatever came next in Marion County? When the hug fell flat, Greg held out a fist and Darren tapped it with his. Greg smiled and said, "I'm happy about you and Lisa, man."

So not only had Greg and Lisa run into each other at the courthouse, they'd spent enough time together to get into Darren's drinking and the state of his marriage.

Outside the hotel, Clyde, Rosemary King's driver, was leaning against the driver's-side door of her silver Cadillac, waiting. Darren checked his watch, wondering if Rosemary's dinner party had finally broken up or if Clyde had been sent to fetch one of her guests. Either way, he was happy to catch the man alone. He'd spoken to so few black folks in Jefferson proper that he had no sense of what all they knew of Hopetown, what the old slave settlement meant to them. "Lot of folks think they all gone by now," Clyde said when Darren asked.

Through the cracked window of the car, Darren heard a husky, swinging blues, music Clyde played when no one else was around. *I believe my soul's found a happy home.* Ruthie Foster. Darren knew the tune, knew she'd once recorded with Jessie Mae Hemphill. The music reminded Darren of being in Mr. Page's kitchen this afternoon, called to mind the second verse of the hymn Jessie Mae was singing then, lyrics he'd never heard in any other version. *I make heaven my home, I shall not be moved.* Black music, Darren thought, so often points hearts and minds to a higher plane. The musicians know that faith is more important than terra firma, that it has to be, for the material world is full of trials and tribulations, transgressions against body and soul, against our right to any piece of this country, its fields and prairies that we once tilled until our backs broke and bled.

"Naw, it's some folks still out there," Clyde said of the old slave settlement. "They keep to themselves, never seen one myself. The old-timers used to say they was all runaways, scared to come into town. But my understanding of history, of Jefferson, ain't no way a white man was just gon' let his niggers walk off to Shangri-la and not come hunting 'em. It's so many tall tales in this town. You can't put stock in half of it. I don't even know if that place is real and not a story some of us made up long ago, a fantasy of slipping free of white folks."

Darren nodded sagely at the Southern logic. He thanked Clyde for talking with him. The driver looked twice over his shoulder before giving Darren a piece of advice. "Be careful," he said in a near whisper. "Rosemary don't play."

Darren would have asked the man what he meant, but his phone rang.

It was his wife calling.

They hadn't even spoken since he'd left Houston this morning.

"Hey," she said once she knew he was alone in his hotel room, her voice husky the way it got after eight p.m. She'd be in one of his old sweatshirts by now. He could picture her collarbone peeking out where the fabric slid off her shoulder, and he felt a pinch of longing. It was there for her too. "I was thinking," she said. "Maybe this time I could come see you."

"I'm working, Lisa."

"I know. It's just the hearing in the Madison Holdings deal got pushed another week, and I could take a day or two, drive up there, give you a hug."

"You want to drive four hours to give me a hug?"

"Well, maybe more than a hug." There was a pause on her end of the line, and then she whispered, almost as if she were ashamed of it, "I miss you."

Darren flipped on the overhead light in the suite's front room. It seemed smaller than when he'd left it, everything swallowed in an oxblood velvet. It was hanging from the windows, it was woven into the wallpaper, and it was in the upholstery of the chesterfield sofa where Darren sat down to peel off his boots.

"I miss you too. But I'm just here for a few days."

"It's just, you heard Dr. Long, we're in a good place right now, and the last time we were apart, the distance, it got between us, it changed things —"

She was talking about his time in Lark, of course, the days and days he'd spent closely with another woman. Randie's name had come up only once during their counseling sessions. Still, she sat at the edge of his consciousness, a watery light in the distance, a beacon of him at his best self, and Lisa knew him well enough to understand some new thing had a hold on him, had taken up residence in an ill-lit corner of his heart, a place where perhaps she, his wife, had never been welcomed. She'd never accused Darren of laying a hand on Randie but, more cruelly, of him being unsatisfied with a wife who didn't need him the way the widow had. It irritated him to hear Randie reduced to *the widow,* but he knew instinctively it would be unwise to say so. His job in that suffocatingly warm therapist's office was to listen. He never told her that Randie had invited him to be with her when she buried her husband's ashes in Tyler. Or that just a few weeks ago, Randie had sent a postcard to his office, a picture of the arch at the Freedman's Memorial Cemetery in Dallas, where, despite her professed distaste for all things Texan, she'd taken a job for a start-up fashion label. She'd be in the state for another week, she'd written in an artful script. Nor did he tell his wife he'd actually thought of driving up to Dallas to see Randie, just to know if she was doing okay. He kept it all to himself. It was, all of it, better left alone. He'd never responded to Randie's voice mail or the postcard, but guilt lingered, which was why he told Lisa now, against his better judgment, that it might be okay if she came to Jefferson for a night. "Dinner, maybe. But I can't promise anything else."

Lisa let out a throaty chuckle and said, "I can."

It was playful flirting, and what man didn't want his wife throwing herself at him? But Darren registered something pushy in it too, something slightly heartbreaking about the desperation in his wife's willingness to drive four hours to hold him, as if she wasn't sure their marriage could withstand a few days apart. She wanted now what she'd so casually tossed aside when she'd kicked him out of their home in the fall: the music of Darren's breath at her back, his body pressed against hers in the dark of night. But even four sessions with Dr. Long had left him with a sharp pill of resentment he couldn't quite swallow.

He had trouble falling asleep. He kept hearing voices outside the bedroom window, women giggling and even a few girlish shrieks. He crossed the room in the dark and pulled back a corner of the heavy drapes to see a gaggle of middle-aged white women, their double chins lit by the candles they were holding. They were staring directly into Darren's room. Naked except for his boxers, he quickly ducked back into the darkness of his hotel room, which apparently was a site of great interest on the town's famed ghost walk. Another tour group came by forty-five minutes later. The same deal — candles outside his bedroom window, women staring gape-mouthed at the Cardinal Hotel, at Darren's room in particular. Bored and unable to sleep, he pulled one of the hotel's brochures from the nightstand and read about the Cardinal's grisly past. He was startled to discover a whole page dedicated to the very room he was staying in, the Garden Suite, a room that also showed up in the other ghost-tour brochures fanned on his nightstand by hotel staff. Apparently, a Penelope Deschamps, née Penny Deckard, of Acadia Parish, Louisiana, shot herself with a pearl-handled derringer in this very room, heartbroken over the death of her husband and the loss of her favored slaves. Her ghost was said to reside in the famed Garden Suite, occasionally showing herself at the bedroom window to passersby. Darren hadn't truly appreciated the breadth of Rosemary's distaste for him until he remembered she'd arranged for him to stay in this very suite, knowing he wouldn't get a lick of sleep. Jefferson billed itself as the most haunted town in Texas. There was no part of its past it wouldn't turn over for a dollar; these ghost tours could go on all night. He made a dive for the minibar, seeking obliteration. He ate a tube of Pringles and drank two beers back to back, praying the alcohol and starch would knock him out. Sleep finally came on him like a black wave; it moved up his body until he felt a heavy comfort on his chest, felt his eyes give in to the weight of it. He dreamed of slaves and Indians, of the water on Caddo Lake, moss-choked cypress trees crowding him on all sides. He thought he saw Levi King behind this one; no, that one. The boy was hiding. He just had to catch him. He just had to move faster. But the water was heavy. His clothes were soaked through as he tried to navigate the swamp, the toes of his boots scraping the lake bed. And then he was back in the bayou in Lark, Randie standing on the shore watching him. She was leaning against a post oak tree, wearing that white coat and nothing else. Darren averted his eyes; even in the dream, he seemed to know he'd conjured her half naked, and he felt shame, hot and pink as his insides, flush through his entire body.

He woke up hard.

It confused him almost as much as the realization that something had woken him — a crash coming from somewhere inside the room. He sat up and felt a cold dread, the hairs on the back of his neck standing up as straight as a tiny army at attention. He saw the gun first, gripped in the hand of a white woman wearing a ruffled white dress buttoned to her throat, her eyes as black as pellets of buckshot. He was so sleep-deprived that at first he thought it was Rosemary King pointing the small pistol at him. A derringer. That's what it was. The story of Penelope Deschamps popped in his mind just as he turned on the bedside lamp and the woman vanished. He was still dreaming, wasn't he? He had to be.

He heard a faint thud overhead, followed by a woman's muffled voice. Darren realized now the noise that had woken him was coming from the room above his. He heard what he imagined were two bodies in a tussle and what sounded like furniture being pushed against walls, and then everything went quiet save for his own rapid breath. And then a woman's voice, raised in pitch: *Wait,* he thought he heard her say. Unless it was *Rape.*

He grabbed his gun and ran into the hallway outside his room.

His feet were bare and the carpet was rougher than it looked. The needle above the single hotel elevator put its car on the second floor, and Darren didn't imagine the woman who was in the room above his had time for him to wait for it. He opened a door onto an unadorned and vaguely foul-smelling stairwell. It stank of rotting flowers and urine, though neither was in evidence. The second story of the hotel had an open floor plan; it was essentially a gallery that looked down over the first-floor parlor, the lobby's enormous crystal and brass chandelier at eye level from where Darren was standing now; it threw dagger-like prisms of color on the door to the room that was directly above his, room 207. He banged on the door, then knocked into it with his shoulder to test the sturdiness of it, wondering could he break the lock. But for all the dated elegance of the Cardinal Hotel, the lock was part of a modern key-card system; the door didn't budge, nor did anyone open it when Darren said, "Police!" He pressed an ear to the door but heard only a soft silence that felt more ominous than the commotion that had woken him earlier. "Everything okay in there?"

The door to the adjacent room opened and out stepped a man in his sixties. He was wearing a white hotel bathrobe, his belly wrapped as tight as a Christmas ham in butcher's twine. He had the thick hair of a teenager, and without the pomade in it, Darren almost didn't recognize him. But when the man pushed a lock of it from his face, Darren blinked, and it came back to him at once: it was the man who'd escorted the brunette woman into the hotel earlier this evening. He remembered thinking that they'd been coming from Rosemary King's place and that they'd been drinking. The man looked stone sober now. A bemused expression on his face, he stared at Darren, who realized he was wearing only his boxers. "Well, if you don't look a sight," the man said.

"Heard trouble in your neighbor's room."

"Don't see how. There's nobody in there."

"How do you know that, sir?"

"I always rent the rooms on both sides of me when I travel. Else what the hell am I working this hard for, right?" He gave Darren a faint smile. He was ruddy . . . or flushed. His lips were plump and cherry red, even though his skin was spotted with patches where melanin had fled his face, like ghost freckles on his skin. "I don't sleep too good, and people play their TVs too damn loud."

"I'd like to search the room," Darren said, indicating 207. "Both, actually."

In the end he searched all three of the

rooms rented to the man and found nothing. No woman in distress, no sign of a struggle, nothing out of the ordinary except for a pair of pink sponge curlers resting on the nightstand by the bed the man had been sleeping in when Darren's "banging and shouting" had woken him. He took the loose lock of hair in front — a good three inches longer than the rest of his hair — divided it into two sections, wound each one around a pink foam roller, then snapped each roller into place. Darren, half naked, watched with utter bafflement the careful work the man made of it and wondered vaguely why, if he'd been asleep, he was just now putting up his hair for the night. "And you didn't hear anything?" he asked. "No commotion in any of the rooms?"

"Not a peep. But I threw back quite a few this evening."

"Where were you coming from, sir?"

"Dinner party."

"At Rosemary King's house?"

"Yes."

"And who was the woman I saw you with earlier?"

"Well, Ranger, let's just say I pick up all kinds of friends on my travels, and I rarely inquire about names so I can claim ignorance when the wife asks." He was sitting on the edge of the king-size bed, close to swinging his hairy legs back under the covers, clearly waiting on Darren to leave. "That all, Ranger?"

His cool indifference in the presence of law enforcement also bothered Darren, but he couldn't rightly say why. There didn't appear to be a single thing the man had done wrong, but the whole exchange left Darren unsettled. He'd heard something. Hadn't he? He actually doubted himself for a moment. Could he trust anything he'd seen or heard this evening? Between exhaustion and the cheap hotel-room beer, he'd conjured a ghost in his room. Maybe he'd imagined the noises too. Maybe he'd drunk more than he thought. Maybe this backslide was more dangerous than he realized. It was two o'clock in the morning, and he was standing in a strange man's room in his underwear. "I didn't get your name," Darren said.

But it turned out he already knew it.

"Sandler Gaines," he said.

The man who was buying Hopetown.

12.

First thing in the morning, Darren checked the man's story.

The woman working the front desk was wearing a frilly white shirt tucked into a slim black skirt, and she had a red velvet ribbon around her ponytail that looked like it had been snipped right off the curtains. She typed into a rather large gray desktop computer and within a few seconds confirmed for Darren that rooms 209 and 207, the two flanking Mr. Gaines's suite, were indeed both empty last night. "And all three rooms were rented to Mr. Gaines?"

The desk clerk, who was in her twenties, stared at the screen and then frowned. "Well, no," she said slowly, eyes scanning the computer's monitor. "Room two-oh-seven was rented to another guest."

And yet Sandler Gaines had had a key to the room.

"And the guest's name?"

198

The clerk shook her head, the swirl of her honey-colored ponytail swinging. "We're not allowed to give out that kind of information, sir."

Darren set his badge on the counter and smiled. "It's okay."

Seeing the shiny glint of the five-point-star badge, the girl let out a tiny *Oh* in surprise, a gasp of excitement, and for a moment Darren thought he had her.

But then the clerk gave Darren a sweet, pitying frown, like a kindergarten teacher telling her kids to stop jumping down the slide, that rules keep everybody safe. "I believe you'd need a court order or something like that to see private hotel records. Discretion is one of the pillars of service the Cardinal Hotel prides itself on," she said, rattling off chunks of text from an employee-training binder.

"And you're sure the room was empty?"

"Oh, yes, sir, she checked out around nine o'clock last night," the clerk said, not realizing what she'd let slip. *She,* Darren noted. He'd still been at the bar with Greg at the time. He wasn't sure what he'd heard last night, but in any case, Sandler Gaines had lied to him, and he wanted to know why.

"How long has Mr. Gaines been staying at the Cardinal?" he asked.

This she answered excitedly, forgetting herself and the sense of propriety she'd held so dear only moments ago. "Oh, he arrived with the *Jeffersonian.*"

"The what?"

"The steamboat," she said. She pointed to a display of brochures for various local attractions, everything from the Jefferson Historical Museum to the Jefferson General Store to garden walks and ghost tours and plantation restaurants to a *Gone with the Wind* museum to several ongoing Civil War reenactments. From the display, the desk clerk plucked a green-and-white brochure and handed it to Darren. There was a picture of a boat that resembled a wedding cake but with a large paddle wheel and two black smokestacks attached to the back. COME SEE JEFFERSON'S NEWEST ATTRACTION, the caption read. The brochure had pictures of slot machines and blackjack tables on the boat and an image of a well-dressed and well-tanned couple standing on the deck of the *Jeffersonian,* their two glasses of champagne kissing as the sun set behind them on Big Cypress Bayou, the main artery from the town into the wilds of Caddo Lake.

Darren didn't understand what he was looking at or what Gaines was selling.

"Gambling's illegal in Texas," he said.

"Oh, that's just for show," the clerk said. Her name tag said SHAWNA, Darren saw now. She had wide brown eyes and nails both bitten and polished. "It's just a boat right now, a prototype, Mr. Gaines said when he had a crew bring it in. Can't even ride on the thing yet. But you can go see it. It's just a few yards behind the courthouse, parked right under the railway bridge. It'll cost you ten dollars, though," Shawna said. "And was everything okay with your room?"

It was smaller in real life. He'd walked down a small hill of grass, past a plaque that identified the spot under the rusted railroad bridge as the Jefferson Turn Basin, the place on Big Cypress where ships could turn during the heyday of Jefferson's days as a port city. The "steamboat" docked before him — essentially an oversize double-decker pontoon boat in elaborate disguise, the smokestacks and paddle wheel in back tacked on as decoration — certainly called to mind the era when Jefferson was the crown jewel in Texas trade, a time of local wealth and glamour when steamboat travel was considered the height of sophistication and comfort, *the* way to get to Texas from New Orleans or St. Louis or anywhere else along the Mississippi River. There were candlelit dining halls and elegant ballrooms, smoking salons and rooms for men to wager money on card games. And there was danger too. Only a few hundred yards behind Darren was the faded mural of the *Mittie Stephens,* homage to a ghost ship.

It was one of the deadliest steamboat crash-and-burns in history, some sixty souls perishing on a cold night in the middle of Caddo Lake nearly one hundred and fifty years ago, after the vessel caught fire and then grounded in shallow water. Though the wreck of the *Mittie Stephens* was the one everyone remembered, there'd been crashes before that, and there were crashes after, until steamboat travel through Caddo Lake dried up for good in the 1870s. Why Sandler Gaines was trying to build a new entertainment industry on such rusted history was beyond Darren. And there'd be no time to dissect the business venture now or even take a peek inside. He heard footsteps coming fast behind him, and then Deputy Briggs's voice. "There you are." Darren turned and saw the young deputy gnawing on a piece of white sandwich bread wrapped around a link sausage with dill pickle chips hanging out of it. "Was waiting out front of the Cardinal from six this morning," he said. The sun was still on its climb to the east on the other side of Big Cypress Bayou, the light sprinkling gold across the greenish surface of the water. It was only a little after seven, but Briggs was hyped. "Guess you musta slipped past me somehow. The news came down just fifteen minutes ago," he said, nodding toward the yellow brick court-house.

Darren took a last look at the *Jeffersonian,* then turned and started away from the water and up the hill toward town. "War-rant come through?" he said.

"Big time."

Gil Thomason was already in cuffs in the back of a squad car by the time Darren made it back to the trailer park. There were several deputies gathered, plus Sheriff Quinn, all of them trying to calm down Marnie King, who was walking in circles with her eyes down, as if divining something in the pattern her bare feet made in the dirt. She shook off a deputy who was trying to stem her plum-faced rage and snotty tears. She was crying, telling anyone who would listen that the shit wasn't hers. "The credit cards, rocks of crystal, you're crazy if you think I'd ever have that shit around my kids." She jabbed a finger against the back passenger window where Gil was tied up and said, "You can lock the son of a bitch under the jail for all I care. Just leave me and my kids out of it. Take me in too, I don't care. I'll tell you every goddamn thing this SOB's been up to, all the shit he promised he wasn't bringing into my daddy's trailer. I'll cut a deal right now. I just want my boy back." She banged her hands on the squad car's window as if, given enough time and effort, she could make contact with Gil and his "goddamn, fucking hard head." Quinn finally grabbed her by the arms, practically lifted her off the ground, and dragged her away from his cruiser before she could do any real damage. The palms of her hands were as red as if she'd set them on hot coals.

A crowd had gathered. Marnie and Gil's neighbors, the white couple living out of the van decorated with the DON'T TREAD ON ME flag and dixie beach towel, were standing closer than Darren might have allowed if it were his crime scene. Bo, the dude with the beard, the one who'd offered to posse up against Darren if Gil gave the say-so, was standing with his arms folded tight across his chest. His wife, girlfriend, sister — Darren had no clue — had a cigarette dangling from the corner of her dry lips. With her right hand she held up a cell phone, filming the police activity while providing running commentary between puffs on her smoke. "You see this shit, you see what it's like out here, what it's come to in this country when white folks is drug out they home. You see how these turncoat fake-ass cops are doing good white folks minding they own business."

Darren told the woman to back up a few feet, and when she spit in the dirt at his feet, he told her he was willing to give her the same treatment black folks got from cops if she thought she was getting the raw end of this citizenship deal. "Though, bit of advice, you may want to get your affairs in order first."

"You hear that, Sheriff? The nigger just threatened me."

Quinn turned, his arms still holding Marnie in such a way that she was nearly cuffed by the sheer strength of his will. They both saw Darren at the same time. Like a bull from a pen, Marnie threw off the sheriff and ran through the red dirt to Darren, looking at him with begging eyes. She grabbed his arm, digging her fingers through his shirt, digging through to bone. Darren felt like a stone in mud, hammered in place by her hurt. "Did you find Levi? Did you find my boy?"

Bo scratched his reddish beard and nodded toward Darren. "Why don't you ask him what he was doing talking to Leroy Page about the boy last night?"

Sheriff Quinn shot Darren a look that cracked what easy camaraderie there'd been between them yesterday. Quinn was furious. "You talked to Page?"

"Wanted to be clear he knew what he saw Friday night."

Marnie looked from Darren to the sheriff. "Mr. Page? He saw Levi? Does he know where my son is?"

From the back of the cruiser, Gil hollered through the glass, loud enough that his breath fogged the back window, "I never laid a hand on that boy."

Marnie screamed back, "You whipped him just two weeks ago, left welts the size of bloody slugs. He couldn't hardly sit right for days."

"Shut the fuck up, Marnie!"

"Fuck you, Gil."

"It's Page," Gil said, nearly obscured by the fog of his breath in the back of the cruiser. "Can't y'all see that? The old man had it in for Levi since he tried to burn the church, red hot over the fact that he tagged up the old man's house."

"Ask the Ranger here if he's protecting one of his own," the bearded man said while his wife, girlfriend, whoever, kept filming the scene with her phone. Darren edged away from the two of them, from the cracked camera's lens, aware of the potential hazards that being filmed carried for him as a Ranger who'd only recently gotten his badge returned. He turned his back to the cell phone camera and asked Quinn, "You arresting him on the kid?"

"No," Quinn said, nodding toward the open door to the trailer. "We got stolen credit cards, a drug stash and paraphernalia, plus a buncha shit boosted from the Walmart in Marshall. I'm gon' hold him on that while we try to figure out what happened to that kid." He glanced back toward the green hills on the other side of Hopetown. "Not feeling hopeful, Ranger, I'll tell you that."

Darren lifted his hands in an apology. "I was truly only trying to help. Just wanted to get a sense of the man, Page, see how he reacted to a picture of Levi."

"Aw, hell, he's known that boy his whole life."

Darren nodded. "I keep coming back to the water. We sure the boy didn't get lost out there? Maybe he ran into some kind of trouble with the boat?"

Quinn stared at the weather-beaten boat shed fifty yards or so near the shore, wood feathered gray with age, rotted across the roof, and shook his head.

"The boat was returned, Ranger. Everything says Levi made it back to shore, including Page's own statement. If he says he saw him, I got no good reason not to believe him. And that makes him the last one to see the boy alive. Period."

In the end they carted them both away, Gil for the credit cards and drugs and Marnie for whatever the Texas penal code for acting a damn fool, hollering and swearing and mouthing off to anyone in a fifty-foot radius. The show over, Bo and his wife, girlfriend, sister, or whoever stopped filming and returned to their van. Darren watched as it listed sideways, as they climbed in one after the other. The dusty lane that ran between the trailers, vans, and houseboats grew quiet then. There were still a few deputies who'd been ordered to stay behind while Darren got his look inside the trailer. And the white residents of Hopetown seemed content to let the drama trail up the road behind the two cruisers carrying Marnie and Gil. No one seemed interested in drawing the curiosity of cops anywhere near their patchwork abodes. Darren heard doors behind him slam shut. Heard locks click. Alone, he walked up the stairs of Marnie's trailer.

Inside it smelled of lemon Pledge, of the effort to make something pretty of a thirty-year-old trailer, six hundred square feet of matted carpet, ripped and fraying in places. There were two tiny bedrooms with hampers doubling as dresser drawers, the plastic cages filled with clothes and stacked nearly to the ceiling. The sheriff's deputies had tossed the place. There were books, VHS tapes, photocopied papers and messy piles of receipts, old toys, and a few loose car parts strewn over the floor and on every open surface. But damn if those surfaces weren't gleaming. Someone had white-washed the wood paneling, giving the trailer a vaguely beach cabin–like feel. And with great care, someone had sewn curtains made of blue cotton printed with tiny conch shells.

"Levi made those." Darren turned to see a doughy teenage girl standing in the doorway to one of the bedrooms. Behind her, he saw the one double bed and its two twin-size comforters, one an aging fleece with a picture of Hannah Montana on it, parts of her peach-colored skin flaking off the fabric, the other with Pokémon on the cover. "He got kicked out of gym class, and his coach made him take a home-ec class as punishment. But I think they look nice." Softly, she said, "I'm Dana."

"Your brother seemed to get into his share of trouble."

"He's just a stupid kid, bored out of his mind out here."

"Lot of bored kids don't terrorize folks." He turned away from her then, continued his inspection of the trailer, finding no more connection to the Aryan Brotherhood of Texas than a copy of *Mein Kampf* that no one had so much as cracked the spine on, dixie-flag tea towels, and a few sketches of SS Bolts and the ABT crest on the back of a bill for a refill of the family's propane tank. Gil Thomason was a poser, it seemed, a wannabe ABT tough who didn't seem to hold much connection to the organization's inner circles of power. The photocopied papers in the folders he found weren't member rosters or notes from meetings but song lyrics and sheet music. Someone was learning to play "Cry, Cry, Cry" by Johnny Cash on a guitar that Darren saw nowhere in the trailer. He'd seen enough. The rest of his work would take place inside an interrogation room back at the sheriff's office in Jefferson. In fact, the blankness of Gil's association with the Brotherhood might make it all the easier to use him to tie Bill King to Ronnie Malvo's murder. *Maybe justice is poetry,* he told himself again, maybe it was whatever art you could make of it.

"I was the only one here, you know," Dana said behind him.

He turned and caught her looking down at the tips of her shoes, cheap boots with peeling pleather. "They lied to the sheriff. That whole mess about them waiting up all night? Bullshit. They were out to Jefferson or Marshall or wherever the hell and didn't come home until two in the morning, drunk off their asses, both of them. Took till sunrise for Mama to sober up and understand Levi was gone. By then I'd already called Rosemary. So I knew he wasn't there."

And Rosemary must have been the one to call Bill.

Hence his letter to the governor Sunday.

"This is my fault," Dana said, tears forming, making black rivers of her drugstore mascara and a shallow pool of pain where they landed in the hollow of her throat. "I sent him on the water. I gave him the boat key. And when my company left . . . ." It was such a strange, formal word coming from a girl in cheap boots and raccoon eyes. Darren felt a pity that shamed him. She was trying so hard to get this right, to get this man with a badge to see past the tiny trailer, the messiness of her mother and her boyfriend, to get this black man not to look at her and see white trash. He respected the fact that she was smart enough to wait until Marnie and Gil were gone to tell the truth.

"When my friend left, I was the one who waited, watching as it grew dark," she said. And here she grabbed him by the arm, startling him with a grip as strong and desperate as her mother's, and pulled him toward a small rectangular window above the trailer's kitchen sink. There was a clear view of the boat shed; Quinn's deputies had confirmed the boat was there. "And I'm telling you the old man is lying. I woulda seen something."

"But you admit you missed seeing your brother returning the boat."

"Mr. . . . Ranger, I didn't see anybody. Not Levi. Not Leroy Page on patrol."

"Is it possible you missed Mr. Page?"

"Missed a black man on a horse with a forty-five on his hip? Around here" — she tried to say this next part gently, not wanting to offend Darren — "that's not the kind of thing goes unnoticed. When Mr. Page and them Indians do their patrol, soon as you hear the clip of those horses, folks in the trailers come sit out on their front steps with their own weapons showing. Been known to pop a few warning shots. You can't miss it when they get started." She looked down at her hands, chipped black polish, nails bitten and torn. "Leroy is lying, got to be."

13.

"I want eyes on Page," Quinn was saying to a couple of his deputies as Darren walked into the tiny office of the Marion County Sheriff back in Jefferson, his first time inside. The whole outfit wasn't much larger than the suite he was occupying at the Cardinal Hotel. There was a white woman in her seventies sitting behind a reception desk. She had a jar of strawberry candies set out, as if this were a real estate office or a pediatrics practice and not a place for the sifting through and sorting of criminals, a workspace that was directly attached to the county jail. The receptionist, chestnut-and-gray hair teased and sprayed into a perfect dome, took one look at Darren and said, "The rest of 'em is back there."

"The rest" included Greg Heglund, wearing the same black suit from last night, and another federal agent, slightly older than him and dressed as stiffly in a black suit and black tie. The two had their heads together as they trailed Sheriff Quinn and his deputies into the hallway. As Darren approached, Quinn, who'd cooled toward him considerably in the past twenty-four hours, gave him a terse nod and said, "Thomason's all yours." They were moving with such clarity of purpose that when one of the deputies offered to escort Darren to the interrogation room, where Gil Thomason was waiting, Darren actually hung back to try to get a word with Greg, whom he'd never seen with another federal agent, never seen walk and talk in the clipped and stiff way that he did now.

Greg was telling Quinn, "We'll work to get a warrant to search Mr. Page's home on our end. If this is what we think this is, the Bureau is ready to put in the time and resources to bring about a federal indictment."

"What's going on?" Darren asked his friend, who, in the presence of the local sheriff, made a show of giving Quinn the floor and fairly ignoring Darren.

"Mr. Thomason has signed an affidavit detailing acts of harassment by Mr. Page against him and Marnie King and threatening violence against the boy, Levi King. Nobody's seen hide nor hair of this kid for

215

four days, and it's time to call this what it is. Agent Heglund here is looking to head up the homicide investigation for the FBI, and we'll assist in any way we can."

Greg finally looked at him, and Darren saw something sheepish in his expression; the direction of the case seemed to have shaved years of fraternal affection and closeness between the two men down to something so thin Darren could see straight through what was left of it, could feel cold air breeze through the new holes in their relationship. "Leroy Page is our number-one suspect."

So you got your hate crime.

He kept the words to himself, wouldn't call out his friend like that. But a gulf had opened up between them. After twenty-some years of friendship, had race finally dumped a swamp of quicksand at their feet, making it impossible for either man to reach the other without the threat of losing himself in the process? Or were they just doing their jobs the best way they knew how? "What about Thomason?" Darren said. "What about the drugs?"

"Oh, he ain't going home no time soon," Quinn said.

"And you don't think he knows that? He's saying anything, trying to save his own ass."

Wasn't that, in fact, what Darren had been counting on? Using a criminal's natural instinct for butt-preservation to get Thomason to name Bill King in the Ronnie Malvo homicide? Lazy police work could cut both ways, he guessed. "He's telling tales on Leroy Page just to save himself on the drug charges he knows are coming."

"It's not just him," Greg said. "Marnie King confirmed Leroy Page has been terrorizing folks out in Hopetown, riding with an armed posse, and that he had a particular dislike for her son. The two had had words, a grown man cussing a kid."

"A kid who'd spray-painted *nigger* on his house, who'd tried to burn down what the Indians hold as sacred, their place of worship."

"All of which is going in the indictment," Greg said. "Goes to motive."

Darren felt like he'd walked in at the tail end of a horror movie, the plot of which he couldn't quite follow. But he was sure everyone on-screen was making a terrible mistake. *Stop this,* he wanted to scream. "Talk to the daughter. Dana, Marnie's other kid," he said, speaking directly to Greg now. "She says Gil and Marnie weren't home all night. She was the one looking for Levi and she says Leroy Page wasn't out that night, that

217

there's no way he saw Levi."

"So the old man lied about seeing him alive?" Quinn said. "Well, that sure as shit don't clear him."

Darren said, "The only way you got to Page as a suspect is him saying he'd seen the kid. If he was confused, got his nights mixed up —"

"Sorry, D., but that's just not true," Greg said. "We have the old man's own statements about Levi King and now corroborating stories from the boy's mother and her boyfriend, also living in the house." He looked at Darren, wanting some reassurance that things were okay between them. "Don't worry — we are going to handle this carefully, every rock overturned, before we go anywhere near a grand jury. We know we can't afford to fuck this up." *Trust me,* his eyes were saying. *It's a tactic. The long game is for the greater good.* But then he went and ruined it by saying in front of the other federal agent and Sheriff Quinn, two white men: "You know if the races were reversed and some black kid came up dead and his white neighbor had threatened him, that neighbor would be a suspect." Greg using Darren's race — and his assumption that he had a right to do so in mixed company to make his point — hurt Darren in a way

218

that nothing else had.

" 'Came up dead'?" Darren said. "There's no body. There's no case, Greg."

"We'll see," Quinn said, putting a supportive hand on Greg's shoulder.

Darren's time in the box with Gil Thomason was as unproductive and unpleasant as a trip to the bathroom after a hard bender, and his head ached just as much. He was admittedly distracted by the turn this case had taken, by Greg's cocky assurance that he was doing the right thing, and by Darren's own doubts about Leroy Page. He believed Dana and her tears for her brother. But why would the old man have lied about seeing Levi the night he disappeared?

Gil wasn't exactly cooperating. He alternated between stony silence — arms crossed tightly across his chest, wooden chair leaned back on its rear legs — and launching race grenades at Darren, as if he'd grown bored and wanted to see how they would land. *Nigger. Coon. Nigger-coon. Roach. Monkey with a badge.* "Did you know that on average, black men have IQs twenty points lower than white men? So chances are, badge or no badge, I'm a hell of a lot smarter than you, Ranger."

"If you tell me you can spell *IQ,* then I'll

believe it," Darren said.

Gil actually paused for a second, thinking. The answer was so simple, as was the joke embedded in it, that Gil had to search hard in his brain for the trick, and it left him gape-mouthed and looking as dumb as driftwood. And that only made him madder. *Nigger. Coon. Burr-head. Buckwheat motherfucker.*

There wasn't a single visible tattoo on his tanned and ropy arms. His neck likewise bore no marks save for acne scars and shave bumps along the hairline. Darren wasn't sure Gil Thomason knew who Hitler was, let alone could explain the significance of the seminal text *Mein Kampf* that was in his trailer. And after fifteen minutes, Darren decided he'd wasted enough of his time on Gil and lost his appetite for dirty dealing; it was a fire you could start for a single good reason and end up turning a forest to ash. He was on his way out of the station when he was informed by one of the deputies that Marnie was asking to speak to *him.*

The headquarters of the Marion County Sheriff didn't have two interrogation rooms, so Marnie had been locked in Quinn's office this whole time, a sliver of a room overheated by a radiator with flaking paint under the window. Case files were stacked every which way, and Quinn had a bunch of leftover yard signs from his most recent campaign leaning upside down against a wall, their wooden stakes pointed in the air like church steeples. But it was a MAGA hat sitting on the edge of Quinn's desk next to a jar of buffalo nickels that drew Darren's attention; it was red like a siren, a warning signal. The sheriff was done with Marnie by then, but it was clear he had no intention of leaving Darren and Marnie alone in his office. He sat behind his desk, fingers linked and resting on his slight belly, watching Darren, who stood while Marnie, who'd been dragged to the station barefoot, ran her dusty toes along the flat gray carpet. Even with the heat, she was shivering as she sat in the chair across from Quinn's desk. Neither man acknowledged her discomfort. Despite Darren's irritation over her probable exaggerations of Leroy Page's behavior toward her family, he was curious enough to be courteous. He crouched down to keep her from having to crane her neck to meet his eyes. Her tears had dried, but her eyes were puffy and makeup-smeared. "I'm sorry about Gil" was the first thing she said. "All that *nigger* this and *nigger* that. He just talks tough, ain't nearly as hateful as he pretends

221

to be. You'd see if you got to know him."

"Well, ma'am, I usually take people at the first *nigger,*" Darren said. "I find it saves time that way."

"I don't hate Gil, I don't."

"Well, good for you."

"I just don't want y'all thinking I'd have all that mess around my kids," she said, running the back of her hand under her nose to wipe a lingering drop of snot. "I never even let *Bill* keep drugs and guns around the house. There's safe houses for that stuff. But Gil ain't been jumped in yet, and he's an idiot."

"But surely you knew what Bill was up to back in the day," Darren said.

"I know a whole hell of a lot," Marnie said. "I'll know whatever you want me to know if you find my kid. Please, Ranger Mathews, I am begging you to help me find my kid." She had the same despairing look her daughter, Dana, had had in the trailer today — she looked at Darren as an unforgiving mirror, saw the wretchedness of her life choices through his eyes. She too needed him to see past all that, to see past the bitten nails, the teeth yellowed with nicotine, the skin pocked with time and poor nutrition. She wanted him to see her as a woman, as somebody's brokenhearted mother, not *trash,* as Rosemary King had so crassly put it. "I'll remember anything you want me to about Bill King, sign anything."

There it was, Darren thought, his for the taking.

She lowered her head then, her face pinking as the tears started again. "I just want my son back," she said. "I'm a good mom. Fuck Rosemary."

Quinn leaned forward, his chair squeaking slightly. "Ma'am, we are doing everything to find out what happened to your son."

"You think he's dead."

Quinn wouldn't correct her statement, so she turned to Darren. "I can't explain it, but I just don't think my baby's gone."

"It's important to have hope," Quinn said. "But as law enforcement, we have to be pragmatic, ma'am. We can't let evidence slip by while we're hoping."

To Darren, she said, "Please find him. Please." And then she added, "I'll give you anything you want on Bill," like she knew his real reason for being here, as if she didn't believe an agency as important as the Texas Rangers would actually be worrying over her trailer-park kid.

"You ever heard of a man named Ronnie Malvo?" he said, the words jumping out before he could stop them. "ABT, out of

223

San Jacinto County?"

Marnie looked at him with her swamp-green eyes, searching the brown of his for how much this might get her. "Yeah, yeah, I heard Bill mention him."

"So I guess you know he's gone?"

"Gone?"

From his desk, Quinn watched the back-and-forth volley with a frown, trying to follow the turn this interview had taken right under his nose.

"Dead," Darren said. "Murdered, a couple months back."

Slowly, Marnie nodded, committing to no more than that.

"And Bill?" Darren said. "He ever mention any beef with Malvo, any reason he might have wanted to harm the man or see him gone?"

"You know, he might have," she said carefully, nailing her gaze to his so he would understand the deal she was cutting. "But my hurt over Levi, not sleeping at night, worrying over my son, I just can't think of nothing else. But you find my son, and I'm gon' think on it, and I bet it'll come back to me."

Darren sighed and straightened to his full height.

Marnie looked panicked then, fearing

she'd lost him, her last hope. "Please," she said, standing too. "He's alive." She narrowed her eyes at Quinn. "He don't believe me." She looked back at Darren. "I can't explain it, I just . . . day my daddy died, his heart give out while he was sitting in his chair watching reruns of *Hogan's Heroes*. It was still on the TV when I come home. But I knew. I knew before I hit the door he was dead. I can't explain. I just felt a bolt run through me in town and I rushed home." Tears sprang up, making her green eyes wet and making Darren think again of the great Caddo Lake. "My boy, Levi, he's still alive. I know it."

14.

He teased Wilson with it when they spoke by phone about a half an hour later. Finally something for his actual mission, something real they could pin on Bill King, ABT captain and a missing piece in the joint task force's collection of indictments on the Aryan Brotherhood of Texas. "Ronnie Malvo?" Wilson said over the phone. This was followed by a *hmph* sound, as if he couldn't quite believe it. Darren was careful to play just the tease, not to commit to anything he couldn't change his mind on later. He'd been ready to let the whole thing go until he'd met a like mind in Marnie King: "Find my son and you can keep Bill King's ass in prison for the rest of his life," she'd said as he was leaving Quinn's office. "She knows something for sure," Darren told his boss. "But the thing with the kid, she's distracted, not ready to talk about all that right now, you understand."

"That's some find, Mathews." Wilson sounded vaguely proud, but he was unable to mask a fog of suspicion that rolled out of his mouth on a sigh that colored the whole conversation gray. "I mean, if there's something to this, it not only explains what happened to Ronnie Malvo but also sets a potential capital murder charge against Bill King, plus conspiracy. And again, you're sure you haven't mentioned anything like this to the San Jacinto County DA? I mean, with them trying to solve this thing and still asking questions about you, and then this here falls right in your lap . . ." He paused, allowing Darren the opportunity to fill in the silence with something that would make sense to Fred Wilson. Darren could tell he wanted it to be this simple, but he needed Darren to sell it, to help him wave away the pinch of stink that was hovering in the fog over this whole conversation.

"Don't know about you, but I was raised not to look too closely in a horse's mouth, especially not when its gifts might wrap up a federal case."

Wilson chuckled softly. Darren heard the creak of his office chair and pictured the older man leaning back, head nearly bumping the framed commendations on the wall behind him. "Well, this gives me a reason

227

not to call Vaughn back on the Malvo case. I'll wait until we see if we really got something here."

Darren swallowed a lump in his throat. "He called again?"

"No matter."

Something heavy seemed to have lifted off the lieutenant. Wilson's voice came back lighter, damn near buoyant. "This is good work, Ranger," he said. Darren felt a wave of nausea over how easy this was, how far he'd wandered from how he was raised. He thought of his uncles, both of whom were men of truth, in all things. Could there ever be honor in lying, even when it might save an elderly black man from prison, even if Ronnie Malvo deserved no more than knockoff justice, a cheap facsimile? Could anything really justify what he was doing? He immediately wanted to take it all back.

He made Wilson promise to keep the information close to the vest until he could dig a little deeper. And of course there was still the business with the kid. It made sense, he said, for him to stick around Marion County for a while. "Sure, sure," Wilson said, adding that he was still working on getting Darren inside the Telford Unit in Bowie County. "But I'm having a hell of a time."

"What's the holdup?"

"Someone dragging his feet at the Department of Criminal Justice. But don't worry, I'm going to get you in front of Bill King one way or another."

Darren couldn't think of anything he wanted less in that moment. But he bit through the stress of the mess he'd gotten himself into and said, "Sure thing, sir."

He hung up with Wilson, already halfway back to Hopetown.

The old man didn't answer his front door. The horses were stabled and the Buick was parked on the grass out front, but there was no other sign of Leroy Page, not a window cracked open nor the sound of his old radio coming from anywhere in the house. There *was* music, though. Harmonica, drums, and a flute of some sort, the sound reedy and thin but also warm, the drums almost welcoming, as familiar to him as the rhythm of his own heartbeat. It wasn't his beloved blues, but something holy was in the air, and his first thought was the church, the conical hut that sat a little above the rest of Hopetown on a mound of packed dirt — the only part of the original settlement that wasn't green with freshly clipped grass. Music like that had to be coming from a house of worship. He was walking in a semicircle around the hut, searching for a way in, when behind him he heard a man's voice call out a warning, deep and sudden. "Got no place in there, you or none of the other pig deputies."

Darren turned to see Donald Goodfellow on the porch of his mother's yellow house. He'd casually laid a rifle over the drum between his legs. Beside him sat his son Ray, who was holding a wooden flute, and a Caddo man Darren didn't recognize who'd tucked a harmonica in the front pocket of his denim shirt and likewise had produced a weapon, a Buck knife a good six inches long with a hickory handle so polished it caught the sun and sent a shard of light into Darren's eyes. He squinted, stepped toward the men with deliberation. There were some things he needed to make real clear real fast. "Not a deputy, sir, don't answer to the sheriff. You're talking to a Texas Ranger, who's gon' ask you one time nicely to take care with those weapons. No cause for none of that." The knife found its way into a leather sheath. Darren stopped squinting long enough to see that Donald Goodfellow hadn't stowed his rifle yet. "I'm looking for Mr. Page," he said.

"You and them other cops that been by here."

Darren understood then that they were guarding the place, protecting Mr. Page's property. "Wasn't none of that my doing, Mr. Goodfellow," he said.

Ray glared at Darren. "You got no right to be here."

"I got a right to be anywhere that's under the rule of Texas law —"

"Tick tock, tick tock," Ray said, jutting out his chin with swagger. "Just you wait." His father shot him a look, and Ray's chin disappeared like a turtle's.

"Now, what's all this here?" Margaret Goodfellow opened the screen door and poked her head out. Her eyes scanned the scene — the tense Ranger, her son with a rifle out. "Donald, put that thing away this instant." His mama's words evidently carried more weight than a Ranger's, because Donald took the gun from his drum and set it at his feet. "We've got *dush'-cut* and *dah-bus* for lunch," she said to Darren. A clear invitation that riled young Ray Goodfellow.

"He's hunting after Leroy, *E'-kah,*" he said.

"He's fishing," she told Darren. "But you welcome to join us while you wait."

She looked at the others and said of Dar-

231

ren, as plainly as if she were saying the sky was blue and they were fools to quarrel with her about it, "I like him. He's got kind eyes. Music later. We eat."

Darren Mathews had never been offered food on a woman's front porch and refused. It was simply unheard of the way he was raised. So he spent the next hour or so in Margaret Goodfellow's dining room, his long legs folded up under him at the low table around which the family sat on the floor. They were joined by Donald's wife, Virginia, and his sister, Saku or Sadie — Darren heard both names used — who was much younger than Donald and a new mother. She held a chunky, barely walking toddler on her lap through the meal, feeding him by scooping a few beans from a decorative clay pot on the table onto a piece of golden fry bread, blowing on it, then easing the bean-soaked bread into his mouth. It was faintly sweet, the bread, and of a texture that was a feat of culinary physics: crisped with oil on the outside and as soft and chewy as a doughnut on the inside. The bread paired with the smoky beans was perfection, a simple meal that rivaled any of the Creole food he could get in Jefferson. The men mostly ignored him, but Margaret asked about his family, where he came from.

In turn, she told him she'd been born in Hopetown, as had everyone sitting around the table except little Benji in Sadie's or Saku's lap. He'd been born at the hospital in Marshall, the first hospital delivery in a generation. "We lost our midwife year before last," Virginia said with an air of mourning as she poured Darren a second glass of sweet tea mixed with sliced apples. "So Ray was the last one to be born in Hopetown. Well, Ray and Leroy's daughter Erika."

"She the one encouraging him to sell?"

The room grew so silent and stayed that way for so long that Darren could actually hear the lake behind the house, the music of warblers and the sound of wood storks nesting and braying up high in a cypress tree somewhere. Finally, Margaret spoke with the same firm knowingness with which she had told her people to trust Darren. "Leroy will protect us," she said. And when Darren asked how, he counted a good twenty seconds before she said, "It's all being taken care of."

"May I ask how your people ended up here?" Darren said.

"Leroy's ancestors invited our ancestors to Hopetown near the turn of the last century," she said, the lines around her eyes crinkling warmly as she played some picture in her mind, Caddos and blacks living side by side. "We're family."

"I meant how did your people end up here in Texas?" Darren said.

Margaret gave Darren a sly look as she reached into the pocket of her dress for a pipe and a packet of tobacco. Sadie or Saku took the baby from the room rather than telling her mother she couldn't smoke in her own house. Margaret watched Darren as she packed her tobacco. "So they give you this badge with no history, is that it?" She lit the pipe with a kitchen match; the burning tobacco smelled faintly of cherries. "Texas is our ancestral home," she said with a careful patience that embarrassed Darren. He sounded as much a fool as the white folks who asked the Mathews family where they were *from* from. *I know Texas, but before that* — A question to which Darren's uncle Clayton would offer caustically, "We grew ourselves whole here, passed one set of ribs around a cotton field until we had made a tribe of black Texans called Mathews. Before Texas, we were dust."

Darren hadn't meant to sound ignorant about state history and forced migration; he'd only been trying to put the Goodfellows within the political context of most

234

Texas Indians, who'd been pushed out of the state in the middle of the nineteenth century. "I thought most of the Caddos settled in Oklahoma. On a reservation there, yes?" He looked at Margaret, who smiled faintly, puffing on her pipe.

"My family has never seen Oklahoma," she said.

Donald Goodfellow tossed an embroidered napkin onto his mother's table and finally spoke. "There were many bands of Caddos from this part of the country. The Kadohadacho around the Red River in northern Texas and Arkansas, some in southeastern Oklahoma, and the Natchitoches in Louisiana. This family, we're Hasinai, and East Texas is our true home. The legend of this family is that a small band of Hasinai, led by a stubborn *caddi,* or chief, simply never left Texas. No treaty, no plans by other Caddos to surrender land, no murderous white folks could make them go. We are the last of that band of Hasinai Caddo Indians."

"I'll tell you one thing about this badge," Darren said, feeling the weight of it tugging uncomfortably on the thin fabric of his shirt. "The Rangers were used by landowners and government officials to clear out Indians from so-called white land," he said, willing to tell the truth about the Texas Rangers' racist past in a way he never would if he weren't among people nearly as brown as he was. "How did your family, your ancestors, avoid being captured and sent up north?"

Donald looked at his mother. She puffed on her pipe and said, "Oh, there are ways of hiding in plain sight." The wrinkles around her eyes seemed to wink at Darren as she smiled. He waited for her to say more, but then he heard the squeak of what sounded like a barn door but was really the door to the boat shed behind Margaret's house. She set down her pipe suddenly and stood, the hem of her dress rushing to the floor like a waterfall. It was blue, woven through with red strips of cloth, studded with yellow beads. "Leroy is back."

Darren stood, thanked Margaret for the food, and even nodded a polite goodbye to the mostly mute men around the table who hadn't exactly been warm to him. He was sliding his Stetson back on his head when Margaret told him what she needed him to know. "You understand he didn't hurt that boy, don't you? Leroy is my friend for sixty years. I *know* him. He would never do this."

Darren was waiting on the old man's front

porch when Mr. Page came up from the boat shed lugging fishing gear without a cooler or a single catfish in sight. Darren asked the man point-blank why he had lied about seeing Levi Friday night. "They're going to use that against you now," he said. "Look, I don't know what you did, but if you were serious before about getting a lawyer, now's the time."

"Aw, I just said that shit to get you out of my house."

Darren raised his hands in exasperation. *Don't say I didn't warn you.* "They're getting a warrant on you. They're going to search your place."

"Good," Leroy said, pushing past Darren into his house, where he unceremoniously dumped the fishing gear in the front parlor. "They had to get a warrant to get into them white people's trailer down the way, they gon' have to do the same for me. Wasn't about to let a black man with a badge use his East Texas bona fides to trick me into letting the law search my house. I want the same rules the white man gets."

"So that's it?" Darren said. "That's why you kicked me out?"

"That ain't good enough?" He walked down the hallway to his kitchen. Within moments he had the radio on and the refrigerator open. He popped the top of a Miller High Life, then pulled a premade bologna sandwich from a stack of at least two dozen just like it, all of them wrapped loosely in wax paper, lunch for a month, maybe two. The sight saddened Darren in a way he couldn't explain. There was a bluesy zydeco on the radio, Beau Jocque on the accordion, singing about coming home, another song trying to pin that elusive idea to a place and time. Darren didn't think he'd ever heard a blues song consider the place currently under the singer's feet *home*. No, home was always a long walk on a dusty road, a stowaway ride in a boxcar, or a slow train to Jordan. *All you need is faith to hear the diesels humming.* For Beau Jocque, home was where his mother was. *'Cause that's where I belong,* he sang before one of the meanest guitar solos in zydeco history, more East Texas than western Louisiana, the black coloring the French. The longing in his throaty tenor was familiar to Darren, who'd been raised on this music, who set a blues record on his uncles' hi-fi the second he walked into the house in Camilla, every time, because even there, even in the house where he'd grown up, home was always a reach back in time, glassed as it was in memory. It was still an idea he couldn't exactly touch. Food could sometimes reach it, a pot of peas and ham hocks on the stove. Stories too. But music did it every time. Texas blues were the way home.

Darren asked, "Did you or did you not see Levi King Friday night?"

"Not gon' be called a lie in my own home."

"Dana, Marnie King's daughter, says you weren't even on patrol that night."

"You see what trash she come from?"

"Don't make her a liar."

"But you gon' take her word over mine, a homeowner and a man who never caused nobody no trouble in his whole life, a vet who served his country?"

"She says she never saw you."

"She's wrong," Leroy said. He guzzled half the bottle of beer.

"Then walk me through it again. What were you doing when you saw the boy?" Darren asked. Leroy Page paused so long that Darren could hear the soft patter of water, as light as tears falling on sand, coming from somewhere in the kitchen. He glanced down and saw that the rolled-up bottoms of Mr. Page's dungarees were sopping wet from the knee down. What the hell kind of fishing was he doing out there that got nearly his whole body wet? Thin beads of water, cloudy as crocodile tears, continued to patter onto the linoleum floor. The old man downed the rest of his beer and belched softly. "I was walking," he said finally.

"Walking?" Darren said. "No horse, no patrol?"

"I don't believe I ever said I was on patrol."

Darren was sure he had. But five seconds later, he couldn't remember if Quinn or Page had used the word *patrol.* He cursed himself for not taking the time to write up a few notes after that first encounter with Page and Donald and Ray Goodfellow. He'd been so focused on getting info for the task force — and on his own plans to use Bill King's incarceration and messy family life for his own ends — that finding the kid had almost been an afterthought. But Levi King felt real to him now. He still had the boy's picture in the pocket of his shirt.

"And so you were just taking a stroll . . . down by the trailers?"

"My property still," Leroy said with a huff of indignation.

"Unarmed?"

"Didn't say I was stupid."

"And you saw the boy?"

"I saw the boy," Leroy said. "He was locking up his granddaddy's boat in Lester's old shed."

"You two speak?"

"Naw. I reckon he'd grown kind of scared of me, the way I cussed him after the mess with Margaret's church and blackening my door with ugly words. Naw, Levi didn't say anything, and neither did I."

"Did you see Dana, Levi's older sister, in the window of his trailer?"

"Didn't look toward the trailer, just kept on with my walk."

Darren sighed, removed his hat, and scratched at an itch at the back of his head. He didn't like the fact that the story sounded slightly different than the one Leroy had given before, just as he didn't like the part of himself that was clearly trying to protect the man. He thought of sitting with Greg in that bar, remembered his best friend of twenty-something years trying to get Darren to own up to his blind spots when it came to black folks, the feelings of deference that shot up through him like roots through fertile soil — the instinct to protect and serve that came over him around black folks, especially those of advanced age, men and women whose challenges and fortitude had made Darren's life

241

possible.

"Why don't you just tell the sheriff, the FBI, that you're planning to sell?" Darren said, his old legal training never too far from his mind. "If you're planning to sell and get out of this place soon, leaving behind all the mess with the white folks down in the trailers, there'd be no motive to harm Levi King."

"The FBI?"

"This is serious, Leroy. Folks want to make an example of you. It's more than just the sheriff's department in this thing now. Just tell them you have a deal to sell the land to Sandler Gaines, and it might shift the investigation."

The old man opened the fridge and pulled out another Miller High Life. He offered a golden sweating bottle of it to Darren, who hesitated and then refused. "Never heard of him," Leroy said, popping the top of the beer. His hands were dry and ashy since he'd come in off the water, and Darren noticed scratches on them that he hadn't seen before. They were at least two, three days old.

"Sandler Gaines, the real estate developer. The man buying Hopetown."

"I've sold my land to a trust, something Rosemary King put together with some preservation society she's on the board of. The Marion County Texas Historical Society, something like that. This is a sacred site for the Caddo Indians, and it will stay that way. Rosemary made me that promise."

Darren shook his head; too many contradictory pieces of information coming at him fast, like he'd walked into a swarm of horseflies. He needed to see clearly, to make sense of what he'd just heard. "So in this deal with Rosemary and her trust, she's essentially going to force her grandson, his mother, and his sister off the land? Just kick them out with no place to go?"

"Oh, them people ain't kin to her," Leroy said. "The only one in all this that Rosemary gives a damn about is her boy."

"Levi?"

Leroy shook his head. "Bill, her son."

Darren gave in and asked Leroy to go ahead and give him one of those beers. He watched the old man lift the bottle opener from where it hung on a string by the Frigidaire and noticed a bent, cream-colored business card that was taped to the wall next to it. It was, Darren could just make out, a card from a law firm. So the old man *had* contacted a lawyer after all. He thought to comment on it but liked the idea that the old man maybe didn't realize he'd seen it.

Leroy Page was right about one thing, Darren thought. Rosemary King seemed infinitely more concerned about the welfare of her son, Bill, than about the whereabouts of her nine-year-old grandson. But how Leroy knew this was itself a mystery. "How do you know Mrs. King?" Darren asked. The moss-draped, swamp-side hamlet of Hopetown seemed a world away from Rosemary's Victorian colonial in town. "I mean, how did you even come to know her well enough to reach out for her help on this deal to put Hopetown into a private trust?"

"Oh, it was Rosemary who reached out to *me,*" Leroy said, eager to make that piece of it crystal clear. He set down his beer and started in on his bologna sandwich, talking with food in his mouth. "Like I said before, black people are the most forgiving people on earth."

There was so much bitterness in the way he said it this time that Darren made a face, not understanding what the man was getting at, realizing that he didn't actually understand Leroy at all. From the moment Darren had arrived in Hopetown, he'd looked into the man's elderly black face and seen his own uncles, his grandparents and great-grands past; he'd seen Geneva Sweet and the black folks in Lark, and he'd seen Mack, the longtime family friend he was trying to save from prison. But he didn't know Leroy Page, not really, and he definitely didn't think the man was being straight with him now, hadn't been since they met. He nodded toward the scratches on his hands. "How'd you get those?" he said.

Leroy looked down at his hands, then looked up at Darren in his pressed slacks and ironed shirt, the shiny badge pinned to his chest, and said with a tiny kernel of scorn he didn't bother to hide, "I work with my hands, son."

For the first time, Darren felt a profound dislike for the man. "It's Ranger."

Maybe it was the beer that was making him cranky. Sure as shit wasn't enough alcohol in it to do anything but make Darren want to suck down something real. He cursed himself for not keeping a pint in his truck anymore. He repeated his advice to Leroy Page to think about getting a lawyer, and then he got the hell out of there, regretting the visit almost as soon as his boots hit the porch.

There were two cruisers parked in front of Leroy's house, a pair of Marion County Sheriff deputies watching him walk out of the suspect's home. Beyond the police, white men and women from the trailer park had lined up a wall of cars, all facing Leroy Page's front door. There were rifle racks in pickups, handguns glinting on dashboards. They were armed and ready for battle, several loudly accusing the sheriff's department of protecting a nigger who'd messed with one of theirs. The deputies did nothing to stop them, but neither did they let a single man or woman come closer to Leroy's house. By now Margaret's people had returned to her front porch. They had reclaimed their weapons, and even Margaret had a pearl-handled pistol tucked into an apron tied around her waist. The whole of East Texas history set out like figurines in the Civil War reenactments on Rosemary King's lawn, the air resonant with a threat of violence; you could hear it in the rumble of all those car engines, in the sound of the shells Donald loaded in his gun. Darren thought it was altogether possible someone might die in Hopetown before Levi King was ever found.

15.

Leroy Page was lying, Darren thought.

At least, he didn't believe the man when he said he'd never heard the name Sandler Gaines. His plan had been to return to the Cardinal Hotel in town and see if he couldn't track down the real estate developer and get a clearer idea of what was going on with the sale of Hopetown. Maybe it would reveal more about Mr. Page, what kind of man he really was. Levelheaded and sanguine about the potential sale of his homeland? Or angrier about it than he'd let on? Had Levi's harassment, along with that of his mother's boyfriend and his barefoot, red-faced goons, driven Mr. Page to sell against his heart? And had that driven Leroy into a fit of rage? Darren pictured the blond boy in the photo, tried to quantify in his mind the amount of grace owed a child, one who was merely copying the grown men around him. And that's all it was, wasn't it?

He hated to think the country was growing racists like bumper crops, full of piss and venom, as bitter as the dirt from which they came. Levi King deserved the benefit of the doubt, didn't he? Did Darren really want to live in a world where a nine-year-old wasn't worth his hope?

He needed to find Sandler Gaines at the hotel.

Maybe change his shirt and freshen up a bit first.

But when Darren opened the door to his hotel room, his wife, Lisa, was sitting on the king-size bed, a few legal files spread out on the bloodred velvet duvet. She wasn't wearing lingerie exactly, but her hair was down and the slip she had on was black and lacy and decorated with tiny bone-white bows, making her look like a present left for him on the bed. He was confused for a moment. First, if he was being honest, he'd forgotten Lisa had said anything about driving up to Jefferson. And second, why was his wife dressed for debauchery but also wearing reading glasses and flipping through a manila file folder with a Bic pen clamped between her teeth? He had the fleeting thought that the security at this hotel was troubling enough that he should consider a change of venue, as now two people had walked into his room without a key.

She looked up and saw him and smiled sheepishly, then quickly scooped up the papers and set them and the pen on the bedside table. "I didn't know when you'd be back."

She got off the bed and stood on her tiptoes so she could kiss her husband. The brim of his hat got in the way, and with a smile she tore it from his head and tossed it, something she knew Darren would never do. It missed the dresser and fell onto the floor. It took everything in Darren's power not to stop her hands, already reaching for his belt, and set his Stetson the proper way, brim down, on top of the dresser. But he knew this show of passion was a gesture from his wife, that it would be rude and hurtful to hold her off, to not play out the scenario she'd surely been scripting on her nearly four-hour drive to Jefferson. He hardly had time to catch his breath, the way she went at him. He wanted to slow down, to taste her, not just her mouth but the skin on her neck where her hairline tangled into a tiny mess of curls between sessions at the salon, the place where she was most raw and tender — he wanted to take his time with all of it. But again, he was afraid to offend her. So he let it play out like something she'd seen in a movie, some idea she had of the perfect picture of passion, which wasn't to say that Darren didn't enjoy himself. He'd only been with a few women in his life, but Lisa was always home, the first girl having eclipsed the ones who came after, girls from undergrad and law school he saw in the years when he and Lisa were separated by their academic choices, when they'd made an unspoken pact to ask few questions. He hardly remembered those girls or the brief, sloppy nights on dorm-lounge couches, one time up against the dryer in the laundry room. He spent his years in Princeton and Chicago only ever wanting to get back to Lisa.

They lay sweaty after, crushed velvet all around them. It made creases in the skin of Lisa's back that Darren traced with his fingers. The room was soft with the dew of the effort they'd made of it, and he kissed the salted moisture on Lisa's shoulder and thanked her. She'd never once joined him on the road, something that wasn't forbidden by headquarters so much as it was just a terrible idea.

"I'm glad you came," he said. He was actually touched, deeply so. He pulled her toward him and kissed her and said he loved her for doing this, for driving two hundred–

plus miles just to be with him. She basked in that for a moment, a twinkle of pride in her eyes, which ruined it a little for Darren. He knew Lisa well enough to sense when she was keeping score, savoring a victory. She had now made the greater show of devotion and had gained the upper hand somehow. And with that leverage, she posed a question that carried the dead weight of a declaration. The drive, the lingerie, her legs wrapped around his waist minutes ago — it all seemed a setup now, a dollop of honey before the bitter medicine went down. "We're not keeping secrets anymore, right?" she said, turning to look into his eyes. A worm of dread writhed in his insides. His first thought was Randie. Did she think something had happened between them? They'd been over that, hadn't they? Or was it Lisa who had something to confess? Darren came up on his elbows and then sat up completely, his damp back against the headboard. The heat in the room had cooled, so it felt clammy in here now. The moisture in the air had exhumed some long-buried scent from the room's carpeting. It was cloying, like rotting fruit.

"What's really going on with you and Bell?" Lisa said finally.

Darren felt relief at first. But it lasted

about as long as it took Lisa to sit up in bed and say, "Clayton says you've been giving her money?"

"Why have you been talking to Clayton about my relationship with my mother?" He now felt the scoreboard flip in his favor, as he could avoid telling Lisa the truth about the missing gun and his mother's blackmail if he focused on *her* transgression: talking about him to his uncle Clayton behind his back. This had come up no less than fifteen times in just four sessions with Dr. Long, and Lisa had acknowledged that this made Darren feel like she and Clayton were ganging up on him — over his choices about law school, the Rangers, and, especially, his relationship with Bell. Clayton wanted Darren to cut his mother out of his life. Lisa was breaking a rule they'd negotiated in the safe space of the therapist's office.

"I'm not sure that's the important thing here," Lisa said coolly.

"I'm not sure that it isn't."

"This is not about Clayton." Darren gave her a look and then she said, "Yes, he called me, worried that your mother was scamming you or something, saying you'd asked him to get some money to Bell, to pay her rent. And I kind of couldn't believe you didn't think you could tell me. And then

Frank Vaughn came by my office and —"

"What?"

"The DA from San Jacinto County."

"I know who he is," Darren said, feeling angry and panicked at the same time. "What was he doing coming to your office in Houston? You didn't say anything, did you? Nothing about the night I went out to Mack's place?"

"Two days before Ronnie Malvo was killed? No, Darren, I did not tell a district attorney about you riding out like a cowboy in the middle of the night without calling for any backup to talk Mack down from shooting a man." She swung her legs out of bed and stood over him, arms crossed like swords. "So that's one lie, Darren. That's one lie I have now told to an officer of the court."

"He asked you about it? Directly?" Darren stood too. Did Vaughn already know?

"No."

"Well, then, it wasn't a lie."

"Quit acting like you didn't clear two years of law school, Darren. Interfering with a murder investigation is obstruction. I could be disbarred."

"That's not going to happen. Mack's not going to say anything. And I won't let anything happen to him or you, I promise you, Lisa."

"Did he do it?"

"What did Vaughn ask you?"

"Answer the question, Darren. Did Mack shoot Ronnie Malvo?"

"I don't know."

"I don't believe you," his wife said. She lowered her arms, baring herself, making a show of her defenselessness. "And if I don't believe you about this, then I don't trust you, and if I don't trust you, Darren, what are we doing?"

"I was trying to protect you," he said. "And Mack."

"I love Mack too," she said, but Darren knew it was a lie. She didn't know Mack like he did, hadn't grown up with the man. A Houston girl, she didn't know the bonds of rural black folks, the way the earth and its seasons made family out of strangers, how folks helped each other out, surviving by sharing food or shelter; she didn't know the way black East Texans lived or died by the stories they shared, warnings of which towns and which back roads to avoid. Her professed love for Mack was to mitigate the utter harshness of what came next. "But if he killed a man," she said, wrapping her arms around herself again like armor, "I don't care who it was, don't you dare get yourself or your career tangled up in any of it."

"Too late," Darren said.

He felt the pull of flight then, of surrender, the desire to leap off this cliff and confess. He asked her to have a seat on the sofa and then sat down across from her on the bed and told her about Mack and the missing gun. Told her about his suspicion that Mack had hidden it at the Mathews family homestead in Camilla, a suspicion that Darren had kept to himself for weeks. Told her that by not saying anything about it, he'd damn near committed perjury in front of a grand jury. And the cherry flambé on top: Bell Callis had the gun. Lisa sat in stunned silence for what felt like an eternity but was probably only two minutes of her bull-like breathing, two minutes of her unwillingness to look him in the eye. She stood suddenly and started to dress, covering the lacy slip that now seemed to belong in a different marriage with a dark gray silk shirtdress. She looked up from buttoning it and said, "Okay."

"Okay what?"

"Okay, you fix this," she said with cool pragmatism. "Vaughn ain't letting this drop. He asked if we kept any guns in the house, if I'd stumbled across one that didn't

255

belong. He could get a search warrant, Darren."

"He won't find anything."

"You know once they get in, they can find any damn thing they want to."

She turned her back to him, slid on a pair of yellow Tory Burch flats.

"You're leaving?"

"I told Greg we'd have dinner with him," she said.

"Hmph." It was a grunt of surprise. He didn't know when Lisa and Greg had spoken, how she even knew he was in Jefferson. Beside the bed, the phone rang. Darren answered and heard a woman's voice on the other end, soft-spoken, a lilt of inquiry in every syllable, as if she were apologizing for the intrusion or for her gender: "I'm looking for Monica Maldonado," she said. Darren told her she had the wrong room and hung up just as Lisa was starting for the door. She glanced over her shoulder at Darren, who was still naked on the side of the bed. "I'll wait for you downstairs," she said, still barely making eye contact, leaving Darren exiled in his own shame. "You could go to prison, Darren," she said. "Fix this."

Once she was on the other side of the door, Darren stood, naked and shriveled in body and spirit. He felt immediately queasy from all of it. The fight with his wife, her abject disappointment in him and her fear that he'd made decisions that put their life together in jeopardy. The prospect of dinner with Greg, who was right now moving the Levi King disappearance in a direction that Darren couldn't get behind, even though he didn't trust Leroy Page. And there was something else. He'd hung up on the caller before he had a chance to register her words. There was something familiar about the name of the woman the caller was looking for. He waited for a while before getting dressed, hoping it would come to him. But in the end he couldn't recall where he'd heard it or what it was supposed to mean; it was an itch he couldn't reach.

The restaurant was Greg's choice, a steak house in a former bank that had been built at the turn of the last century, just a few blocks from the Cardinal Hotel. They had a table on the second-floor gallery, linen white and crisp against the darkening sky and the swirl of iron detailing on the balcony. It was a long way from Froggy's, where Greg and Darren had met last night, and he wondered if the posh setting now was for him — a gesture of reconciliation — or for Lisa. His wife did look beautiful in her surroundings, her brown skin like dark honey by the light of the candles and the string of tiny white bulbs decorating the garland of plastic holly on the balcony. The restaurant had hired carolers to sing for dinner patrons. The singers stood on the street, necks craned up to the second-story balcony as they sang "The First Noel" in seventy-two-degree weather. Darren had a view of Jefferson's town center, and from this height, he could see where the prim tameness of the town gave way to the rawness of the piney woods that surrounded it. Cypress Bayou, which emptied into Caddo Lake, was behind the restaurant, not far from Sandler Gaines's mock steamboat. It was hard to believe that the worlds of Jefferson, with its antebellum grace, and Caddo Lake, with its thorny, untamed waters, were only a handful of miles apart, just as it was hard to picture nineteenth-century women in petticoats and parasols traveling through an overgrown swamp.

Something else that didn't fit in downtown Jefferson: the rust-streaked yellow van from the trailer park in Hopetown. Darren saw it across the street from the steak house, saw the dixie towel spread across the windshield, and through the driver's-side window he saw Bo, red beard aflame at sunset. His eyes, shadowed beneath the brim of a ball cap, were trained on Darren, watching his dinner party on the balcony. Darren instinctively reached for his pistol, made a show of slowly lifting it from its holster and setting it on the white tablecloth in full view. Bo gave him a little shrug, may have even winked at the gamesmanship; Darren couldn't tell from this distance. Only thing that was clear was that he was being watched. Lisa flinched when she saw the gun. Greg made a face but ignored it.

There were other, weightier things on his mind.

Before the first glasses of water were poured, Darren made it plain to Greg that he wasn't going to piss on his investigation or interfere in any way, that he wasn't sure about Leroy Page anymore either. But he held out hope that he wasn't a killer, that the boy might even still be alive. "I know you want to make a point with this case in order to stir the Justice Department about the truth of hate crimes, but if that boy is actually still alive, your investigation is going to stop anyone else from looking," Darren said. "I still think his grandmother ain't exactly telling all she knows in this. And Dana, Levi's sister, said she never saw the boat come back, which means Leroy

259

couldn't have seen it either."

"I know, you told me," Greg said.

"I just keeping coming back to the water is all," Darren said. "Maybe the answer lies out there somewhere. Maybe this was a simple accident."

"Water's too shallow. Everyone from Sheriff Quinn to the game warden says that's unlikely."

"Don't mean he wouldn't be gator bait. Who knows? Maybe something happened to the boat, and the boy's hanging on to a cypress tree out there somewhere, waiting for someone to come save him."

Greg shook his head, even going so far as to glance down at the menu to show his lack of interest in Darren's line of thinking. "If something happened to the boat, if Dana never saw it come back, then why the hell was it sitting in the boat shed? It's more likely that Page is telling the truth about seeing the boy return the boat . . . which makes him the last one to see Levi King alive."

Lisa sighed then. She hadn't spoken to or touched her husband since they'd arrived. Even the air kisses she gave Greg carried more warmth than Darren was getting. If Greg noticed the arctic chill between them, he was gracious enough to keep quiet about it. Lisa shook the paper menu in her hands, suggesting that they move on from talk of potential homicides and federal crimes. Within minutes, a waiter was by her side, a slim white man trained to read a table, to identify the guest who was playing host to the others, and he seemed flustered not to understand the dynamic at the table. *You ain't the only one,* Darren thought. Lisa ordered the étouffée and Greg the grilled catfish. Darren put in for a Kansas City strip steak, which was oddly the nicest cut of meat in this Texas steak house. But of course, Jefferson was still a small town, and despite its rococo architecture, the Victorian and grand colonial homes, its play at glamour and sophistication, nothing could hide its small, hard, provincial heart.

And speaking of hard-hearted provincialism, Darren looked over the balustrade to the street below and saw Clyde opening the back door of Rosemary King's silver Cadillac, saw the older woman emerge in a crisp navy dress that was belted in silver. As she started for the restaurant's front doors, her guest exited from the other side of the car. Darren recognized the hair first, that dandyish swirl on the top of his head. Sandler Gaines entered the restaurant just a few feet behind Rosemary. Darren tossed his napkin

261

on the table and excused himself while Lisa and Greg were reminiscing about their time together as undergraduates at Southern Methodist in Dallas, retelling a story that involved a burst pipe in Boaz Hall and an RA literally caught with his pants down in the second-floor men's toilet, a story that Darren had heard too many times to count. He couldn't remember when the three of them had last been in a room together, let alone seated at the same table. Darren, Lisa, and Greg. Now might have been the time to ask how Lisa knew Greg was in Jefferson, when the two had spoken about it, and how and why this dinner had been arranged. But that string of questions felt weighted, anchoring something in his mind that was just floating out there in the blue, harmless and without aim.

He was glad for the distraction of Rosemary and Sandler Gaines.

They were seated at a private table, behind a dark curtain; a black server was standing against the wall at attention in anticipation of their every need. Darren asked the brother to bring him a bourbon neat but to otherwise leave the three of them alone. Rosemary half rose from her chair to object to the intrusion, but Darren showed his badge to the black waiter and that was all it took — he slipped behind the curtain. Darren sat in the empty seat across from Rosemary and said, "So you two are buying the land out in Hopetown, is that it?" Rosemary slid back into her seat. Darren noticed a sudden flush of pink across her skin. It whitened the pearls around her neck so that they resembled a second set of teeth at her throat. She pinched her lips together and reached into the leather satchel on the chair next to Darren's for her cell phone. Without saying a word to either of them, she dialed a number, pointedly ignoring Darren.

Gaines turned to him with a lank smile and said, "I looked at the property, that's true, but I'm afraid I was outbid in the end." He gave a tiny shrug that was nearly lost in the puffy flesh around his shoulders and chin. "My loss, I guess."

"And the fact that you're breaking bread right now with the actual buyer is just, what, a coincidence?"

Gaines raised the glass of burgundy he was drinking. "I believe you're mistaken, Ranger. That land is being put into a trust."

"That you arranged," he said, addressing Rosemary.

She was whispering into her cell phone, so low that Darren couldn't see how anyone on the other end of the line could make out

263

a word she was saying.

Gaines spoke for her. "Rosemary and I have known each other for years."

"Don't say anything," she said to him. "Not till Roger gets here."

"You called your attorney?" Darren said, almost impressed by the move.

"Sheriff Quinn is next if you don't see yourself away from my table." She dialed a new number on her phone, finally looking at Darren directly, her blue eyes nearly as dark as the blue-black color of her dress in the dim cove of their private room. "I know my rights. According to Sheriff Quinn, I am in no way under investigation in the disappearance of my grandson, and I am not obligated to say so much as *boo* in your direction, Ranger." Someone must have answered on the other end because she went back to speaking as softly as a person could and still be talking. She was right. The Levi King case was Quinn's or else the FBI's by now. But it wasn't wholly Darren's business.

He threw up his hands to show he was backing off and glanced over his shoulder in search of the bourbon, his tongue already burning in anticipation of it. Then, as offhand as he could, he turned to Gaines and said flatly, "Why did you lie to me about renting one of the rooms next door to yours at the Cardinal?"

Rosemary looked up right away, the flush in her neck deepening.

"Room two-oh-seven was occupied by another guest, a woman," Darren said. "Not, as you told me, by you. And yet you had a key."

"I believe we discussed all of this in the wee hours of this morning, when you burst in like a crazed man, half naked, chasing ghosts and phantom noises and the like. The story is as simple as it is unremarkable. I met a lady, we had a dalliance, she left when the transaction was complete. That is all. That she let me hold on to her room key may be testament to my generosity."

Was Darren missing something or was Gaines insinuating that the woman was a prostitute? He thought of his drive past Rosemary's house the last night, of seeing the lit chandeliers inside, the sense of grandeur and old money. "What would a hooker, a call girl, even, be doing inside your house, Ms. King?" he asked. Then he looked at Gaines. "I saw you two leaving together." Rosemary set down her phone.

"If this has nothing to do with Levi, I'd like you to leave," she said.

The sheriff arrived before the bourbon.

He was still in uniform and out of breath, as if he'd run straight from his office. He put his hands on his hips and looked around the table like a harried mother who'd walked in on a mess and was unsure which child to scold first. Darren made a show of rising to leave. He would go before he had to watch a local sheriff embarrass himself by dressing down a Texas Ranger in public. But he used the presence of the sheriff to put a little heat under his next question to Sandler Gaines. "And the commotion I heard in the room next to yours last night?"

Gaines looked at the sheriff and then at Darren with an affected expression of befuddlement. "What commotion?" he said. "You saw the room. If it was goings-on like you say there was, there'd have been show of a struggle, wouldn't it?"

Darren noted that it was Gaines who used the word *struggle*.

But he had nothing else to go on, just a feeling that everyone in this little county excelled at obfuscation and misdirection. Marnie King and Gil Thomason, Rosemary and Sandler Gaines, Leroy Page, hell, even Margaret Goodfellow. *Not nary a one of 'em will tell you a story straight,* he thought. There was something shrouded about the place, like the grayish moss hanging on the cypress

266

trees in Caddo Lake. It was impossible to untangle the truth, to follow a local's response to a simple inquiry in a straight line. But he did believe Marnie King's desperation. He did believe Dana's tears about her brother. Even Bill King's pleas for help felt as real to Darren as the same man's history of racial vitriol and violence. Darren didn't respect a one of them, wouldn't cross the street to spit on Bill King, but he knew Bill and Marnie and Dana loved Levi King, and they wanted him home.

When he returned to his table, it was empty, the entrées barely touched. The herbed butter on his cheap steak had melted and was now running in a cloudy river toward the edge of his plate. Pools of grease had opened in Lisa's bowl of étouffée, staining the accompanying white rice an acid orange. Darren was about to summon their server to ask where his fellow dinner guests had gone, find out how and why they'd fled so quickly, when he heard his wife's voice float up from the street below him. "No," she was saying, a hint of bass, of force, in her voice. "We are not doing this right now. We're barely holding shit together as it is." Darren glanced over the railing, saw Greg reach for his wife's arm, and heard him call her name in a way that wasn't so much possessive as petulant, as if he believed she owed him something. "We were just kids then anyway," she said.

When Darren made it downstairs to the front steps of the restaurant, Lisa and Greg were no longer touching. In fact, they were no longer standing anywhere near each other. Greg gave him a limp pat on the back and said they'd talk soon and then walked off in the direction of the blue Ford Taurus he was driving. Lisa turned to Darren, reflections of the Christmas lights twinkling in her watery eyes. Her earlier fury with him was now drowned in whatever these tears were about. "Don't hate me," she said. He reached to embrace her, ready to absorb whatever she was about to say.

Lisa stood stiffly in his arms and lied to him. "I have to be in court tomorrow. We finally got a hearing in front of Judge Caselli, and I have to prep my team before we present oral arguments."

"You're leaving?" he said. "Now?"

"I have to."

"Lisa . . ." He searched his wife's face. *No secrets, right?* But she had already pulled out her phone. She apologized for needing to make a call — that minute, apparently —

268

and then stayed on her cell phone through all the time it took to pack up her things in Darren's hotel room and have him walk her to her car in the lot around back. She hung up in time for him to say, "Drive safely, Lis. And call when you get home." She nodded and gave him a cool, dry kiss on the cheek. Without saying anything about it, he followed her all the way out to Highway 59 and past Marshall as she headed south. At some point in the evening he'd lost sight of Bo and his rusty van, and he wanted to make sure his wife wasn't being tailed.

There was a hurt coming, he knew that, a rumble of dark clouds that had gathered strength when Darren wasn't looking, when he'd left Lisa and Greg alone at the table with their secrets. Still, he felt an odd gratitude for the pain on his horizon, for what it signified, for what it freed him to do.

16.

He'd had her phone number for weeks.

There'd been contact since Lark, since their goodbye in Dallas, when he'd touched her for the first time, holding both of her hands outside the medical examiner's office where the body of her estranged husband waited to be claimed. But it had always been *her* reaching out to him, leaving a message to let him know she was burying Michael in his hometown of Tyler after all, that she'd brought the East Texas boy home, and asking if Darren would like to be at the service. It would just be the two of them, she'd said. His parents were gone, his uncle Booker too, of course, and the memorial service with law-school friends and colleagues from his firm had been at the North Shore home of his managing partner, a kind man who wore a dark cardigan instead of a suit and didn't know enough about Michael to even utter the word *Texas* in his eulogy. That's

270

what sold it for Randie, the moment she decided Darren had been onto something about letting Michael's soul rest in East Texas. And then there was the postcard she'd sent just a few weeks ago, writing that she was working a gig with a designer in Dallas. Which was only a couple of hours from where Darren was sitting, alone on the edge of a hotel bed that still smelled of the last act of his marriage, rank and faintly sour. *Fermented* came to mind, a sweet that had turned. He looked down at the cell phone he'd been holding for ten minutes.

And then he called her.

He didn't recognize the voice at first and thought maybe all this time he'd actually had the number wrong. But he'd woken her, that's what it was. She was not, in fact, still in Dallas; she was across the world in Florence, Italy, where it was at that very moment four o'clock in the morning. Darren was mortified. He began apologizing profusely — feeling also a quiet disappointment over the distance between them — but Randie stopped him and said, "It's okay. I'm glad to hear from you." Her voice was rough with sleep, but it took him back. Boy, did it take him back. To that juke joint just over the Shelby County line in the town of Garrison, the night they'd gotten drunk and talked about their lives and loves. He could still see the colored bar lights playing across her skin as she told the story of Joe and Geneva Sweet, the tale of a love that was fate or happenstance, depending on your point of view on that sort of thing. Either way, it was the story of two people whose lives crossed unexpectedly in the town of Lark, Texas, and the love that had pulled them off the road they'd been living on, sat them down, and whispered, *This. Pay attention to this here.* Through the phone, he could hear her moving around in the bed, could picture her in her hotel room reaching over to turn on the lamp, something porcelain and hand-painted, then sitting up and resting against the padded headboard. "You called," she said. And with no hint of playful rebuke, nothing to suggest she wasn't utterly serious about having been made to wait for him, she added, "Finally."

"Can I ask you something?" he said, speaking quickly, before he lost his nerve. "And you just answer me and not ask me anything in return?"

"Yes," she said in a way that suggested she'd been waiting for this. This question, this phone call, this moment.

Darren lowered his head to the floor until he found his voice again. "How did you know Michael had cheated on you?"

"Oh boy." It was a whisper followed by a length of silence so devoid of breath and speech that Darren thought he could hear the sounds of early-morning delivery trucks on some Florentine street below her room. "Oh no."

"Greg," he whispered.

"Your friend?"

And then, because he felt ashamed — not just of the possibility of being a cuckold but of the quiet knowledge that he'd used this as a pretext to call another woman — he said, "I don't know." What did he know, really? Only that he'd walked into this hotel room alone and wanted to talk to Randie.

"I don't think I can do this, Darren."

Darren shook his head and apologized. "I wasn't thinking," he said. "It must be painful to talk about, all of it." It had been only a couple of months since the investigation in Lark, when she'd had to reveal that Michael had been unfaithful while also trying to deal with the gut-punch reality of his sudden death.

"No, I mean I don't think I can talk about your wife," she said.

She was quiet on the line for a while. Darren saw flickers of candlelight between the velvet curtains, heard a few giggles through

273

the glass. The ghost tours were starting up again. So . . . he told her about them instead, about the whole business of selling the past that made up a good portion of the economy of Jefferson, Texas. He even flicked back a corner of the curtain to describe the current tour group, which included one woman who was dressed in full antebellum regalia, a butter-yellow cinched-waist confection that on second glance might actually have been a Halloween costume for Disney's *Beauty and the Beast.* This made Randie laugh. And so he kept talking. He told her about the ghost that supposedly haunted his room, told her about waking up from the dream and thinking he saw Penelope Deschamps standing with a gun at the foot of his bed — anything to break the tension that had sprung up between them, which he found he could bear no better than she could. She talked about where she was staying, a boutique hotel near the Ponte Vecchio, talked about the leather goods she was shooting for a spread in French *Vogue* and the fact that she'd eaten her weight in gelato the first few days she was in town, lonely and trying not to pick up her old habit of smoking, difficult when there were so many people around her looking impossibly beautiful and glamorous while smoking in every piazza, in every street. She remembered how he used cigarettes in Lark to play a part, to look harmless and insignificant, to gain entry into places like the parking lot of the icehouse in town, where they'd been shot at, "for fuck's sake." Darren groaned, but there was something playful in it, the pleasure of recalling an improbable survival. He reminded Randie of how ridiculous she'd looked driving his truck, and they both laughed until the silence crept up between them again, the air charged with things that weren't being said.

"But you never smoked for real?" she asked. "Not even in college?"

"No. My mother smokes. That killed the idea of glamour right there."

She asked about his mom, a woman she'd never heard him mention. He told her about his childhood, of the uncles who had raised him and why. He didn't have to go so far as to tell her about Bell hiding a potential murder weapon for her to get the gist of his complicated relationship with his mother, for Randie to understand Bell and her petulance, the danger of a grown woman who felt she was owed shit that deep down she knew she'd never have. Randie's parents were still living, divorced, but both in DC, and there was distance there on all sides, she said. "They must be proud of you," Darren said. Randie grew quiet again, and this time there was a note of melancholy in her voice when she changed the subject and asked why he was in Jefferson. He told her about the missing kid and the tangled aspects of the case. "His dad's a killer, a known member of the Aryan Brotherhood of Texas." He told her about Hopetown and the little bit of history he understood so far, the mix of Negroes and Caddo Indians living together for generations. Randie said she'd like to film it. "Before it's gone." And this saddened Darren so much that he opened up the room's minibar, hoping it had been replenished at some point during his absence today. But by then they'd been talking awhile and Randie said the sun was rising in Florence. Somehow his body felt more connected to her room in Italy, where he'd been picturing her for the past hour and a half and where it was just after dawn, and he lost his taste for the liquor. After she described the rush of gold that was lighting up the Arno at that very moment, this country boy tried to best Europe with a description of the sunrise from the back porch of his family homestead in Camilla, how dawn started in the pine tops in the surrounding woods, light the color of butter freshly churned eventually rolling down to brighten the East Texas thicket, the rising sun making diamonds of the dewdrops on the lush green lawn of the back eight acres, where on any day of the week you might see a fawn poke its white-capped head out from the trees, eyes a glassy green, its black button nose sniffing at the same honey-sweet scent of wet grass and pine as you, or you might hear prairie warblers in the trees or find a bluebird perched on the porch railing if you were lucky.

"I'd like to see it someday."

"Yeah," he said slowly, the word like air leaking out of a balloon, the fantasy losing its shape almost as soon as it was spoken. They both knew this would never happen. He was a Texas Ranger who'd solved the murder of her husband. What did that make them? Friends? Certainly no more than that. "Thought you hated Texas," he said, pushing away even the thought of seeing her again, reminding himself there was no reason for it. He'd done his job, and that was the end of it.

The hotel-room phone was ringing now. He tried to ignore it at first, but it kept going and eventually Randie said, "Darren . . . do you need to get that?"

"Yeah, just give me one sec."

"Actually, it's kind of getting late here. I have a seven o'clock call time."

"Right," Darren said, feeling a squeeze in his chest. He wanted to keep talking, but the moment had passed and the hotel phone wouldn't stop ringing.

"It was good to talk to you, Darren," Randie said. "Really."

He nodded and smiled, though she couldn't see him. "For me too."

Then she said softly, "Darren."

Hearing his name on her tongue broke through their shared pretense that this conversation was harmless. It was nearly inexplicable to him, but no less real, how utterly safe he felt talking to this woman. And he could no longer ignore the desire that was tangled in that fact.

"You should forgive her, whatever it is," Randie said. "I wish I'd had the chance to do the same with Michael. I wish I hadn't held it over him like I did."

He hung up one phone and answered the other.

The woman on the hotel line started talking before he could say hello. "I know this isn't room two-oh-seven, I know that. But I'm not getting anything out of anyone at the front desk, even though I've been call-

278

ing for two days."

At the mention of room 207, Darren immediately stood from the bed. That was the room right above his, the one from which he'd heard those startling noises the other night, the room about which Sandler Gaines had told him a bald-faced lie. "Slow down," he said. "You called before, didn't you? This afternoon?"

"That's right. I was wondering if I had the wrong room number or something or if there's some other explanation for why I can't find her."

"Who?"

"Monica Maldonado."

"What do you mean, you can't find her?"

"We had an appointment and she never showed. Isn't answering her phone either."

"What's your name?" Darren said, reaching for a pen and the pad of hotel stationery on the nightstand. It was embossed with a vine of roses across the top.

The woman hesitated. "I'm not looking to cause trouble, I just —"

"Ma'am, my name is Darren Mathews, and I'm a Texas Ranger, and you're not the only one who thinks something is wrong."

"Gail Combs," she said then, almost sighing her own name in relief. "I run a notary business here in Jefferson. Ms. Maldonado

279

reached out to me when she arrived in town a couple of weeks ago about using my services for some legal documents she needed signed. I asked for payment up front, since she mentioned something about having to travel some distance to the signatories, and I wrote up an invoice for my services. I sent it to her office . . ." And here it seemed like she was carefully reading the name off of her own paperwork. "Chafee, Humboldt, and Greene in Alexandria, the one in Virginia. I never received payment or acknowledgment that they'd gotten the invoice, and like I said, she never showed for our appointment. Maybe I'm a nosy one who ought to mind her own business, but I think it's weird that she won't answer her phone, and even though this is the hotel she told me she was staying at, the front desk keeps telling me they never had a guest by that name, even when I told them the room number she gave me as her contact info when she first called me."

And when Darren had asked about room 207, he'd been told that the guest had checked out the same night he'd heard strange noises coming from the room, the same night Darren had seen Gaines escort a possibly inebriated woman through the Cardinal's front doors, a woman he now believed was Monica Maldonado. "I just hope she's safe," Gail said. "I mean, my husband tells me I watch too much *Dateline,* but a woman traveling alone, and now missing . . ."

Missing.

Darren let the word settle in his head. It seemed an extreme assessment of the situation, seemed statistically improbable that there were two missing-persons cases in Marion County. He considered the situation. He had a notary's admittedly alarmist fears, fueled for all Darren knew by the fact that she hadn't been paid, and he had a woman he'd hardly glanced at who had apparently vanished. Assuming the drunk woman with Sandler Gaines and Monica Maldonado were one and the same, Darren couldn't have given a sketch artist anything more than the dark shade of her hair. He was almost tempted to believe that he'd made this whole thing up, that Monica Maldonado had never been to Marion County, or had never checked into the Cardinal Hotel, or maybe didn't exist at all. Almost. But there were two things that rushed at him the second he ended the call with Gail Combs. One, he remembered her first call, when Lisa had just left this room, how he'd sat for a while trying to understand what the name Monica Maldonado meant to him, why it tickled some recessed corner of his brain, like he was holding his breath for a sneeze that wouldn't come. And two, he remembered where he'd seen the name of that law firm. That's what ultimately put it together. The names Chafee, Humboldt, and Greene had scratched at his memory because he'd seen them earlier today, in black ink on the bent business card that was taped to Leroy Page's kitchen wall. Darren hadn't seen the Virginia address on the card, but he'd seen the name. It was Monica Maldonado.

■ ■ ■ ■ ■

PART FOUR

■ ■ ■ ■ ■

PART FOUR

17.

He couldn't get into the room until the next morning, so he spent a good portion of the night looking for information on Chafee, Humboldt, and Greene on various search engines, coming up with precious little about the firm save for their Alexandria, Virginia, address and a note on Martindale .com, the legal directory, that theirs was a general civil practice, which meant that Leroy Page was not in fact a criminal client of Monica Maldonado. After only a few hours' sleep, Darren woke up even more confused; he had no idea why the woman had been in the town of Jefferson, let alone what her current whereabouts might be. Neither the receptionist at her office nor the managing partner he'd asked to speak with after several calls (the second it hit nine a.m. on the East Coast) would even confirm for Darren that Monica Maldonado was in Jefferson, Texas, much less tell him why.

"I'm afraid that's privileged information," the partner, whose name was Dale Godwin, said, not sounding in the least concerned by the fact that a Texas Ranger was asking after one of his employees. For all Darren knew, Mr. Godwin, like many outside the state, did not understand the Rangers' role in law enforcement in Texas; he might have been talking to a park ranger for all the sense of urgency in his voice. He did, at least, confirm that Monica worked for Chafee, Humboldt, and Greene, but he assured Darren that she was *a big girl* — his actual words — who knew how to take care of herself.

"Well, she's not been seen at her hotel in two days and she failed to appear at an appointment she arranged with a local notary, Gail Combs, an invoice for which I bet you have sitting somewhere in your files right now," Darren said. He let that sink in for a moment before adding, "But I'm sure your firm's been in contact with Ms. Maldonado over the past forty-eight hours, right, Mr. Godwin?"

The lawyer blew out a heavy thud of breath, not so much a sigh as the sound of a bass drum, the music in a Western that told of dread on the horizon. "Let me talk to her secretary," Godwin said. "And I'll get back to you."

After more than an hour, Darren still hadn't received a return call.

While breakfast was being served in the dining hall off the lobby, he headed to the second floor, bypassing the front desk altogether and trailing one of the hotel's maids, a whippet-thin black woman with a head of pressed hair and flyaway strands that refused to lie down for anybody. He watched as she knocked on Sandler Gaines's room and announced, "Housekeeping," in a dulcet but perfunctory tone. When she received no answer, she opened the door with her master key. Darren, his fears allayed by the fact that Mr. Gaines was nowhere around, flashed the woman his badge and said he needed to get into room 207.

"It's empty, sir," she said.

"No matter," Darren said with a forced air of authority, speaking at a clipped speed that left little room for questions, "I need to get in there, ma'am. This is state business and as serious as it gets. I'm ordered to search this room."

The maid — BARBARA, her name tag said — shot Darren a look that suggested she thought it was possible it was some bullshit mixed up in this, but Darren was black and

287

carrying a badge so she gave him the benefit of the doubt but also felt she was within her rights to mutter under her breath as she opened the door to room 207, "Better not get me fired over this neither." Then she left him alone.

The velvet drapes were thrown open to a view of the same courtyard garden that was outside Darren's suite downstairs. From a floor up, he saw a few guests taking their coffee outside, one of whom was Sandler Gaines, his pomaded pompadour shining in the golden morning light. Darren stepped away from the window quickly, so as not to be seen snooping in this room, and felt a crunch underfoot. He looked down to see a hair comb cracked into pieces under the heel of his boot. It had been peeking out from under the bed, and as Darren knelt to get a closer look, he realized the hair comb, inlaid with mother-of-pearl, had already been broken. The other half of it was a few inches farther under the bed. Even in shadow, Darren could see hair tangled in the teeth of the comb. He lifted the tails of his white button-down and grabbed both pieces of the comb with the fabric. He dropped them both into a laundry bag from the room's closet, but not before inspecting the clump of hair. It was the same shiny black color as the hair of the woman he'd seen with Sandler Gaines.

He walked all of it the few blocks to the sheriff's office on Austin Street.

The hair comb, the scuffle he'd heard in room 207, the lady he'd seen with Sandler Gaines, the notary who'd called looking for Monica Maldonado, and the fact that after Darren had spent the night calling rental car companies at DFW *and* Love Field, the nearest major airport to Jefferson, Texas, striking out every time, he'd hit the jackpot when he called the Avis car-rental agency at the Shreveport airport, just over the Texas/Louisiana border. It had taken little convincing for the young woman working the desk on the graveyard shift to give up information to a Texas Ranger over the phone. Monica Maldonado, who lived on Russell Road in Alexandria, Virginia, had rented a white Pontiac Sunfire that should have been returned to that airport location yesterday. Inside Sheriff Quinn's small office with the MAGA hat and the mason jar filled with buffalo nickels, Darren also added the fact that he'd seen the woman's business card in Leroy Page's kitchen in Hopetown, offering it as proof that Ms. Maldonado did exist and had indeed been in Marion County at some point.

Quinn, who appeared to be wearing the same clothes as he'd been wearing last night at the steak house, leaned back in his chair and put his hands behind his head, showing two large yellowing pit stains. "So what is it you're trying to say there, Ranger?"

"I think this woman may be missing," Darren said. "And I think Sandler Gaines was the last one to see her. I saw the two of them together."

"You can identify this woman?"

Darren hesitated, then lied. "Yes."

"And Page — what all's he got to do with this?"

"I don't know, but he clearly had some contact with the woman."

"You're saying we got a serial killer in this county?" Something in the idea amused Quinn rather than frightened him. "You sure know how to make trouble out in Hopetown, don't you."

"Excuse me?"

"Mr. Page."

"It was Sandler Gaines who was the last one to see her, I said."

Sheriff Quinn lowered his arms and rested them on his desk, his face taking on a sober quality. "I never had no trouble with Leroy Page before all this," Quinn said, speaking as if he hadn't heard Darren at all. "And truth be told, I never wanted to believe he'd hurt that boy, but the talk out there, the rumors and suspicions now, it's a bell you can't un-ring, Ranger. You'da done well to remember that before you went mentioning his name anywhere near Gil Thomason and his trailer-park posse. You damn near signed that man's death warrant before the feds even had a chance to make an arrest."

Darren felt his stomach drop. He heard a sharp note ringing in his ear, so Quinn's words, when they came, sounded distant. He felt his long legs go weak and wiggly as pepper jelly as Sheriff Quinn said matter-of-factly, "Leroy Page was shot last night."

Darren shook his head, at first in numb disbelief and then in anger. "What happened to the men you had posted outside his place?"

"They got past 'em somehow," Quinn said, a little too businesslike for Darren's taste, as if he were conceding the deputies out front of Page's house had only been for show. "We think they got in around the back some kind of way."

"And who's 'they'?"

"I got deputies going through the trailer park like a tight comb picking for lice. I'm not stupid, Ranger. I put this on the trash out there."

"And Mr. Page, is he —"

"He's alive," Quinn said, suddenly standing. "They got him to Marion County Hospital in time. With his age, though, it's touch-and-go. He got them Caddos praying over him up there on the third floor. He may make it." He shrugged to indicate that he could not understand the ways and means of a narrow band of Caddo Indians who'd lived among black folks for well over a hundred years, but he refused to question their divine authority lest he tempt exemption from heaven by starting any new shit with Indians.

"Talk to Sandler Gaines," Darren said on his way out of the sheriff's office. "He knows what happened to Monica Maldonado. I'd bet my badge on it."

Quinn wrote the name down but insisted he had bigger fish to fry and wasn't prepared to drop everything to find a grown woman no one was looking for save an unpaid notary. "I'm not gon' let you run over me the way you done the sheriff down to Shelby County." So word about the arrests in Lark had gotten to Marion County — especially the fact that the sheriff in those parts was damn near arrested for the collusion Darren had unearthed between him and Wally

Jefferson over the murder of Geneva Sweet's husband. Sheriff Quinn looked at Darren with an irritation that was threaded with grudging respect and something else he was fighting against: fear. Darren felt again the particular power that the badge on *his* chest held and wondered if Quinn was right. Had his asking about Leroy Page in Hopetown put the man's life in danger?

If Darren ever caught a bullet in Marion County, he hoped that someone would have sense enough to take him over the border to Shreveport or, Jesus, just the few miles south on Highway 59 to Marshall, both towns bigger and better equipped than Jefferson, he would think, to handle a gunshot wound. But Leroy Page was in a double room in a medical facility that did the bulk of its business coaching stubborn diabetics through the lifestyle changes necessary for their survival, all within twenty feet of vending machines that sold Dr Pepper and Twix bars on every floor.

Darren had been directed to the unit where longer-term patients were housed. He went past cheaply framed paintings of blue-bonnets and dogwood trees, the heels of his ostrich boots clicking on the vaguely sticky tiled floor — the sound like the peeling of a bandage off skin, over and over again — and finally found Mr. Page's room near the third nurses' station from the elevator. Mr. Page shared the room with a white man in his forties who was eating something out of a Whataburger bag and talking on his cell phone. He did a double take when he saw Darren and the badge but otherwise could not be distracted from his food or his phone. Behind a gauzy curtain on the other side of the room, Mr. Page was asleep, or at least his eyes were closed. His body seemed to be twitching of its own accord, and the black woman sitting on a stool next to his bed had a hand laid across his body, pinning his arms at his sides. She turned when Darren stepped inside what counted for a private room at this small hospital. He saw the resemblance immediately — the same deep hickory skin tone, reddish in parts, hair black with a loose curl pattern and thick, bow-shaped lips. Mr. Page's were dry and crusted with some white substance at the corners; hers were painted a deep pink that had faded and left her lips looking cracked and bleeding. She glanced at Darren, taking in the hat and the badge, the whole Ranger uniform, and then she went back to watching her father with great intensity, as if she could see through flesh and bone to where he was hurting, as if she could kiss the pain away with the force of her caring. "Erika," Darren said, because that's what Margaret had called her when he'd eaten at her home. This was Leroy's younger daughter. Along with the yeasty odor of damp skin where Leroy had sweat through his blue hospital gown, Darren smelled pipe tobacco.

He turned and realized he hadn't seen Margaret in a back corner of the room. It seemed the tobacco had cured her tawny skin, so much was the scent a part of her; he hadn't noticed it in her house, but it struck him full on now. It was sweet, this smell, like baked cherries and damp tree bark, and Darren found it vaguely comforting, though he noticed Erika cutting her eyes at the spectacle of Margaret Goodfellow, red-and-blue shawl over her shoulders, head lowered as she murmured hushed words, almost breathing them into her own chest. She was praying fervently but privately.

"I don't think Daddy would want you here." Erika was looking at Margaret, but she was talking to Darren. "You think he's a killer."

"Why's he shaking like that?"

"Fever," she said. "I've asked them every

twenty minutes to do something. They said if it hits one hundred and five, they'll get the ice blanket."

"I tried to help your father. I told him to get a lawyer."

Erika was wearing a thin gold cross that caught sunlight through the sliver of a rectangular window on the other side of the hospital bed as she turned to Darren to speak. "My father didn't do anything wrong. This is ridiculous. My father would never hurt Lester's grandson. He loved that man."

"Can I ask you something?" Darren said, feeling awkward on his feet, his height making him seem freakish and too removed from the human beings around him. He lowered himself near her stool, crouching on his sore legs. "Who is Monica Maldonado and why was she working for your father?"

"Who?"

"Does this have something to do with the sale of Hopetown?"

"There is no sale."

"What do you mean?" Darren asked. "Your father said this whole thing was your idea."

Behind him, he thought he heard a *hmph* cut through Margaret's praying.

"I mean," Erika said, "he hasn't signed

the papers. I found the whole lot of them sitting on top of him and Mama's chest of drawers. I don't know what's going on, but he's waffling, or he's changed his mind . . ." Her voice faded as she turned back to look at her father in the bed. Leroy's eyelids fluttered at the same time that the spasms in his body found a softer rhythm. "Oh, Daddy," she said.

She took a towel from the bedside table, dipped it into a plastic cup of water, then used it to gently moisten her father's dry mouth. "Either way, he's not staying here after this. I don't care what happens out there. I'm not risking his life on some place that hasn't been a real town, a real community, in fifty, sixty years. Hopetown is a memory, an idea that's long past its time."

Now there was a cluck of the tongue from Margaret, who was clearly listening to every word. Erika, who'd had enough, stood and turned to face the elderly woman, pointing a finger in her direction. "He would have been gone years ago if it weren't for you. As soon as Lester's awful family moved in and took over, he would have left Hopetown if he weren't trying to protect you."

Margaret opened her eyes. "Your father is an honorable man."

"My father is an old fool who lost control

of our ancestors' land."

"Your ancestors?" Margaret said, a curl of amusement in her eyes. "You understand so little of your own history, my girl. Between my ancestors and yours, the debt of gratitude goes both ways. Your father understands that."

At that moment, Leroy's eyes popped open and he sat straight up in bed, his face twisted in either pain or terror over something he was seeing in his mind. He threw off the covers and yanked the IV from his arm while Erika screamed, "Daddy!" He tried to stand up but his legs immediately buckled beneath him; Darren swooped in and kept him from collapsing onto the cold floor. He could feel the heat coming off the old man, his skin as tight and hot as one of the Goodfellows' drums left out in the sun. Leroy Page grabbed Darren by his upper arms, whether to steady himself or move the Ranger out of the way, it was hard to tell. His eyes were wide and red, and he was looking with desperation over Darren's shoulder toward the door.

"I've got to go, boy," Mr. Page said. "I can't stay here. It's things I got to do out there. You've got to help me get out of here, before it's too late."

Mr. Page's roommate must have rung for

help because the door suddenly burst open and two nurses ran in; they were followed by an orderly who carefully but forcefully put Mr. Page back in bed and then stood over him as one of the nurses replaced the IV. By now, Erika was crying, saying, "I told you he's not okay. He's not making any sense. That's the second time he's tried to leave."

Leroy was back to shaking in his bed.

Erika laid her arm across her father's body again.

But it wasn't until the hospital staff had left that Leroy's body stilled. He looked at his daughter, then at Margaret, a kind of peace coming into his eyes so that he almost seemed lucid. Darren stepped forward, gently placed a friendly hand on the man's leg, and asked, "Did you see who shot you, sir?"

"Rosemary," he said. But he was not looking at Darren, did not appear to have heard his question at all. "Rosemary could stop this anytime she wants to."

"Stop what, Daddy?"

Then he looked at Darren directly. "You can't trust them."

"Who?" Darren asked.

"None of 'em," the old man barked, spittle boomeranging from the corners of his mouth and back again. "There is no re-demption, there is no future free from their past sins. You give 'em an inch, they'll take a town."

Darren couldn't tell if the distorted apho-rism was a result of Leroy's fevered brain misfiring or if there was something he was trying to tell Darren. "Mr. Page, who is Monica Maldonado? The lawyer? You had her business card."

Before he could answer, the door to the hospital room opened again, this time with enough force that Margaret Goodfellow gasped and dropped the prayer book that Darren hadn't realized she'd been holding. He saw Erika stand, saw something electric run through her whole body, her hands curl-ing into two tight fists, before he turned and saw two men in dark suits enter the room with several Marion County Sheriff's depu-ties behind them. Greg huddled by the door, not making eye contact with Darren, as he watched one of the men in suits — a federal agent, Darren now understood — inform Mr. Leroy Edwin Page that he was under arrest for the murder of Levi King. As they handcuffed the man to his hospital bed, Erika collapsed over his body. "What is it, Kiki?" Leroy said, dazed. "What's going on?" The agents and deputies crowded around the accused's bed, so that Darren was completely squeezed out of the way. He ended up against the back wall near Margaret, the murmur of her renewed praying a hum of refuge amid the clink of handcuffs, Erika's weeping, Leroy's moans of confusion, the angry beep of the cardiac monitor as his frantic heartbeat lit up the room like a firework.

18

In the hallway, Darren nearly grabbed Greg by the collar and pulled him to the farthest nurses' station, out of earshot of the other agents. They'd directed the deputies to watch Leroy on rotating shifts. The two agents were on their cell phones right outside his door. Leroy's roommate was in the hall asking anyone who would listen for a different room. Darren could not exactly name what he was feeling. Betrayal? But by whom? By Greg, for arresting Mr. Page? Or by the old man for maybe, just maybe, being guilty?

"We found them in the search," Greg said. "Several articles of the boy's clothing, including Levi's underwear."

Darren winced at the image. "And you found the kid's blood, hair, something? Did some kind of testing to prove that they're his?" he asked, knowing that even the FBI couldn't have turned around a DNA test that fast. It felt rushed, this arrest, and Darren wondered if Greg might be trying to get as much out of the headlines as he would out of a conviction. Maybe that had been his plan all along. Show the incoming Trump Justice Department that the FBI meant business when it came to crimes against the white heartland and then hope they forgot about it once they were trying to find the light switches in their new offices. "You don't even have a body."

"We're working on it," Greg said. "But right now we've got Page's own statement that he was the last one to see the boy alive, and we've got the boy's mother and sister making a positive ID on the clothing." He shoved his hands into the pockets of his suit pants, which made his shoulders scrunch up toward his ears, made him appear self-conscious and unsure of his standing with Darren. "We weren't aiming to make it come out this way. We weren't, D."

"Come on," Darren said. "I know you better than that."

Greg grew silent for a moment. "Look, about last night —"

Darren stopped him before he had to hear his wife's name come out of Greg's mouth. And, anyway, the thought of Lisa gave him an idea.

■ ■ ■ ■

"Chafee, Humboldt, and Greene."

"Never heard of them," Lisa said.

"They're out of Alexandria, Virginia, no other offices that I could find."

His wife sighed. He'd caught her in the hallway of the civil courthouse in Houston and nearly everything around her echoed through the phone. The click of high heels, the ding of an arriving elevator, the voices of court staff and attorneys, and the weight of Lisa's annoyance about this phone call. But some part of Darren couldn't help noting that she was exactly where she'd said she would be this morning, that maybe her abrupt departure last night hadn't been a lie.

"What is this about, Darren?"

"It has to do with this case," he said. "Kind of."

"I have to be back in court in like ten minutes."

"I just want to know what kind of business they're in, the firm's bread and butter. I had a hard time finding anything concrete online. And away from my Lexis account, I'm kind of stuck trying to understand what they do."

"So I'm your secretary now?" There was something playful in her tone, a reach toward a repair of whatever had been broken and weird between them last night. "Give me a second," she said, and he pictured her sitting down on a bench in the hallway. "Actually, let me look into it, and I'll call you right back."

Darren was in the Marion County Hospital parking lot, leaning against his truck. The air was as cool as it had been since he'd arrived in Jefferson, but still strangely damp and humid, an affront to the large bells and red and green ribbon the hospital had affixed to the light fixtures in the parking lot. They were only a few weeks out from Christmas now, a time when he would normally be in Camilla. But nothing about Marion County said home to him. It was zydeco where he wanted blues. It was boudin where he wanted hot links. It was swampy cypress trees where he wanted pines, which always made him think of the holidays at home, even in the dead of summer. He was ready to get out of this county, but something had rooted his boots in place, some bits in this story that didn't add up, that played like Russian nesting dolls — open one mystery and find another and another and another and another.

He was thinking of the fact that he'd yet to buy Lisa a Christmas present, which allowed his mind to wander back to last night, to feelings he'd easily avoided by calling Randie Winston halfway around the world. What was that between Lisa and Greg? They were his oldest friends; they'd known one another since high school. There was no way he would have missed something going on between the two of them, would he? The evidence was light and circumstantial, but damn if it wasn't compelling. The look on Greg's face when he grabbed Lisa's arm. The *want* there. Not for sex so much as for forgiveness. Of what, Darren didn't know.

When she called back, he picked up on the first ring. He fought an urge to demand to know what she and Greg had been talking about when he'd walked out of the steak house last night. Instead, he listened to his wife whispering from where she sat in the Harris County Civil Courthouse, as if even mentioning another firm's business was breaking some kind of attorney-client privilege. "Chafee, Humboldt, and Greene is, as you said, your standard civil law practice, nearly identical to my firm. Contract law, tort litigation, some IP lawsuits. But Brendan Chafee, before becoming a founding partner, was a DC lobbyist, so I can only imagine that some part of that business spilled over into the current firm's work, even if it's not being advertised."

"Like what?"

"People who need shit from the government probably," she said, breathing more heavily. He imagined her standing and gathering her things. "Look, Darren, I really, truly have to get into Caselli's courtroom right now."

"What about nonprofit work? Trying to get a historical landmark set up?"

"Shit like that usually happens at the state level. Chafee's work was federal all the way, dealing with the Treasury, HUD, Department of the Interior." She paused here, thinking, hmming under her breath. "That could be it, where you would go to protect a federal site. But I don't know about a firm like Chafee, Humboldt working for a nonprofit. You're talking about Texas?"

"Yes."

"I don't know, Darren, but really, I have to go."

"Thanks, Lisa," he said.

She stayed on the phone long enough to say, with what he took for soft sincerity, "You're welcome," adding with a lilt of uncertainty, "We'll talk later, right?"

"Lisa," he started, wanting to reassure her or himself of something.

But by then she had already hung up.

Since he had nothing else to go on, he tried to find a phone number or an address for the Marion County Texas Historical Society, but nothing came up on either Google or Bing, which for a small-town nonprofit didn't surprise him much. He slid his phone into the pocket of his slacks and walked back through the hospital's sliding doors, feeling the rush of disinfectant-scented air-conditioning as he went hunting for a county phone book. He'd found them to be more accurate than anything online. For small-town business folks, it was still a point of pride to be listed in print; it made you legitimate in a way that a computer — which not everyone had access to — just couldn't.

Beyond the reception area was a row of pay phones, each partitioned by finger-smudged panels and each with a small cubby underneath that was filled with various items: gum wrappers, smashed paper cups that were flaking curls of wax, and, in one, a tiny plastic doll the size of Darren's pinkie. Only the last phone "booth" held a Marion County phone directory. Darren opened the business listings starting with the letter *M*. He ran his long fingers down the names, searching through the businesses twice before accepting that it wasn't there. No listing for the historical society. But his finger stopped on the spot just above where Marion County Texas Historical Society should have been. He actually smiled at the familiar name, at the jaunty moniker the man had chosen for his enterprise: MARCUS ALDRICH'S TRUTH AND TREASURES. His uncle Clayton's old college friend with a PhD in history was still, as Clayton would say, messing around in an old, dead town, wasting his talent and time.

Maybe not, Darren thought.

The storefront was on East Austin Street, past the Jefferson General Store, which sold everything from moonshine jelly to locally made maple syrup to cowboy-boot galoshes to dixie-flag bikinis; it was on the other side of the railroad tracks, in the middle of a row of antiques shops that had Lone Star flags flying out front and rusted neon soda signs stacked near their front doors, which were outlined in Christmas lights seemingly blinking in time to the rhythm of the Oak Ridge Boys' "Because of Him" on speakers inside each store.

Marcus's shop was not so festively adorned.

He was early with a Kwanzaa kinara in the front window, each red, black, and green candle dry and dusty, as they'd certainly been sitting out since last December, and there were a few yellowing photos tacked to the windows, paintings of the lake and drawings of Caddo Indians, plus early photographic images of slaves, a group gathered in front of a small cabin, their skin scarred, bones gnarled at their joints, but other than that, the storefront and the store itself appeared nearly empty. Darren removed his hat to press his face against the window. Inside, he saw an open cardboard box of books, a table with a calculator, pad, and pencil, but no register, no proprietor, no sign of life at all.

But the door was unlocked.

It smelled of mothballs and incense when Darren stepped inside. There was an air-conditioning unit shaking in one of the windows near the back of the store, though the word *store* seemed not so much to describe Marcus Aldrich's Truth and Treasures as openly mock it. There were more photographs inside, laid out on the long table in no discernible order. They were each encased in a plastic sleeve with a tiny colored sticker in the corner, circles of green, yellow, blue. Darren ran his fingers through the stack of pictures like he was splaying out cards in a saloon. His eyes stopped on a queen: a woman in a daguerreotype was wearing a familiar ruffled white dress, cinched as tight at the waist as it was at her throat, so it appeared these body parts measured the same. He saw black eyes, felt, when he looked at her tight-lipped smile, the same bolt of panic he had when she'd stood over his bed. Although without a derringer in her hand, this was the same woman. A ghost or a dream, who knew, though he couldn't bring himself to believe the former.

"The yellows are fifty," a voice said.

Darren looked up and recognized Marcus at once. His hair was seasoned with considerably more salt than pepper these days, but he still favored wrinkled Hawaiian shirts, Wranglers, and boots worn so thin, Darren could count his toes through the honey-colored leather. He had colorful strips of kente tied around his wrists like bracelets, and he had a pencil tucked for easy access in the tight curls of his Afro. He nodded toward the photo in Darren's hand, which did in fact have a yellow sticker, and said again, "Those go for fifty."

"Dollars?" Darren said, voice cracking at the idea of it.

"Cents," Marcus clarified. "Most people come in here for the book."

He motioned Darren toward a clearly self-published tome with a red cover. The title was in black and green letters. TRUTH AND TREASURES: THE REAL JEFFERSON, TEXAS, BY MARCUS L. ALDRICH, PHD. Besides the surplus stock in the box, there were a few copies on the table next to the photo collection. Darren picked one up, handed it across the table to Marcus, and then added, "I'll take this too." He lifted the picture of the ghost. "Can't beat fifty cents," he said, trying to make light of the situation, his reason for purchasing a photo of an antebellum white woman. Marcus nodded, pausing to take in Darren's badge and hat before ringing up the sale. This was an all-cash type place, and as Darren reached for his wallet to pay, Marcus stared at his face, trying to place him.

Playfully, Darren said, "Maybe you could sign it to my uncle Clayton."

Marcus broke out into a grin so wide that Darren could see his tobacco-stained teeth, the halo of brown in his smile. "I thought that was you, Darren."

He came from around the table and gave

Darren a hug, chuckling at the improbability of the whole thing, running into him here in Jefferson. "Last I saw you, you was tagging along when Clayton helped me move out of my ex-wife's place."

"That's right." Darren smiled at the memory, one of the few times that he and Clayton went on an adventure alone, just the two of them.

"And he was in my face about wasting my good ol' Prairie View education on this here —"

"Pop's got a lot of ideas about what he thinks people should be doing with their lives." Wasn't he always meddling in Darren's? In his marriage, for sure.

"You ain't got to tell me the sky is blue." Marcus looked around his tiny shop, perhaps seeing it through Darren's eyes and therefore Clayton's. "I'm happy here, man. Shit is quiet. The divorce paid for this here shop. I sell my book, write a little something else on the side, fish on the lake when I feel like it."

Darren raised his hands to show he had no cause to judge. He was still holding his newly purchased copy of the daguerreotype.

"Penelope Deschamps," Marcus said. "One of only two known survivors of one of the worst steamboat crashes in this county's

313

history, the *Magnolia*. We're talking before the war started, years before the *Mittie Stephens,* the crash everyone remembers. It was sixty-one died on that one, in 1872, but, ask me, the *Magnolia* was the more interesting in terms of history and influence on this county." He offered Darren a glass of tea. He kept a pitcher of it in a minifridge in his back office, that and a pint of Chivas, he said, that could doctor up a glass of sweet tea real nice. Despite the morning he'd had, Darren accepted just the tea. When Marcus returned from his office, he was carrying the sweating glass of tea clouded with sugar and a chair for Darren.

Then he told a story.

The gist of it Darren already knew, Jefferson as the golden apple in Texas's antebellum eye. A bustling economy made possible by slave labor and timber — always big in East Texas — but also by becoming something that no other Texas city save for Galveston on the coast had been able to accomplish by the middle of the nineteenth century: a first-class port city, made possible by steamboat travel through Caddo Lake and up the Cypress Bayou into the town center. Cotton and other plantation bounties out of Shreveport and New Orleans and towns farther north on the Mississippi — plus manufactured goods, fine linens and furniture for the newly wealthy — flowed into Jefferson across the murky water of Caddo Lake, requiring the relatively new technology of steamboat travel to contend with the thorny swamp culture, which for many years had no law enforcement agency dedicated to policing whatever went on behind the thicket of trees on the many islands that rose up on the water between the cypress forests and tangled patches of bluish-green lily pads floating like small cities. The islands had at one time been famous for concealing outlaws, some fleeing jailers from as far away as New York City, and any other folks who might not want to be found; they took refuge in these pockets of raw woods floating in the middle of the largest lake this side of the Mississippi. There were rumors of Indians on one of the islands, Caddos who for the most part lived in quiet peace but were known to knife any man who tried to ride a canoe up to their island. Darren remembered Margaret Goodfellow's words: *There are ways of hiding in plain sight.*

Steamboats carried commercial goods but also wealthy travelers, including hundreds of New Orleans natives looking to start over somewhere new but with cultural memories of home. This was especially true during the years after the war — which was when the *Mittie Stephens* crashed — but had been going on for some time. That was how the story of Penelope Deschamps started and *almost* ended. She was a poor little thing, Marcus said, born Penny Deckard in Acadia Parish to a white sharecropping family. Her daddy was an angry man, doing the work of niggers and falling farther behind every Christmas. He drank steadily and with only one son to work the fields with him, he saw in Penny merely another mouth to feed and set about finding a way to marry her off. He spent money he didn't have on copies of *Ladies' Magazine* he sent away for and ordered Penny to study them cover to cover, to teach herself to be a lady. "Lord knows you ain't got a lick of that from your mama. She might could show you how to bleed a hog, but that ain't gon' get you out of this house."

Penny was a quick study. She took to bathing more than once every two weeks, started pinning her hair in a chignon, a style she could neither spell nor pronounce — she was functionally illiterate and leaned heavily on the pretty drawings in the magazines — and soon she was ordering her family and the few church friends she had to call her

316

Penelope. Left free of the fieldwork and useless in the kitchen, she began taking constitutionals around the perimeter of the old plantation where her family lived in a cabin that was away from the slaves but hardly any bigger than theirs and with the same dirt floor. She walked from the plantation's schoolhouse, which doubled as the church, to the royal oak around the side of the big house and back again, often carrying books as either props or tools to improve her posture. Her daddy whipped her when he saw her walking around with books on her head like a damn nigger carrying water from the well. "You stop that foolishness this instant." No one knows to what degree Penelope knew what she was doing or how much luck played a part in it, but when the master's son returned from a single semester at Louisiana State University in the winter of 1857, he took one look at Penelope and declared himself done for. Louis Deschamps didn't bother to ask Penelope's father for her hand in marriage, never spoke to him before the wedding. He simply announced his intentions to his own father, seeking *his* blessing, and then told Penelope to prepare herself for matrimony.

They were married in March of 1858. Penelope moved into the big house with her new husband and had borne him a daughter and a son by the time Louisiana voted to secede from the Union, and war was imminent. The master died before the first shots were fired, making Penelope the mistress of the plantation where her father had toiled his whole life. There was no time for either father or daughter to be pricked by the irony of the thing, for shortly thereafter, her daddy and brother were killed in combat, and Louis, her husband and father of her two children, died from scarlet fever, leaving young Penelope Deschamps the owner of a plantation she did not understand the mechanics of running and did not have the intelligence or patience to learn. Besides, Confederate soldiers were trashing the place, commandeering the big house and stealing silver and busting up chifforobes and bedposts for firewood. Seeing no way she was going to come out of this with even two pennies to her name, she contacted a lawyer in New Orleans and made a sale for a quarter of what the plantation was worth, then booked passage on the *Magnolia* for herself, her mother, her two children, and six of her favored slaves — a brother and sister, the sister's husband, and their kids, who served as kitchen help and playmates for Penelope's own children. The

rest had been sold along with the plantation.

The first days of the trip were uneventful,
with most of Penelope's time spent trying
to see a way out of her misfortune. The
money from selling the plantation might be
enough to live on for a while, but she was
still a very young woman and knew that she
would have to create some new industry for
herself in order to survive. There was talk of
purchasing a saloon, maybe one with a few
rooms for rent. She and her mother were
going over various recipes they thought they
could master when there was an explosion
near the boilers. Flames engulfed the *Magnolia* within minutes. Penelope ran for her
children as she watched burning men and
women jump in the waters of Caddo Lake.
She lost track of her mother in the blaze
and never found her son. She and her
daughter were forced overboard, where they
sputtered in the water amid the smoke and
haze until being rescued by a fisherman who
saw the fire from the nearby town of Uncertain, Texas. It was a fitting name for the land
they soon stood on, Penelope dripping and
clutching a carpetbag with all the money
she had in one hand and her five-year-old
daughter's hand in the other. Her mother,
her son, and most of the boat's crew and

their fellow passengers were gone, drowned or killed by the fire, the bodies never recovered. "The slaves were never found again either," Marcus said. "They were presumed dead, but lot of folks around here believed they ran. Or swam, I should say —"

He stopped because Darren's phone was ringing — *again.*

He hadn't recognized the number the first two times it buzzed, but this was his lieutenant, Fred Wilson. Darren motioned to Marcus that he would have to take this. Marcus, sensing he was losing a captive audience, leaned forward over the table that held his life's work. "I'm just trying to provide a different perspective on all the gilded-lily-white amnesia that is the tourism industry in this town. Life was always hard in Jefferson for folks like us; wasn't no belles and balls and all the rest of it. Jefferson threw its hat in with the Confederates, and it deserved everything that came after: The railroads bypassing Jefferson for Marshall. The opening of the Red River that ultimately lowered the water table on Caddo Lake so that steamboats could no longer travel on it. Killed this town almost instantly," he said with some glee. By now he was mostly talking to himself, and Darren stood and angled away from Marcus. He'd answered the phone.

"The Department of Criminal Justice has been trying to reach you," Wilson said. "We got you in to see Bill King, but it has to be today. Don't know why they're making this so difficult, but that was the deal we cut. You have to get up to Telford Unit in Bowie County by three o'clock."

"That's an hour from now."

"Don't mess this up, Mathews. We may not get this chance again."

19.

He bade an abrupt goodbye to Marcus, grabbing his copy of the book and the photo of Penelope Deschamps, but not knowing what to do with either once he got in his truck. He tossed them behind the front bench seat and quickly decided on a route to the Telford Unit prison in New Boston, damn near to the Arkansas border. He hadn't eaten anything all day and so chanced a swing through a catfish place. He gorged himself on the road as he headed north.

He was nervous in a way that shocked him: His hands shook if he lifted them off the steering wheel. He felt a sour damp coming up out of his shirt collar. And the fried fish turned on him before he got twenty miles outside of Jefferson. He'd sat across from killers before, but this was different. Bill King's crimes felt personal. He let out a rancid wet burp as his phone rang again.

It was his mother.

Seething was too soft a word for the blue-black tone of her voice, the hum of rage that Darren could feel vibrating through his cell phone as he exited Highway 59 on the outskirts of Texarkana and headed west to the prison town of New Boston. "So you sent your uncle after me?" Bell asked. "Damn it, Darren, why you gotta make your mama hurt you? I thought we had an understanding."

Darren was confused. "Mama," he said, reminding her of his newfound filial devotion.

"Naw, it's too late for all that. I don't know if I can trust you anymore, which means I just don't know what I'm supposed to do now. I thought we had a deal."

"Mama, what are you talking about? Did Clayton call you?"

"Call me? That uppity nigger showed up at my home. Time I returned from Lake Charles, who's in my yard warning me about taking money from you? He knew about the gun, Darren. He knew about all of it and threatened to make it look like I'm the one tangled up in this murder somehow. I swear, Darren —"

"No," he said, his truck swerving a little too close to the car in the next lane. He was flushed from his sternum up through his neck, and his damp funk filled the truck's cab, fogging the driver's-side window. "I didn't send Clayton to you."

Never told him about the gun either, he thought.

Then he remembered. Lisa. *Jesus.*

He was so angry the edges of his vision pricked with a painful white light, and even though he was behind the wheel, he briefly squeezed his eyes shut. Lisa had done it again. She'd talked to Clayton about Darren, and Clayton, alarmed by the situation, had tried to protect his nephew by going straight to Bell and telling her to back off. Worse, he'd threatened to frame her in some way if she didn't stop messing with Darren and give the gun back. Bell's voice was cracking now. She seemed genuinely hurt that her son had sold her out like this, never mind that she had been low-key blackmailing him for weeks. "When it was just between you and me, it was like it was something special, something only I could protect you from," she said now, twisting logic to turn this whole thing into an act of maternal care and protection. "But Clayton ruined everything."

"No, Mama, no."

"If that DA asks me something now, I

gotta protect myself, son."

"Just hold on," Darren said, his voice rising with desperation. "There's nothing to do. Keep everything the way it was till I can get back to San Jacinto County, and I promise you I can make this right again. You good on money for a while?" His stomach flipped again, and this time he thought he might actually vomit. He was sick of himself, his mother, this whole situation. And he was angry with Clayton and, especially, Lisa in a way that made his brain feel like it was on fire. He turned up the A/C in the truck. "Did Mack get some of your rent money over to Puck?"

"I don't want that man nowhere near me," she barked. "Does he know?"

"That you found his gun?"

"Yes."

"No, ma'am," Darren said. "I'm trying to protect him from all this."

"You need to be worried about your own damn self, 'cause I'm telling you, I don't know what I might do. If that Mr. Vaughn come calling —"

"Don't do anything, Mama," he said firmly. "I'll make this right." He hung up, hating himself for begging his blackmailer to hold on till he could give her more money, anything to keep her from doing something rash.

By the time he made it behind fences topped with coiled razor wire into the prison's parking lot, he'd left a message for Lisa accusing her of betrayal, had likewise left a voice mail for Clayton telling him to stay away from Bell and stay out of the whole damn thing. *You have no idea what you've done.* And as he turned off the truck's engine and opened the windows so he could breathe again, he called Mack at his home. "You may hear some things," Darren started, "but I want you to be assured that nothing is any different. As long as you don't change your story, we're both going to get out of this unscathed."

" 'We'? Darren, what are you talking about?"

"Nothing I want to get into over the phone," he said, looking out at the reinforced-steel bars around the prison's front doors, the men with guns in the lookout towers. He felt they could hear what he was saying right now, that like hawks, they could sense when fresh meat, a potential new inmate, was close. "It's just like we said, though, there's nothing new with District Attorney Vaughn. Whatever he asks, just tell him the exact same thing you said to him before, nothing about an altercation with Ronnie Malvo at your place."

Mack grunted out of frustration. "It's my grandbaby I don't want him harassing."

"Tell her the same as I told you," Darren said. "I'll be back to San Jacinto County soon, and we'll get it all worked out, I swear." Though he wasn't sure anymore what that meant. He had lost control over this entire mess.

He went into the attorney-client meeting room in King's cellblock hating himself. So he was relieved by the hating of Bill King that awaited him, glad that all the ignominious rage he felt over his own twisted moral compass could be aimed in this white man's direction. For how could Darren be confused about himself in the presence of a man who had hunted blacks for sport? Oh yes, he hated Bill King right now, could taste it on his tongue. He hated the man's ties to the Brotherhood, hated the destruction he'd caused, the lives he'd destroyed, and for what? He'd murdered a man who hadn't done anything to him, a man whose name he didn't even know, just to prove to other white folks that he was loyal to a toxic ideology, that it was safe to make and sell drugs with him. Keith Washington, the man he'd killed, had had a wife and two kids, one of them just about Levi King's age, both of them growing up in Longview right now without a daddy. Darren relished the chance to sit across from Bill King and have his own humanity reaffirmed.

Bill King had ceased to be a man to him.

When he was escorted into the small, square room with walls made of concrete blocks painted a slick gray, sticky with maybe hundreds of coats of paint over the years, covering everything from crude drawings to piss and shit, Bill King was standing with his head down. There were two COs on either side of him, so there were six men in the small room, and Darren could smell their coffee breath, the stale Juicy Fruit gum one of them was popping between his long teeth. That one pulled a chair from the round table in the center of the room and shoved Bill King down into it. His cuffed hands banged on the wood-laminate tabletop, making a faint pinging sound, like a starting bell. His hair had grown back in, covering the tattoos Darren knew ringed his scalp. And he wore glasses. He raised his head and looked at Darren, called him *sir,* and asked if he'd like the officers to stay. "It's whatever makes you comfortable," he said.

His eyes were blue like Rosemary's. Levi had his mother's eyes. Just like Darren, who bore more in common physically with his mother than with the Mathews men in his family. Bill King talked quietly and had a flutter in his expression that spoke of a chronic condition beyond contrition. It was shame. It had carved gray hollows beneath his eyes that made him seem vaguely ill. "If it's okay with you, Ranger, I'd just as soon talk to you alone. In private, if that's all right." The four COs shrugged and headed for the door without even checking if Darren was okay with it. There was a window in the steel door to the room. Bill King would remain handcuffed. Darren let them go.

When the steel door closed behind him, Bill stood from his chair, its legs scraping across the floor, startling Darren. Darren's hand went immediately to his side. But his Colt .45 had been checked before he entered the inner layers of the Telford Unit prison. He backed up and heard the clang of the chains connected to Bill's handcuffs as Bill, realizing he'd scared the man, returned to his seat at the table, sheepish. Softly, he said, "I ain't been much of anything in my life but an angry kid and then an angry man for reasons I didn't even half understand at the time. I caused my mama heartache, and Lord knows I've ruined lives."

"Keith Washington."

"Yes," Bill said. "And Danielle, Keisha, and Jarrod."

He was speaking of Keith's wife and children.

He knew their names.

"I've written them once a week for the past six years, saying sorry every way I know how. They were returned unopened at first, but that stopped a couple of years ago, so . . . maybe," he said, his voice growing wistful. "I'd understand it if they threw the letters away, but I hold out hope that they have heard some of what I've been trying to say, the change in my heart."

"I'm actually not here to facilitate your supposed redemption, and frankly I don't give a rat's ass about the ways you think you've changed."

"*God* knows."

"Well, you're free to work that all out with Him at a later date. I'm here —"

"I need you to help me find my son," Bill said. "Please."

"I'm not here about that either."

"I know, I know, I talked to Marnie."

Darren's ears were nearly aflame; his

blood pressure spiked and that damp, sour smell rose up again from his own body. "You did?" Was it really going to be this easy? He heard the words almost before Bill King spoke them.

"I'll claim the hit on Ronnie Malvo. In exchange, I want you to fight for my son." He looked at Darren, who realized this was why Bill King hadn't wanted the COs in the room, that he and Darren were on the same page. With a resigned shrug, Bill said, "I would have gotten life or maybe even the chair if that first jury had convicted me on murder, so I might as well take what I had coming. I knew Ronnie Malvo, knew what he stood for. I'll gladly take credit for offing him."

"Thought you believed you were getting out of here soon," Darren said, remembering his first contact with Bill King, his letter to the governor.

"I've already told Mama to call off next week."

"What's next week?"

"I'm ready to do my time, all I got coming."

"What's next week, Bill?"

"I'm not trying to get anybody else in trouble here; I just want you to find my son. Levi, that's the only good thing I've done in

331

this world, and I had hoped to go home someday and be a real father to the boy, make sure he don't turn out nothing like me. But the truth is I have been a piece of shit as a human being, and I am willing to sacrifice my freedom for that child. Hell, maybe the best way to make sure he don't turn out like me is for me to stay my ass right here inside."

"What makes you think I can find your son?"

Bill let out a sigh of frustration tinged with hopelessness. "I am telling you, sir, I will take the fall on Ronnie Malvo if you just try. Can you please, sir, just *try* to find my child?" He sounded like Marnie King begging. And Darren was reminded of her and Dana's tears. The love here was real. Bill King was willing to take a capital murder charge to help find Levi. And yet Darren hesitated.

"What makes you think he's still alive?"

"What choice do I have?" Bill said, eyes watering. "That child is my only hope that my time on this planet, the shit I've done, can be turned around."

"But it can't be, Bill," Darren said, feeling a hot stone lodge in his throat so his voice came out hard and mean. "I help you find your son, and who gives Keisha and Jarrod their daddy back? How does that work? You telling me your redemption matters more than theirs? You think that saving your white son — who, by the way, is probably a racist shit just like his dad, so you can clear the little fantasy that he's not out of your head now — you think that will make it all right for Keith's kids?"

Bill ran his grimy fingers through his closely cropped hair; the chains connected to his handcuffs rattled against the table. He seemed beat by this, undone by Darren's withholding of praise for his moral rebirth. He so badly wanted this black man to pat him on the back for what millions of people managed with ease: not hating every black person they saw. Bill pleaded for grace. "I am laying my body on the line for my sins, man. Every day. Every day."

Darren looked directly into Bill's watery eyes. "And it still ain't enough."

Darren didn't agree to anything in the room, but he didn't have to. He already knew what he was going to do. But it would take a couple of drinks to screw up his courage. He pulled over at the bar nearest to the prison, a rough-looking roadside joint in a building made to look like a barn. It was called Bucky's, and inside the place was filled with COs just off duty. Darren had removed his hat and badge in his truck to cut down on the spectacle, and at the bar he ordered six fingers of bourbon in two glasses. He wanted them lined up, back to back on the bar top, so there would be no lag between sips, no room for him to contemplate changing his mind. The lights in the bar were as low and warm as the feeling in his limbs when the liquor took over and muzzled his cerebral cortex. He didn't want to think or feel anything, just let the words roll off his tongue when he climbed in his truck later and gave Lieutenant Wilson the news.

"He says he ordered the hit on Ronnie Malvo."

"No shit," Wilson said, his voice full of wonder.

"You'll need an affidavit, of course."

"It's more than we even hoped for, Mathews." Then, almost as if he couldn't believe their good fortune, couldn't believe it at all, he said, "Conspiracy to commit murder, tampering with a federal witness, this is it."

Darren, feeling a strange pull in his chest, almost like he owed Bill King something for taking the heat off Mack, said, "He thinks his son is alive."

"Looks like he's the only one," Wilson said, then he tried to steady his breathing for all that came next. They would need to get that affidavit right away, either by sending Darren back or getting a Ranger stationed out of Texarkana to do it. "And we all have to take a close look at the implications of what this means for the task force — if Bill King knew Ronnie Malvo was a snitch, who else knows? Speaking of which —" And here he called out to the secretary who organized his calendar and helped type up his reports. "Get me on the line with Frank Vaughn down in San Jacinto County when you can. We need to tell Frank that the task force will lead the investigation from here."

The mention of Vaughn reminded Darren of the deal he'd made with Bill, pinched at a sense of duty he didn't want to feel for the former ABT captain. "Bill has concerns about the investigation of his son's disappearance."

"Well, that ain't on you anymore, Ranger. Darren, look, you did a hell of a job, pulled pee from a tree, worked a miracle, son. You owe yourself a drink and a drive home."

Darren smiled bitterly, knowing he had already doubled down on the former and wasn't ready for the latter. "There's more to this, though," he said.

He told Wilson of Rosemary King's odd behavior, the attorney she'd had nearly attached to her hip from the time Darren had met her, which stopped all manner of questioning, including that involving Marion County's latest mystery. He told Wilson about Monica Maldonado, the noises in the room, the run-in with Gaines, the lies, the notary who couldn't find her, and the fact that she seemed to have completely disappeared. Wilson chuckled faintly at the end of it, as if he thought Darren were reaching for something else to do out there to avoid leaving town. "Thought you said things were good at home."

"A woman who was at Rosemary King's house was seen with the man who is somehow tangled up in the sale of Hopetown, where Leroy Page lives and Levi King went missing. Now that woman is *also* missing," Darren said with a certainty he really didn't have. Could he say for sure that the woman he saw with Sandler Gaines outside the Cardinal Hotel was Monica Maldonado? No, he couldn't. But he was sure there was more to this story. "I find that worthy of further inquiry."

"You already done what you could, Ranger. You brought it to the sheriff's attention; beyond that, I can't say that this is one for the Texas Rangers to take up. Stop wasting time and get out of Jefferson and get back where you belong."

20.

He got properly drunk by way of a fifth of
Jim Beam he'd picked up at a liquor store
before heading to his room at the Cardinal
Hotel, where he lay on top of the bloodred
velvet duvet and ignored a dozen phone
calls from Lisa, Clayton, Greg, even from
Mack, for whom Darren theoretically had
good news. The only person he didn't hear
from was his mother, but Bill King's "confession" seemed to neutralize the threat
there, and Darren felt he could breathe
again, could sit in silence for five minutes in
a row without being jolted by his terror of
the .38 in his mother's possession and its
ability to ruin lives — his and Mack's.

He thought about calling Randie again,
but he stopped himself, tender and embarrassed over the possibility that he had gone
too far on the phone call last night. She had
to know now that he felt things for her, even
if they had yet to be named. But what if she

338

didn't feel the same? The whole thing had created an ache where there wasn't one before. He should have left her alone; they should have remained just two souls passing each other in this lifetime.

And something else was humming at the edge of his consciousness.

As the sun set, wrapping Jefferson in coral and purple and dimming to a blue haze the light in the hotel room, Darren left all the lamps off and drank in the coming dark. The bourbon melted his first set of cares like butter, but it set a yellow flame to the new shit that was knocking around in his brain, bringing other concerns to a rabid boil. He thought of Bill and Marnie's belief that their son was still alive, their desperate need for it to be true. He thought of his hard-hearted feelings for Levi and then pictured the face in the school photo, remembered that he was just a kid. He thought of Leroy Page's arrest, his daughter's coldness toward Margaret Goodfellow. He thought about Rosemary and her lawyer, of Sandler Gaines's greasy smile and dodgy manner, and he wondered again if he was right about Monica Maldonado. Was this woman really missing, and if so, why? He remembered her business card in Leroy Page's kitchen. Page's odd, rambling words this morning at the hospital when Darren had tried to ask the delirious man how and when he'd met the woman. *Rosemary could stop this anytime she wants to,* he'd said. Just like Bill King had said, *I've already told Mama to call off next week.*

Why did both men seem to believe that Rosemary held some master key that would open so many of the different locked doors around this mystery?

Next week, next week.

Darren mumbled the words over and over to himself, marveling at the slurred sound. His tongue was thick and slow, but even behind the bourbon curtain, his mind was working. They had been talking about Bill King's earlier belief that he was getting out of prison. *Soon,* he'd written in his personal letter to the governor, underlining the word, Darren remembered. On a hunch, he got on his phone and started looking into Bill King's prison history. He'd been in lockup since 2010 on drug charges and aggravated felony robbery — he had robbed a rival drug dealer's safe house, and the other guy had been shot in the process. He'd been up for parole in 2012 and in 2014. Both times, he was denied. According to his testimony at the parole hearings, Bill had already begun his transformation. There were signed

340

letters by prison clergy attesting to the change. Bill King had segregated himself from other members of the ABT, even committing multiple small infractions so he could get sent to solitary, which prevented him from fraternizing with his now enemy. He was studying the Bible and also trying to get his GED, and he was reading works by Nelson Mandela and Dr. King. *Letter from Birmingham Jail* had changed his life, he said, as he sat in his own jail cell, made him understand that part of what he'd hated about black people for years was their neediness, their steady complaints of I-ain't-gots; it made his eyes go red with rage, he'd written the parole board.

It was whites in need too. Why did everybody forget that? Where were our marches? Not for me, I mean, I always had a little something growing up Rosemary King's son. But I saw friends in my county scratching at dirt for food and some kind of way to make a living and here come the blacks talking about *me first,* and *y'all owe us this* and *y'all owe us that.* I carried around that anger for a long, long time 'cause I ain't had cracked no kind of books, didn't have anyone at home who acted any better, and I didn't understand, until I read Mr. King's book and looked into some other stuff, that they was right. We did owe them for all they got their asses kicked since God was a boy, for all we done treated folks bad. And the ones marching and hollering about *we want to eat here* and *we want to vote* and *we need good jobs,* they was really just trying to raise their families like anybody else. I mean, it was kids in that Birmingham deal. Did you know that? It must be something to have kids my son's age have to fight for what we was given at birth. Kids, man.

It was all bullshit.

Or it wasn't.

That was the thing about second chances — it was impossible to know what was real or what wasn't; every act of forgiveness was a leap of faith. Leroy Page said he'd been burned before, as had every black person in this country. But Darren needed Bill King now, needed his false confession in the Malvo homicide.

He heard the words again: *Next week, next week.*

Darren kept pushing, kept searching.

According to a site that tracked the actions of the state parole board, there was a panel at Telford Unit next Thursday, December 15, and Bill Avery King was due to go before the board. Was this the reason *soon* had been underlined in his letter to the governor? What made him so certain he might be home by Christmas? And what exactly was he telling Rosemary to call off?

By then the fifth of bourbon was whistling with empty air when Darren turned it up to his mouth, wasn't but a few swallows left, and he set it down on the nightstand and grabbed the florid hotel stationery. He tore off five sheets and at the top of each one he wrote the name of each member of the parole board that was set to gather and decide fates on December 15. Pam Sadler, Rita Montes, Arturo Valle, Austin Collins, and J. P. Graham. Then under each person's name he wrote down as much information as he could find online, looking for any connection to Rosemary King. It wasn't until he realized that Austin Collins was a Dallas banker who worked with several Texas real estate developers, including a Gaines Properties out of Longview, that Darren saw he'd been coming at this all wrong. It wasn't Rosemary who had the connection to at least three members of Bill's parole-board panel (a clean majority). She wasn't the one who could rig the results of the parole hearing. It was Sandler Gaines, it seemed, who was willing to commit a felony for Rosemary's son.

21.

It wasn't until he woke up the next morning, still in the same clothes from the night before, that he realized the mistake he'd made. The bourbon, the fact that he drank on an empty stomach washed in fish grease, the call to Wilson, the deal he'd made with Bill King — he stood up regretting all of it.

He also couldn't remember if he'd called Randie or if he'd dreamed it, but he'd told her everything, had confessed to thinking he might just turn in his badge over all this, that he didn't entirely know anymore who or what he was fighting for or how to do it without breaking the very laws he'd sworn to uphold. And he'd told her he'd like to see her again. A dream. God, he hoped that was just a dream, that he hadn't revealed himself so completely to a woman he hardly knew. He felt bricked in by his drinking, could only see the few inches in front of him, could only remember waking up.

But the papers were there.

The information on the parole-board members and his notes about Sandler Gaines were scattered across the velvet duvet, which he'd slept on top of, curled into himself, boots still on his feet. He read them all by the light of day, poured what little was left of the Jim Beam down the bathroom sink so he wouldn't be tempted. It was so easy to be good at dawn, to swear you'd never touch another drop. Then he took a cold shower and waited until he thought cafés in town were open, until he thought he could get a warm bun and a coffee away from the Cardinal Hotel, until he thought Marcus Aldrich was inside his shop.

"So you've lived here, what, twenty, twenty-five years?" he said as he handed Marcus a takeaway cup of black coffee. He'd bet that he didn't go in for the morning fuss of creams and syrups but then watched as Marcus poured six sugar packets from a stash in his office into the cup and stirred it with the eraser end of a pencil.

"Thirty," he said with a disbelieving shake of his head. "Moved here to work on my dissertation, what was supposed to be just a few months, met a girl, fell in love, and never left. Argued my dissertation on a twenty-four-hour turnaround and then came back to Jefferson and moved in with Betty." He was wearing another Hawaiian-style shirt, banana yellow with red hibiscus flowers all over it. And he hadn't shaved.

"Betty?"

"My ex. She runs the Dogwood Inn over on Bonham, one of dozens of B-and-Bs in Marion County. I mean, we both ran it while I was working on the book. We shared a love of Jefferson, but for different reasons, it soon became clear, and what can I say, the marriage couldn't survive two different views on history."

"What was yours?"

"That this whole town is a lie," Marcus said, belching with a heat that seemed to gas him forward. "Perpetuating and profiteering off a fraud — the fiction of bloodless prosperity, an antebellum life of civility and grace — while conveniently forgetting the lives that made this town possible. Let me ask you this, son. On any of the ghost tours in town, they got a stop for the slaves that were killed on plantations in town, the men who were lynched? Hell naw," Marcus said, answering his own question. "It's all white ladies in distress, roaming halls, wrenching their hands over spurned lovers or losing their slaves."

"Penelope Deschamps."

"Your girl," Marcus said teasingly, as if Darren were a fanboy who'd bought a much hyped baseball card instead of a photo of a slave mistress. Darren didn't know why he'd done it other than being unnerved by what he'd seen in his room, wanting to make sense of it by holding something tangible.

"So what's the deal with Rosemary King and Sandler Gaines?" Darren said, switching subjects and getting to the real reason he'd come by this morning.

"You talking 'bout ol' boy rolled that glorified duck boat into town?"

"The *Jeffersonian,* yes."

"Huckster," Marcus said, blowing on his coffee before taking another sip.

"He's got a development company out of Longview. Seems legit."

"You have any idea how many men have come through here believing they could return Jefferson to its former glory or at least try to tap into its tourism industry with a surefire moneymaker? Outlet malls, race-tracks, bingo halls, casinos, amusement parks, you name it and somebody's tried it."

"Gaines seems to be in the pocket of Rosemary King, or she's in his, can't quite figure which," Darren said. "Maybe she's

348

someone who can finally make things happen."

"She is queen bee around these parts."

"So what's this Marion County Texas Historical Society she's running?"

Marcus tilted his head and made a face. "Never heard of it."

"You sure?"

"We got the Jefferson Historical Society, the Historic Jefferson Foundation, and the Marion County Historical Commission — could you mean one of them?"

"No," Darren said, pushing back a little in the chair he was sitting in. He felt the coffee burn in his stomach, felt flushed throughout his whole torso. Had he gotten it wrong?

"This is Rosemary's deal?"

"The Marion County Texas Historical Society is supposed to be buying up Hopetown, out on the lake —"

"I know exactly where it is," Marcus said, a grave expression on his face. "I wrote my dissertation on freedmen's communities in the state of Texas. Hopetown is part of a larger historical story of what black freedom looks like."

"Rosemary is setting up the land in some kind of a trust, or at least that's the deal Leroy Page said he was signing." Documents his daughter said he hadn't bothered to sign, even as Leroy was saying they didn't have much time. *For what, Leroy?* "But I'm fairly certain the thing is a ruse, that she's going to turn around and sell or give that land to Sandler Gaines." In exchange for getting her son out of prison maybe. "What I don't understand is why Leroy would do that, why a man who's lived most of his life shut off from white folks would make a deal with Rosemary King. What's the connection there?"

"Well, you were holding it in your hand," Marcus said.

Darren actually looked down at his empty hands, which had held nothing since he walked in but the coffee cups. And this made Marcus laugh, a short little bark followed by a wide grin; he was enjoying the tale he was about to tell.

"Penelope Deschamps," he said, "is Rosemary's great-great-grandmother. She bought the Cardinal Hotel just after the war and spent years building it up, helped along when her daughter married a timber magnate named William Thaddeus King. Once her daughter was set up with a proper marriage and home, ol' Penny Deckard ate the business end of a pistol."

Darren sat stock-still for what felt like minutes, heat beading into actual sweat across his brow. He remembered Marcus's story of what brought Penelope to Texas from Louisiana, the tragedy that struck on the water, the deaths of most of the *Magnolia*'s crew and passengers, including her mother and son, and the loss of property. Six of her favored slaves presumed perished along with the others. And he remembered Marcus's talk of rumors that the slaves ran. *Swam.* For there was land dotted all through Caddo Lake if you could just get to it. Margaret Goodfellow's words about hiding in plain sight found him again, as did Leroy Page's profession that he owed Margaret and her people everything.

"You've got to be shitting me," Darren said.

Marcus's smile widened. "History is a funny thing, ain't it? So much more interesting in the flesh than what passes for truth in this state's history books. This is the thing your uncle Clayton either doesn't get or isn't capable of understanding. He lives his life's work in a college lecture hall, inside a world of brilliant, purposeful ideas not tested in the heat of the real world."

Since his uncle William's death, Darren hadn't heard anyone criticize Clayton's comfort in the world of academia. He might have scolded Marcus if not for the strange feeling of pride rising in his own chest. Say what you would about Darren's struggles with what the badge meant to him, he was at least living out the question every day. He was in the struggle right now.

"So there were Caddos on one of the islands on the lake?" he said.

"Gogo Island," Marcus said, nodding. "So named for what folks heard from the Indians living there if they tried to trespass. Screams of 'Go, go.' Followed sometimes by a shot from an arrow or, later, a pistol they somehow acquired. They actually traded with some white folks living on the water out there, locals who kept their secret, who had a live-and-let-live attitude. It was a change in leadership in Austin that later started the trouble. The Indians, yes, they took in the small family of Penelope Deschamps's slaves. The old-timers in Hopetown, some I interviewed myself, talked about it freely, how the Caddos felt a kinship of circumstance with the black slaves, had a shared understanding of the reach for true freedom, the Indians from being shipped out of their homeland and into Indian Territory in Oklahoma and the blacks from being returned to enslavement."

The slaves stayed for years, Marcus said, sharing agricultural ideas and learning to build housing from the scantest resources. They shared everything, and there was some mixing, of course, new bloodlines carved into the land, creating a love and trust that had endured for five generations. "They owe each other everything." Which was why Leroy Page would do anything for Margaret and her family.

But in the summer of 1865, word reached them that the war had ended, and many of the former slaves wanted to leave the island, an option the Caddos didn't feel was available to them. There were new families that were split as the blacks migrated to the land where Hopetown sits now, eventually using the Homestead Act to acquire the lakefront property. But they still ran supplies out to Gogo Island, still protected the Indians from the outside world. These were Leroy Page's ancestors. And over time, they built a thriving community that existed outside of the white world completely. There was a school, a church, a small bank, a community garden, and small businesses. For years, they went into town, into Jefferson, only out of absolute necessity, to file papers or to purchase goods they couldn't grow or get on their own in Hopetown. The old-timers told Marcus there was a deep and maybe not-so-irrational fear of having their lives stolen from them again. Even though the war had ended, they had committed a crime, and they weren't sure that Penelope Deschamps and her people would easily forget that. No one likes to admit the fear that was built into Hopetown from the very start, the sense of their freedom being as fragile as the shell of an egg, something that would crack if you held it too tightly, if it weren't handled with the utmost care.

"But how did the Caddos end up there as well?" Darren asked.

"What you got to understand is Caddo Lake, back in the day, was just buck-ass wild, a playground for all manner of criminals, rumrunners and thieves and murderers, but Texas law couldn't really do much about it, or it simply didn't choose to. But in the late 1800s, the state created what would eventually become the fish and gaming commission in order to stop the overfishing of catfish and bass and the men who were making a fortune harvesting oysters for pearls till there wasn't hardly none left. Whatever started it, there were suddenly lawmen on boats, combing every bayou and strait, every island and cypress stand on the lake. It was Page's people that got the Caddos of Gogo Island safely out of there, inviting them to make a home in Hopetown.

Ain't another bit of history like it. I believe them when they say they are descended from a band of Hasinai Caddo Indians who never left the state of Texas, no matter the white man's laws." Marcus slapped his knee, pleased with the outcome of his tale.

"So selling to the trust," Darren said, "assuming it's real —"

"Big *if.*"

"That would have been Leroy's way of honoring his ancestors, the ones who were saved by Margaret Goodfellow's people. His way of making sure, like he told me, the Caddos would have a home where they always should have been, in this stretch of East Texas. He would have made Rosemary promise that was part of the deal."

"But you think Gaines is trying to get his hands on the land?"

"Yes," Darren said. "He admitted he tried to buy it and got outbid."

Marcus sucked his teeth and stood suddenly. He walked to the windows at the front of the store, looked out toward the railroad tracks. "It's a shame, really, to lose all that history to lakeside housing."

Darren shook his head. It no longer rang true to him. "So he builds vacation housing and people spend, what, sixty, seventy thousand dollars to live by the water and go

355

into town to look for ghosts? There has to be some bigger attraction." He pictured the steamboat replica docked out on Cypress Bayou. What had the brochure said? *Come see Jefferson's newest attraction,* something like that. He saw the brochure again in his mind, the cheap photography. There had been a couple smiling, toasting before a sunset on Cypress Bayou. But there had also been images of blackjack tables, roulette wheels. Darren stood too now.

"Before, you said something about casinos," he said.

"Just rumors," Marcus said. "Like I said, folks have floated all kinds of ideas about drawing people back to Jefferson from Dallas or Shreveport, something besides historical tourism. But I never put any stock in that one in particular. Gambling's been illegal in Texas for as long as I can remember."

"Right," Darren said. *Unless.*

22

He'd heard they tried something like this in Louisiana once, Darren thought as he stood on Margaret Goodfellow's front porch, hoping she was home and not still at the hospital. He'd texted Greg to ask about any change in Mr. Page's condition and got back a terse Holding steady. On the drive into Hopetown, Darren had tried to remember the details of the scandal that erupted when the tiny Jena band of Choctaw Indians attempted to establish a reservation in Louisiana for the purposes of applying for a gaming license from the National Indian Gaming Commission; their reservation had to be recognized by the Bureau of Indian Affairs in Washington before they would be granted a license. The infamous lobbyist Jack Abramoff pushed senators and congressmen to whom he and his firm had made generous campaign donations to write letters to the Department of the Interior accusing the tiny group of Choctaw Indians of "reservation shopping," trying to set up shop miles from their actual homeland. It turned out that the real reason for Abramoff's push to end their gaming bid was that his lobbying firm already represented rival Indian casinos in the area. The only Indian casino in the state of Texas that had slots and table games was the Kickapoo Lucky Eagle Casino, all the way down in the border town of Eagle Pass, where you could sneeze and your DNA would land in Mexico. But if Sandler Gaines established one in Jefferson, he'd have a monopoly on casino gambling across the entire eastern part of the state.

Darren knocked again on the screen door with the chipped yellow paint, listening for the sound of footsteps. The baby was home, at least. Darren could hear his squeals and the cheerful chirping of some children's TV program. He hoped it would be Margaret who opened the door and not Donald or his son. But it was Virginia, Donald's wife. She had her sister-in-law Sadie's baby on her hip. She gave Darren a terse smile, and sucked her teeth as she said, "*E'-nah* is inside." She stepped back to let Darren through, eyeing him as he took off his hat inside the house. The dining-room table and every piece of furniture in the front parlor were covered in fabric in some stage of transformation. Dresses nearly done, shawls with fringes being mended, the baby's moccasins that his mother was sewing up the toes on. Even Ray, Donald's son, had a sewing machine in front of him and was carefully sewing a strip of ribbon across a man's turquoise shirt. He looked at Darren but didn't speak. The colors — oceanic blues and buttercup yellows, rose pinks and the red of life itself, of the dirt of East Texas — and the bustle of activity looked festive at first. But it was the slow, mournful tuning of Donald's guitar that kept the energy in the house down to a low pitch. Margaret's son was tucked into a corner with a few other cousins and friends, preparing instruments, waiting for something to start. Margaret emerged from a back room wearing a brick-red dress and carrying a fringed white shawl embroidered with red flowers and bits of blue and green. Her graying hair was pulled into a single braid that was crowned by a round silver comb that wrapped around the back of her head. The braid itself was threaded through with ribbons, bits of leather, and beads. She looked at Darren and put her hand to her chest. "Leroy is okay?"

"Last I heard, yes."

"If he will hold on, the spirits are coming. We start the Vine Dance at sunset, borrowed from our Cherokee brothers and sisters to bring health and wholeness for Leroy, the last of his tribe. We will dance for days in prayer."

"Mrs. Goodfellow."

"Margaret, please. Or *tayshas* . . . for friend," she said with a smile.

"*Tayshas,*" he repeated, hearing his whole world in that one word. Texas. Friend. "What exactly did Leroy tell you about the sale of this land?"

"That we would be protected."

"By having the land established as a Caddo reservation?"

Margaret turned to Donald and said, "Go get the papers from above my bed, son." As he stood, the notes of his guitar faded like fog at dawn.

Darren heard the buzz of Ray's sewing machine and also someone banging pots and pans in the kitchen. He smelled roasting squash and again the smoky scent of those black-charred beans, the onion and chili powder.

When Donald returned to the room, he didn't retreat back to his corner but instead crowded his body near his mother's, as if

360

whatever she and Darren were discussing, it damn sure involved him too. His mother took a sheaf of paper from his hand. "It was the woman who explained it all. She came to us from Leroy, who I guess got her name from Rosemary."

"Monica Maldonado."

The name didn't immediately register for Margaret. But her son nodded.

Darren said, "Latina woman, about five six, long black hair."

"That's her," Donald said. "She walked us through the paperwork."

Darren took the document from Margaret and saw a petition to the Bureau of Indian Affairs for federal recognition of the Hasinai band of Caddo Indians of Marion County, Texas. Attached was a historical narrative of Margaret Goodfellow's family and their connection to the land. The word *ancestral* was used more than once. Darren flipped through the pages, which held a story similar to the one Marcus Aldrich had told him but with a great deal less emphasis on evading the Texas law that had required them to relocate to Oklahoma. The whole thing seemed like a long shot, and yet someone had hired Chafee, Humboldt, and Greene, a firm that Lisa had assured him still had enough ties to Washington to push

361

something like this through.

But none of the pages were signed.

Darren asked why.

"She said she was coming back," Donald said.

"We sat right in this room and drank hibiscus tea with honey," Margaret said. "A sweet little thing but nervous-like, fiddling with her watch, looking at the papers over and over like she was sure she was forgetting something."

"It was something on the last page," Donald said. "She kept asking us were we sure, saying she wouldn't feel right if she left and then found out we didn't really understand what we were signing. That's why, she said, she wanted to talk to us first, and then she said she would come back with a notary in a few days. Maybe, she said, maybe some things in the document could be changed."

"She kept looking at the document and shaking her head," Margaret said. "She actually asked to use the washroom and came back looking like she'd been sick."

"Or like she'd been crying," said Virginia, who had wandered into the room.

Darren asked if it was okay if he sat down. He didn't want to mess up any of the preparations for the Vine Dance, as they had called it. Virginia lifted a bundle of fabrics and clothes, and Darren sat in a leather armchair, brown but for the worn spots on the arms, which were as pale as the belly of a farm hog. He opened the document to its very last page, his eyes falling to a section at the bottom. BE IT KNOWN THAT EACH MEMBER OF THE HASINAI BAND OF CADDO INDIANS OF MARION COUNTY, TEXAS, RENOUNCES ANY CLAIM TO FUTURE IN-COME AS A RESULT OF INDIAN GAMING RELATED TO THIS TRIBE. ANY APPLICA-TIONS MADE ON OUR BEHALF TO THE INDIAN GAMING COMMISSION DO NOT NULLIFY THE INTENT OF PARAGRAPH 11.2. Darren looked up from the petition to the Goodfellow family. "And did you under-stand what this means?"

"Of course," Margaret said, "but we told her we were happy to renounce gaming if that helped our petition get approved. We only want the land. That's what we told the woman lawyer, but she didn't want us to sign this."

"This was never about money for us," Donald said.

But it was about money for somebody, Darren thought. And Monica Maldonado knew it, knew she was helping to cheat them.

"And what do the actual terms of the sale

say?" Darren asked. "In terms of which part of the parcel would belong to you and which parts might have been set aside for other use?"

They were all standing over him now, sensing something was very wrong; even Sadie or Saku had come in from the kitchen. She was holding the boy, had a tea towel draped over her shoulder. Margaret actually dropped down on top of some of the dresses Virginia hadn't moved from the couch.

"Other use?" Donald said.

The baby fussed, teeing up for a cry. Sadie set him on the floor.

"All of that is being handled by Leroy," Margaret said before asking Virginia to go get her pipe and a flask of whiskey she kept in a kitchen drawer. "He is working with Rosemary King on the particulars of the sale. The historical society, they're putting the land in a trust to preserve it and our place here."

"She's cutting you out," Darren said, seeing it all now. "Rosemary."

"But this," Donald said, grabbing the petition for federal recognition for the tribe right out of Darren's hand. "This would make us a sovereign nation."

"On land you don't own."

No one said a word until Margaret yelled

at Ray to stop all that noise. He took his foot off the sewing-machine pedal, and the house fell quiet, except for the sound of the baby scooting across the floor with a feather he'd found; Virginia knocked it out of his hand before he put it in his mouth.

"And once this trust, if that's what it is, owns Hopetown, they can sell off part of the land?" Virginia said.

"So it's a trick," Donald said.

You give 'em an inch, they'll take a town.

Margaret shook her head in disbelief. "Does Leroy know?"

"I think that's why he hasn't signed the papers yet," Darren said, remembering Erika's irritation the day before and her father's other delirious statement that now made a hell of a lot more sense. *Rosemary could stop this.*

Mary, Mrs. King's maid, tried to block Darren at the door.

"But you don't have an appointment, sir," she said as a piece of pure performance, throwing her voice to the back of the house. Quietly she said to Darren, "Go while you can." He would realize too late that it was more than Rosemary's wrath she was warning him against. But at the moment, he removed the thin black woman — who had smudged the bright white of her apron pressing against the heavy door to keep him out — from his path as gently as he could. He had a badge, he said, all the appointment he needed, and he stalked through the house calling Rosemary's name. He found her in a large study that was lined to the ceiling with books and had several velvet lounge chairs and settees organized in a U-shape in front of a magnificent mahogany desk behind which Rosemary King sat holding a sterling-silver letter opener before a stack of correspondence — all heavyweight paper and embossed envelopes in colors of cream and white. She looked up and saw Darren, and without an ounce of surprise at his presence — wearing an expression that said this was Texas, after all; there were roaches everywhere, no matter how hard you tried to keep them out of the house — she pointed the letter opener at Mary. Her maid was hanging in the doorway of the study, clinging to the doorjamb as she might to a tree in a violent rainstorm, something to keep her from sliding to the floor.

"Get Roger on the phone."

"I tried to keep him from coming inside —"

"Now!"

For some reason Darren expected Rosemary to stand, to defend herself against what she must have known was coming. But she went back to her stack of correspondence, barely acknowledging Darren over the lenses of the reading glasses perched on her nose. She was wearing jodhpurs and a pale blue cable-knit sweater that brought out the ice in her eyes, even as they reflected the glow of the fire that was crackling in the fireplace to the right of her feet.

"So you traded Sandler Gaines a casino for your son's freedom?"

She slit through the top of another envelope with the point of the letter opener. With something resembling boredom, she said, "You don't know what you're talking about. And if you don't leave my home now, it won't be Sheriff Quinn you'll have to contend with. I sense his kind doesn't stir you to action."

"There is no trust, is there?" Darren said. "It's a shell organization, a lie you created to get Leroy to sell to you."

"It's a *rapprochement*," she said before licking the seal of an envelope with the pink point of her tongue. She wrote her name in careful script across the front. "His family stole from me, and I forgave him, and I promised his Indians would be safe."

There was so much wrong with what she'd

367

just said that Darren took a step back and cocked his head, as if to see her from a different angle. Was this woman insane, bloated with beliefs that made her as dangerous as her once violent son? Except that Rosemary's were contained within the gentility of this Victorian mansion. "His people didn't steal from you," Darren said. "They saved their own lives."

"Thereby obtaining property that rightly belonged to my relatives."

"They obtained themselves?"

"Who knows what my great-great-grandmother could have accomplished if she'd had a chance to cash out on her slaves before the war ended."

"And Margaret Goodfellow and her people, they don't belong to Leroy Page any more than his people ever truly belonged to you. They are family to each other. And you used that to try to steal the land right out from under them."

"They are getting their sovereign corner of it. I don't know why that's so hard for them to understand. The whole community, tribe, whatever you want to call it is down to fewer than twelve people. How much space do they need? A lakefront casino with novelty rides from Jefferson on an old-fashioned steamboat, this could be a boon

368

for everyone. Rising tide and all that. There'll be jobs for them at the casino if they want. I will personally make sure of that."

"But it's not going to happen, is it?"

"We've still got time," she said.

"Your son, Rosemary, he said to call it off. He's not going through with parole. In fact, just yesterday he confessed to ordering a hit on a fellow ABT."

Now Rosemary stood, pushing her chair back with such force, its front two legs briefly left the ground. They landed with a scrape on the stone floor. "What did you do?"

"Nothing," Darren said. "It was his idea . . . and Marnie's." He knew that would make her blow her top, and he wanted her this way, rage snipping at the thin membrane that held her tongue in place. "He's not getting out, Rosemary."

She shook her head. "They hate each other. There is no way the two of them cooked this up. He wouldn't. Bill knows how much I want him home."

It was as if her lover had spurned her for another. "I think they want Levi home more."

She let out a brutal gut punch of a laugh. "My grandson is dead."

369

Rosemary returned to her seat at the desk, a show of grief knocking her legs out from under her, but Darren couldn't tell if she believed what she'd said.

"What about Monica Maldonado?" he said. "Did you hire her firm or did Sandler Gaines do it or is there even a difference?"

"I'm not sure any of this is your concern."

"It is if she's missing."

"My, but hasn't your stay in Jefferson given you a sweet tooth for tall tales. Been reading too many of our ghost stories, Mr. Mathews?"

"It's Ranger."

She gave a tiny shrug to suggest she couldn't be bothered with that.

"Are you trying to tell me you never had any contact with her?" he said.

"Not at all, Ranger. You said yourself she was seen leaving my dinner party, where, if I remember correctly, she told several of my guests she was intent on seeing the lake, that she had made plans to rent a small boat from one of the local vendors in the town of Uncertain to explore it before she left Texas."

"A boat?"

"I believe several of my dinner guests can attest to her expressing that sentiment."

"You know what I think? I think Monica

got cold feet about what she was being asked to do out here, talked to you and Sandler about it, and when you realized that she might tell Margaret's family what was really going on and that they would refuse to sign —"

"And what? I murdered the poor girl?"

"I didn't say anything about murder."

He remembered again the noises he'd heard, the deep, repeated thumps. Had someone banged her head against the wall, knocking her unconscious or worse? Was that how her hair comb had broken in two? Darren had come out of his room that night and noticed that the elevator was already on the second floor, so he took the stairs. Was Rosemary already in the process of spiriting her away? It was hard to imagine, unless she'd had help. He got a sudden picture of Clyde parked in front of the Cardinal Hotel, forever at Rosemary's beck and call.

"Ranger, dear boy, do you know how many people go missing on that water? She could have had an accident. She could have eaten some bad oysters, for all I know or care. It will not change what is happening in Hopetown."

"And if Leroy doesn't sign the sale papers?"

"He will," she said. "Or he goes to prison."

Darren stood over her at the desk, feeling the heat from the fire lick from the toes of his boots up toward his thighs. He was trying to make sense of what she'd said when he heard footsteps behind him, caught the smell of English Leather.

"Roger, thank God," she said, coming around the desk. She walked to Roger, reaching to clasp both his hands in hers. "He just barged in here."

"Ranger Mathews, I'm afraid if you don't have a warrant of some kind signed by a Marion County judge, I'm going to ask you to leave the premises."

But Darren didn't leave. In fact, he didn't move. He was playing her words over and over. *Or he goes to prison.* The only way Darren could figure Leroy Page was going to prison was if the charges were really true, if no one ever found her grandson alive and well.

"Oh, for heaven's sake," Rosemary said, returning to her desk. She pressed an intercom button on her landline and barked the word, "Now."

Darren thought she was alerting Mary that Roger had arrived, but some animal aspect of his brain was already at work, knew this didn't make any sense. A moment later a bulky silhouette filled the door frame, and Roger made a squeal-like sound and hollered, "I can't be here. Goddamn it, Rosemary, I can't be here for this." He ducked out of the room just as Bo, Gil Thomason's red-bearded neighbor, burst in. He stormed past Rosemary, lifted Darren, and slammed him onto the desk, causing papers to slide and the silver letter opener to poke Darren's back. He could admit a split second of utter shock. He'd never had a man disregard the fact of his badge with such verve and clear abandon, absent any fear. The guy got in a few licks across Darren's face before Darren could unholster his Colt and stab it into the man's gut. It brought the immense weight off of him, allowed Darren to breathe again as the man stood.

"You're not going to shoot this boy," Rosemary said to Darren, "not in this county, not in my house, and get away with it. I paid for Steve Quinn's campaign. Both of them. And Bo here's got you on tape threatening white citizens out in Hopetown. Your reputation of frequently acting outside the bounds of law precedes you and leaves me a kind of creativity in explaining what went on here tonight. That ought to scare you into sitting your ass down about all of this here in my town that doesn't concern you,

373

hear? You shoot Bo, and I'll say it was unprovoked. I'll say you hollered *Whitey* or *Cracker* or any other damn thing. It's time for you to go now, Ranger Mathews. I want you to leave my home and my town."

Darren tasted blood in the corner of his mouth.

He licked at it, a coppery bloom on his tongue.

He threw his hands up in a show of surrender, but his mind was already out of the room, already halfway to the hospital up Highway 59, where he had to see Leroy Page. "You said if Leroy doesn't sign the sale papers, he goes to prison. Just tell me how, help me understand, and I'll go. Why did you say that?"

"Because we had a deal."

23

Rosemary and Leroy had cut a deal, but it wasn't working out for either of them. She wanted her casino and her son out of prison; he wanted Margaret Goodfellow and her family members to have secure rights to the land.

And someone, Darren believed, had gotten caught in the middle.

When he arrived outside Mr. Page's room at the Marion County Hospital, Greg was stationed out front, sitting on a chair and using a rolling tray from another room as a makeshift desk. There were other agents here too, as well as the deputies who were present during the arrest. One of them was eating a package of Chuckles from the vending machine. The other was playing Candy Crush on his phone. It was Greg who stood when he saw Darren, who actually put his body before the door when Darren tried to enter. Through the small window in the door, he could see the old man still cuffed to the bed, Erika by his side, looking more wilted than before, dabbing her eyes with a tissue.

"You can't go in there," Greg said. He looked at Darren with a pose of great, federally backed authority, but really it was just two friends staring at each other, one of whom suspected the other of having slept with his wife. Greg felt the accusation. It sat on the air like a lead weight, the two men's pointed avoidance of it the only thing keeping it from dropping hard at their feet.

"I have to talk to him. We may not have a lot of time."

"He's in a coma." Greg gave Darren a gentle shove back. "No one but family right now. I can't let you in there, man," he said. Then, seeing the frantic look on Darren's face, he added, "What the hell is happening, Darren? Quinn said you were going on about some missing woman, somebody you saw with Sandler Gaines."

"It has to do with the sale. This whole thing is about the sale."

"What do you mean?"

"The boy is still alive." It wasn't until he said it out loud that he knew it was true.

Greg looked around at the other agents and lawmen, and then, as if embarrassed for Darren in some way, he whispered, "Are you high?"

"The old man was using him as a bargaining chip. Stupid, yes, but he's out there and we've got to find him." Again, he went for the door to Mr. Page's room. But Greg grabbed him by the arm and dragged him a few feet down the hall, well out of earshot of the agents in black suits now wrinkled and stale.

"Darren, I just indicted the man in federal court on a homicide charge."

But if Levi is alive and returned, Darren thought, *Leroy doesn't go to prison.*

This was what Rosemary was waiting on, for Mr. Page to come to his senses about the sale, not realizing that Mr. Page had lost access to his senses.

He slapped his palm against the hospital wall. "Greg, that kid is alive, and we have to find him."

"I'm worried about you, Darren," Greg said, leaning in close enough to smell his breath. Darren knew he must have seemed unhinged. There was still dried blood on his mouth. "We found the kid's clothes at Page's house. It doesn't get any clearer. What's going on with you? Who did that to your face?"

"You can't have gotten the DNA back that fast."

"No, but we're banking everything on the mother and sister identifying the items of clothing. The stuff itself, shirt and shorts, even underwear, had been laundered. The man actually had them folded and sitting on top of his washer. The fucker thought he could wash away all the evidence."

Darren got a sudden image of the dozens and dozens of premade sandwiches in Leroy's fridge on the day he'd returned from a fishing trip with no fish, his pants legs soaked to the knee with lake water, like he'd waded out to something. And Greg said they'd found the boy's clothes washed and folded. He hadn't hurt the boy; Margaret was right about that. He was taking care of him.

Darren thought he knew where.

He left Greg with his mouth hanging open and ran as fast as he could through the halls out to the parking lot. He got into his truck and raced toward the railroad tracks and the Truth and Treasures shop.

"I need a map," he told Marcus. "Gogo Island. Where is it exactly?"

Marcus, who had been sitting with his feet up on his table listening to a podcast on his phone while sleeving new inventory of photographs into plastic, reached to the box on the floor for a copy of his book. He flipped through the pages until he came upon a crude hand-drawn map of Caddo Lake, considerably less impressive than the one Sheriff Quinn had shown Darren when they first met. He ripped it from the book like it was an act of great heroism.

There was no way the map was to scale; it didn't even show the whole of the lake, just the shore on the Harrison County side, the docks near the town of Karnack, part of Goat Island, the largest on the lake, and Horse Island. Between those two islands sat what was called Back Lake, and Darren remembered that the water out there was so wide and unruly that folks had broken it into parts in their minds to be able to make sense of something so massive. Back Lake ultimately flowed into Clinton Lake, on whose shores Hopetown sat, the northeastern-most part of the lake that belonged to Texas.

Somewhere in all that blue on the page, Marcus put his finger on a spot that was about the shape and size of a butterbean, according to this map.

"That's it," he said, his voice low, almost reverent. "Bordered on all sides by tall pines and hickory trees, so that you can't hardly know what all's went on there. But that's it. Gogo."

"You got another one?" Darren said, shaking his head when Marcus reached for another book. "No, a larger map, something they give out to tourists and fishermen, that sort of thing? Between the two maps, I think I can find it."

"How you gon' get there?"

That had yet to be figured out. On the way over, Darren had called Sheriff Quinn three times, each time leaving the same message about needing to get in contact with the game warden. The sheriff had not returned his calls, and Darren thought it was probably time to accept that that bridge was burned and smoldering by now. So he phoned his lieutenant in Houston. "Mathews," Wilson barked as soon as he picked up his desk line. "Why am I still getting calls from Frank Vaughn, the DA in San Jacinto County? You didn't mention the Bill King catch, did you?"

"No." He hadn't. And his mother still hadn't returned any of his phone calls.

"Good, 'cause until we get this thing down on paper, get a notary to witness his confession, I don't want to be putting our business in the street. Frank and his team in

San Jacinto County been working this one for nearly two months now, and I want to be sure we got this in the bag before I tell him we got the killer, tell him to back off and let us run the case from here on out."

"I want the same thing."

"Well, maybe I'll wait to figure out what he wants," Wilson said. He made a wincing sound and then took a swig from something on his desk. Darren pictured another of his wife's concoctions, some buttermilk and mashed-beans brew, maybe; Darren could only imagine. "You on your way back to Houston? I imagined you've done worn out your welcome in Marion County."

"We've still got a missing child."

Wilson belched into Darren's ear. "I don't follow. Steve Quinn told me the feds were moving on an arrest in that case, one of the old-timers in Hopetown."

"I believe the boy is alive, sir, and I need to get an assist from the game warden to get an escort out on the water."

"Water?"

"He's on the lake, sir. He's on an island out there, I'm almost certain of it. An island that's connected to the history of Hope-town. I believe the old man was holding him as leverage to get Rosemary King to change the terms of the sale."

"Mathews, you sure about this —"

"I found a snake pit out here. Thieves and liars. And I think Leroy Page has some misguided idea about how to make things right, and he took the boy. And there's a woman involved, a woman who's gone missing, a lawyer working on the sale, and I think Rosemary King had something to do with that."

"Son," Wilson said. It was rare he didn't call him *Ranger,* though *Darren* often slipped through, given how close Fred Wilson and William Mathews had been when they served in the department together. The *son* here came out tender as a caress, the kind usually followed in these parts with the soft insult of *Bless your heart.* But Wilson was actually trying to communicate something that Darren hadn't expected: trust. "I don't have feet on the ground and can't really wrap my mind around all this, but Darren, if you're telling me you think there's a kid alive out there somewhere, I ain't gon' do a damn thing to stop you from looking. But I can promise you ain't gon' get a lick of help from Marion County. You give me an hour or two to make a few calls, I'll see which one of our regional offices has access to a boat we can get to you."

"We don't have time. It's been almost six days."

"You think he's in danger?"

"Strange enough, I think Leroy's been feeding him, taking care of a kid he openly admitted he couldn't stand." It was Leroy who was in danger of going to prison if someone didn't get this kid before he actually died out there, now that his grandfather's old fishing buddy wasn't around to bring him food and water. Darren said, "It's just time he came home," and left it at that.

"Do what you have to. I back you one hundred percent."

He didn't think he'd ever heard those words from Wilson, and hell if it didn't cross his mind that to save a white child he was being given carte blanche to go around the locals here, that with this one, he had Wilson in his pocket. A match head's flame of anger lit in his chest and extinguished itself just as quickly. Did he think the missing blond boy lit a fire under Wilson? Yes. Did it mean the boy didn't still need his help? No. Could he possibly keep Leroy out of prison? Yes.

He took the torn map from Marcus's book plus a tourist version that Marcus kept in the store, tucked both of them into his pants pocket, and started for the door. He didn't realize Marcus was following him until he was on the pavement outside and heard the door to the store lock behind him. He turned.

"I'm coming too," his uncle's old college roommate said.

"What?"

"You'll never find it without me," Marcus said, sliding his arms into a red faux-leather bomber jacket. He put a hand on Darren's shoulder as if they were partners in some grand adventure, as if he was about to have the time of his life.

Marcus told him they'd find a ton of boats on the docks in Karnack near the Big Pines Lodge restaurant, but he neglected to add that every last one of them would be filled with tourists, men, women, and children who'd paid good money to buy lake-tour tickets from one of the five tour companies running businesses out of shacks sitting like rotting teeth in a semicircle behind the restaurant's parking lot. The air carried the scent of burning boat fuel from the idling engines and the grease exhaust from the lodge's kitchen, where everything from gator to catfish to hushpuppies swam for its life in a vat of hot oil.

The boats were pontoons mostly, each

loading between ten and eighteen people. Darren set a boot on the lip of the nearest boat. He kept a hand on his pistol but didn't remove it from its holster, knowing the stance was enough to command folks' attention. "Everybody off this boat." The boat's captain was a leathery white man who was all skin over bones that looked as thick as carved stones, so he appeared vulnerable and terrifying at the same time. The sides of his head were shaved, and his mullet, bleached white from the sun, bopped up and down as he pushed through his paying customers to the back of the boat to see what in hell was going on. "We got a kid missing out there on the lake and not a lot of time," Darren said. The captain saw Darren's hand hovering near his Colt .45. He saw the badge too. Something flashed in his eyes — maritime duty, Darren hoped. He believed they had an understanding. "This is an emergency. We need to get everybody off this boat."

There was a toddler who started crying when the captain began ushering the tourists off the boat, promising refunds and a free ride later. Marcus hung back on the dock, offering a hand to passengers as they exited the boat, grumbling and grousing as they went, the women holding their children tightly. Once the *Blue Heron* was empty of passengers, Marcus joined Darren in the boat. He put on two life vests, one strapped over the other. Darren pulled the maps from his pocket and told the captain to take them north along the narrow branch of Cypress Bayou that was a passageway to Carter Lake, which would lead to Back Lake and Goat Island and the spot on the map Darren was pointing to. "Gogo Island," he said.

The captain walked to the engine's control panel. It was set in the center of the boat, with seats all around it, built with a tourist's unobstructed view in mind. So Darren left the map with the captain — Jim, he'd said his name was — and went to stand at the front of the boat, the metal railing pressing into his hip bones. Marcus hadn't said a word since they started sailing. He was pressed into the bench seat in back, not moving. "Never heard of it," Jim called to him. "But, hell, you could live in these parts fifty, sixty years and never know every stretch of island, every bayou strait, every duck blind or bootlegging outfit once tucked in these woods. I bet there's stuff in here even God couldn't find with a map."

"A little more optimism, huh?" Darren said, not liking the frank nihilism of futility from a man who was helping him find a child. He asked Jim if they couldn't pick up the pace, then leaned back to see if Marcus thought this was all looking right. Were they headed in the right direction? Marcus either didn't hear him or was more nervous on a boat than Darren had realized. "Seriously," Darren said, turning to the captain. "Not meaning to bust your balls, but could we kick it up a bit?"

"Heading into a cypress forest up here," Jim said. "We race through there and bump up against one of the cypress knees shooting up out the water, and we're liable to tear up this boat. Trust me when I say you don't want to be stuck out here come sundown. They call it 'spending a night in the Caddo Motel.' You picked the quickest route, but a lot could go wrong between here and there."

Behind him, Marcus made a sound, a hiccup of panic.

The sky hadn't even grayed to the ashy purple of coming dusk. They had at least a couple of hours of light, Darren figured. He couldn't understand the captain's odd demeanor, the faint joy he seemed to be getting out of a dire situation of which he was not in control. The scraggly mustache made it hard to tell, but Darren thought the man might be smiling. He was about to tell the guy to quit fucking around and take this thing up to full speed when they entered the cypress forest. Jim actually slowed the engine to a near crawl, and he *was* smiling, Darren could see now. Beaming. "There she is."

"My God," Marcus whispered.

Inside the forest they were floating through, there was no sound beyond the tinkle of lake water against the sides of the boat, no world beyond Caddo Lake. Darren had never seen anything like it. Cypress trees, their trunks skirted so that they appeared like shy dancers at a church social, leaving enough space for God between them, enough space for Jim to snake his way through dozens of trees shooting up to a sky that was darkening after all, Darren thought. That or the canopy of Spanish moss hanging from the trees had steepled the forest, had put a roof over this holy sanctuary on water.

The three men rode in silence for what seemed like an eternity.

It was raw beauty, floating through a forest of trees older than time itself, trees that seemed to stand sentinel against outsiders, against any man or woman who didn't respect the lake's history, who didn't respect or understand what had been here before any of them on that boat had been born, before America was even an idea, before Mexico and Spain had a piece of it, before the French tried it too, before Texas was more than a word of kindness on a Caddo's lips. *Tayshas.*

When they broke through the forest and onto the open water of Carter Lake, Darren was happy to catch a snatch of sun behind clouds that were moving in from the east. They would face night-time or a storm if they didn't get through this quickly. In the open sound, Jim picked up speed, as Darren had asked him to. They moved into Back Lake and skirted along Horse Island and then the southern border of Goat Island, which stretched for a few miles. The *Blue Heron* was closing in on the area on Marcus's map that represented Gogo Island. Darren scanned the water in front of him, staring at the stand of pine trees that seemed to shoot up out of the water but were actually more like a wall around a piece of land that grew bigger the closer the boat got to it. Darren turned to Marcus, who was still pressed into his seat at the back of the boat.

"Is this it?" Darren said.

Marcus was quiet. Darren waved him

forward. "Is this the island?" When Marcus shook his head uncertainly, Darren yelled at him to get up and come look. Jim had started to slow his engine as they approached not so much a shore but a place where the land rose a solid foot out of the water. Darren pushed Marcus against the railing.

"I don't know, man," Marcus said.

"What do you mean, you don't know?"

"I've never seen it."

"You lied to me?"

With an embarrassed shrug, Marcus said, "I can't swim."

Hence the two life jackets, the way Marcus was clinging so hard to the boat's metal railing that Darren could see every ridge and wrinkle on his knuckles. He caught a flash of lightning out of the corner of his eye, followed a few seconds later by a cannon shot of thunder. There was a storm coming for sure. "If y'all finna do this thing," Jim said, "now's the time."

Marcus snatched the map from his book out of the captain's hands. He stared at it for a while, then looked at the open sound behind them. He nodded with less certainty than Darren would have liked and said, "This is it." Followed a few moments later by an equivocal, "Gotta be."

"Can't really pull up on land in this thing," Jim said to Darren. "This is as far as I go."

Darren nodded, then made to climb over the rail. He would have to swim or wade and find a tree root he could grab to hoist himself onto the island. But just as he was about to go over the side, he heard Marcus yell his name and felt an arm around his neck. It was Jim, those stone-like bones crushing Darren's windpipe. Worse, he felt a weight lift at his side and knew the man had gotten hold of his gun. He didn't understand what was happening until his eyes, leaking with the stress of trying to breathe, saw the tattoo on the captain's wrist.

A teeny-tiny dixie flag.

Jim whispered in his ear, "You think Rosemary ain't put out a word or two about you? The mother of Bill King can always count on our support."

"He quit the Brotherhood."

"What's that?" Jim said, squeezing Darren's neck tighter.

"Let him go, man," Marcus said weakly.

In Darren's ear, Jim laughed. "Brotherhood is for life."

"The boy," Darren croaked.

"If this ain't some nigger magic, some

bullshit story about Indian islands, and Bill King's kid is really on this floating bushland, *I'll* go get him."

And then Darren heard a faint metallic thud.

The pressure on his neck was gone at once.

When he turned, he saw Marcus holding the boat's fire extinguisher, which he had used to extinguish the boat's captain. *Or, shit, no.* Darren took a second look and saw that he was still breathing. He took the gun from Jim's hand and held it out for Marcus, who looked scared to touch it. "What'd you say about my uncle choosing academia over real-life shit? Well, this is as real as it gets."

Marcus took the gun and Darren told him both of their lives were in his hands before he jumped over the side of the boat. The water was much deeper than Sheriff Quinn had said, at least out here in the open sound. He was treading water around the side of the land, looking for something he could use to yank himself onto the shore. Eventually he stepped on the root, or knee, of a cypress tree, which gave him enough height to reach the trunk of a pin oak that was sandwiched between two pines. It was small enough for him to wrap his arms around the whole of its base. He pulled himself up and onto Gogo Island.

It was like walking through a park at first or going off trail on a hike, never mind that he could hear the whisper of water surrounding the island. He found remnants of previous lives scattered here and there. Pieces of broken pottery, circles in the ground where dozens, maybe hundreds of pit fires had burned through, changing the landscape forever. He saw birds nesting, squirrels, and nutria rats. It was too cold for water moccasins, but in another season he would have added them to the list of wildlife. He'd been walking for twelve minutes or so before he came upon something that stopped him in his tracks. He stood so still he could hear the water dripping down his pants onto the hard, packed earth. He was staring at a conical hut almost identical to the one near Margaret's people in Hopetown, only this one had rotted through in places, and part of its roof was hanging down. Through the holes in the wood-and-straw wall, Darren saw a flash of movement. He screamed Levi's name and ran toward the hut.

He was within a few inches of it when a rock flew by his head. Another shot out of the hut, this one hitting him squarely on his left shoulder. A third rock hit Darren's hip bone. "Go away," he heard a voice say, one that was choked with snot and raw with rage. "I will kill you. I swear I will."

Darren had to duck his considerable height to make it into the hut. What had been a holy site for Caddo Indians at one point now smelled like piss and bologna and the funk of an unwashed child missing for days. He was scrawnier than Darren had imagined, but maybe nearly a week out here without proper nutrition had whittled the boy down to this; his clavicle was showing through the oversize flannel shirt he was wearing, one of Leroy Page's, Darren guessed. He wore the old man's dungarees too, rolled three or four times at the ankle. He was covered in chigger bites that he'd scratched into angry red welts. Darren saw older scars on his legs too. He remembered Marnie saying Gil had hit the boy before and thought of all the wounds he didn't wear on his skin.

"Let's get you out of here, Levi."

"I ain't doing nothing niggers say do no more."

"I'm here to take you home," Darren said, crouching before the boy.

Levi wiped away snot with the back of his hand. "That's what Mr. Page said and then he brung me here. He a lie, and you a lie too, and you better git before I end your nigger life." He picked up a very large rock, one he'd clearly been saving for a battle up close. He raised it high, beads of sweat forming on his forehead as he bore the weight of it, as he prepared his skinny arms to attack Darren, who didn't flinch. "And then what, Levi?" he said. "Like it or not, besides Mr. Page, I'm the only other person who knows you're out here. And he's in a coma." He watched Levi's eyes go wide before he bit his lip, trying to figure what all this meant. "So no more sandwiches, no more clean clothes and water. No one else is coming for you, Levi. But Leroy, he wanted to get you out of here. I believe he was planning to before he got hurt."

"What happened?"

"Someone shot him. Can't have all the hate talk out there and it not end up in violence some kind of way. It's just human nature. You talk it enough and it carves out a path of permission in your heart, starts to make crazy shit okay."

"I ain't mean nobody to get hurt," Levi said. "It wasn't Gil's ass, was it?" He sounded suddenly like the oldest, world-weariest nine-year-old on the planet. The dark puffy circles under his eyes looked like twists of gray cotton candy.

"Naw, he's in jail."

And that's when he broke wide open, tears and snot raining down his face. "Gil's gone?" Darren nodded and Levi threw his body forward and fell into Darren's arms, nearly knocking him backward. His warm body was almost feverish. He was racked with sobs, and Darren could feel the bones in his rib cage trembling against his hands. "I want Mama and Dana. I want to go home."

Something about Gil Thomason out of the picture released the pain and anger and fear the kid had been holding in for who knew how long. He wiped his nose on Darren's shirt, then looked down at Darren's five-point-star Ranger badge, then back up at the dark skin on Darren's face, then down again at the silver badge.

"Holy crap, is that thing real?"

Despite himself, Darren let out a low chuckle. The kid couldn't even believe a savior who was sitting right there in front of him. Or maybe, Darren thought, maybe he was just a kid seeing a Texas Ranger badge for the first time.

"Yes," he said. "It's real."

24.

Marcus had to steer the boat toward Hope-town in the rain while Darren kept the Colt trained on the boat's handcuffed captain. Marcus didn't at all know what he was doing, and at several points, Levi had to take over to show Marcus which buttons to push, which throttles to toggle this way or that. Levi had never been on a boat that size before either, but he said it was just like a video game. Any time he wasn't at the control board, he was right up under Darren, as if he were afraid to leave the Ranger's side, as if this might all have been a dream and if he couldn't feel the lawman near him, he might wake up back in that hut. *No one else is coming for you.* Darren could smell the musk of his blond hair, could feel the heat in his body rev up the closer they got to the shore. Calls had been made on the way, and by the time they arrived, pulling onto shore not too far from Levi's granddaddy's boathouse, Sheriff Quinn was waiting, as were Marnie King and her daughter, Dana. Marnie, hair slick with rainwater, hanging in limp chunks around her head, ran into the shallows at the shore and reached for Levi before he could even climb over the side of the boat. She kissed his cheeks, his dirty arms, cried as she looked over the top of his head and said to Darren, "Thank you." Once on land, Levi ran to his sister and she hugged him tight and swung him around. Darren left the family to themselves. Marcus didn't take off the life vests until he was safely on land, where he assured Quinn he'd hit the captain in self-defense. The sheriff got a good look at Jim and his mullet lying prostrate on the floor of the boat and let out a whistle. "Oh boy, this gon' be a goddamn mess."

Darren climbed off the boat as well. There was no way he was riding that thing back across the lake. He'd find some other way to get into town. He'd started walking in that direction on the road that led out of Hopetown when he heard the shuffle of tiny footsteps in the red dirt and sand that made up the roads out there. He turned and saw Levi coming up behind him, his face wide open like a daisy drinking in dew, like Darren was the sun that made all things possible. "But what about Daddy?" he said. He must have been chewing on this question the whole ride to Hopetown. Gil was gone. That was one prayer answered. He was back home with his sister and his mama; that was another. "Is Daddy still coming home soon like he said?"

Darren looked at the boy and was for a moment speechless.

Because of Darren, Bill King would likely never leave prison. It was no less than what he deserved, considering the murder for which he'd never served any time. And yet Darren still felt the lie in it, the liberties he'd taken that meant he had to look Levi in the face and say, "No, son, he's not coming home."

Levi bit his lip and kicked a toe in the dirt, confused and hurt.

"Just like Keisha and Jarrod Washington's daddy ain't coming home."

"Who?"

"Ask your mama to look it up for you," Darren said, trying to be matter-of-fact about the information and not willfully cruel. Levi's life was a precarious one. Like a toy ball tottering on a wire fence, he could fall either way. They'd have to be careful with him, his family. "Or, better yet, write your daddy a letter and ask him about it. If

399

he's changed like he says he has, he'll tell you the truth." As he continued his walk out of Hopetown, he heard drums in the distance, the wail of Donald's guitar, could picture Margaret and her family dancing in the rain.

In the end, the only federal case to come out of Marion County that December was the investigation into the conspiracy to commit fraud by Rosemary King and Sandler Gaines, the latter of whom skipped town shortly after the boy had been found. Rosemary, Roger by her side, held a press conference on the manicured lawn of her Victorian colonial and called the whole thing "hogwash."

Monica Maldonado's rental car was found abandoned on a farm road halfway to Longview, but there was nothing to suggest she hadn't parked it there herself and simply walked off — no physical sign that anyone but her and a rental-car employee had ever been inside the vehicle. She had, as Rosemary predicted, simply disappeared, and though Sheriff Quinn had come around to seeing the foulness at the center of the thing, without a body, he couldn't do anything but open a missing-person case with his department and wait for something to change.

Darren stayed in town long enough to meet two of her sisters, who had flown in from Washington, DC, and Pennsylvania; they thanked him for alerting the authorities to her disappearance, but still he felt ashamed there wasn't much else he could do. It was not a case in which the Texas Rangers chose to get involved. It was Quinn's to handle. He told the sisters that Monica had tried to stop something she thought was wrong, that she had prevented good people from being cheated out of their birthright and that it may have gotten her killed. They said they were going to stay for a bit, renting a room in the hotel where their sister was last seen and promising to park outside of Rosemary King's house for days on end; they wanted her to feel their sister's ghost.

When Leroy Page came out of his coma a week later, he was arrested again, this time for kidnapping and child endangerment, but only Sheriff Quinn's men were present. Greg had left town by then, and so had Darren, but not before he'd gotten the old man to sign legal documents that Lisa had generously had a lawyer at her firm prepare, pro bono, for Mr. Page, papers that turned over property rights to Margaret and Donald

Goodfellow with a clause that specifically forbade any subleasing of the land, thereby eradicating the legal and cultural loophole the white nationalists in the trailer park had used to usurp a whole swath of Hopetown, terrorizing Mr. Page and Margaret's extended family.

Lisa had seemed pleased she was able to help.

It was, they both knew, the least she could do.

Greg and Darren had met at the edge of Hopetown to watch while Marion County deputies kicked out every resident in every trailer, van, car, houseboat, and tent, telling them anything they couldn't drive off the land in fifteen minutes would be demolished by a bulldozer. People rushed out barefoot holding picture albums, TVs, one fellow struggling to carry a minifridge. They packed up cars, trucks, and the yellow van that sat next door to the trailer where Gil Thomason had lived with Marnie and her kids. They were all running, all except Bo, whom the deputies had arrested two days before for shooting into Leroy's Page's house and nearly killing the man. Attempted murder, another state felony. Greg, his hate-crime work done, had brought a couple of beers to the show, and they both leaned against Darren's truck, having the most peaceful moment between them in days, both enjoying the spectacle of white folks being run off some shit they'd never owned, had no business touching.

At one point, Greg's expression grew soft, pensive. "We got to talk, man."

Darren shook his head. "Not now, Greg. Soon. But not now."

He never got a chance to say a proper goodbye to any of them.

Not to Leroy, Margaret, Ray, Donald, Virginia, Sadie, the baby, or the other members of the Caddo tribe that Darren had hardly gotten to know. He never talked to Marnie or Dana again, or Gil Thomason, who was looking at a good stretch of time inside the facilities of the Texas Department of Criminal Justice. Their trailer soon to be bulldozed, Marnie had moved her kids into a motel off Highway 59, just south of Jefferson. He drove by it on his way out of town, looking for a towheaded boy with tight, chip-heavy shoulders. He saw Dana watching Levi at the pool, Marnie sitting with a foot dipped into the deep end, not a one of them wearing a proper bathing suit. They were laughing at something Levi had said. Darren took one long last look at the boy, hoping like hell he was right about the kid and Greg was wrong, that after all this he wouldn't one day meet up with a nineteen-year-old Levi King, a man-child with SS bolts inked on his wrist.

■ ■ ■ ■ ■

CAMILLA

■ ■ ■ ■ ■

He was back to staying in the house where he'd grown up, the homestead in San Jacinto County, his beloved Camilla. He didn't put a date on his return, just told Lisa he needed to be close to it for a while. *Home.* She didn't press it, had felt buoyed by her ability to help Darren for once, clearing the interlopers out of what was now the home of the Hasinai band of Caddo Indians of Marion County, Texas, their petition to the Bureau of Indian Affairs going through with new documents that carried none of the mercenary stink of Sandler Gaines. She had shared a part of him, his work, and that was enough for now. If he wanted space — and she was granted a few more days without having to answer any questions — she was happy to give it. It was weird for Darren, commuting into the city to get to the Rangers office in Houston, weirder still to walk into his lieutenant's office on his first day back and find a piece of San Jacinto County staring him in the face.

District Attorney Frank Vaughn was sitting across from Wilson, who was standing behind his desk, arms crossed as tight as if two pythons were taking the breath from a grown man. He was staring at something resting on top of the papers and file folders on his desk. The plastic bag it sat in caught the light and Darren didn't know what it was until he saw the red tape across the top of the bag, the word EVIDENCE. He didn't move, didn't take a step forward. Vaughn turned around in his seat and saw Darren had entered the room. He shot him a grin that could cut glass. "And here come this ol' boy now," he said.

The gun, a snub-nosed .38 revolver, was sitting on Wilson's desk.

Wilson finally looked up at his Ranger, an expression on his face that sat at a crossroads of confusion, betrayal, and disappointment. "Mathews."

"You want to tell your lieutenant why I have the pistol that killed Ronnie Malvo in my possession, same time as you was getting a confession from Bill King?" Vaughn said. "When ain't nobody in my department can put Bill King anywhere near this weapon or anyone he might have hired to

408

do the job?"

"You don't know that," Darren said. He couldn't think of anything else.

"Don't I, though?"

"Darren?" Wilson's tone was hopeful, wanting some easy explanation.

"Where'd you get that?" Darren asked Vaughn.

He could feel his heart pound, a drumbeat at the base of his throat.

Vaughn started, "Not that I owe you any information —"

"It was an anonymous tip," Wilson said, irritated by Vaughn clearly enjoying himself. "But their county ballistics says it's the real deal. It's the gun."

Vaughn looked down at his tie, lifted it like he hoped to divine something in its paisley pattern, then let it fall against the small mound of his paunch. "So we got us a situation here," he said, looking now at the Texas A&M class ring on his right hand. "Trying to —"

"Link that gun to Bill King?"

Wilson shot Darren a look of barely suppressed rage, then came to his rescue anyway. "We'd like to take the case from here, Frank, run the murder investigation out of the multiagency task force, get Bill King on conspiracy."

"Bill King ain't have nothing to do with Ronnie Malvo, and he knows it." He was pointing at Darren. "Tip I got," Vaughn continued, "suggests you've had knowledge of the murder of Ronnie Malvo that you have never disclosed to law enforcement or my office, that you might have known where this gun was since the killing. Hell, might have committed perjury in front of the grand jury for all I know."

"That's enough," Wilson said. "Darren, is any of this true?"

He knew enough not to say a word.

Vaughn fiddled with his tie again and said, "We're investigating you for charges of obstruction. Came down here to let your people know." To Wilson: "You might want to think twice about having this one on the job right now."

"I'll decide what happens in my department, Mr. Vaughn."

"You do what you have to down here, and I'll take care of San Jacinto County, and that includes the investigation into the murder of Ronnie Malvo. My office will continue handling it and any other charges that might come out of it."

He was looking right at Darren as he said the last bit.

"You finished?" Darren said.

"Not even close."

"Am I under arrest?"

Vaughn paused long enough to give Darren a bit of hope. Vaughn knew less than he was letting on. Darren knew where the anonymous tip had come from; now he needed to know what exactly his mother had said. Vaughn tried to recapture the heavy note of danger in his voice, the threat he wanted Darren to feel.

He smiled, showing his teeth again, and said, "Not yet."

She was not in her trailer.

Nothing was.

The whole thing had been completely emptied out. The kitchen cupboards were bare; there was no more than a single plastic fork and a packet of hot sauce in all of the kitchen drawers. The TV, the one Darren had paid for with hush money, was gone, as was the box that connected it to the cable service he'd paid to have installed. She'd left the bed frame and the mattress, but all of her clothes and shoes were gone. Even the small sticky bottles of hotel shampoo she stole from work were no longer lined up along the edge of the plastic bathtub.

Bell Callis had taken the money and run.

She'd abandoned him a second time, he

thought as he walked on wobbly legs down the trailer's front steps, the midday sun pressing down on the top of his head. He fell to his knees in the dirt and crabgrass in front of his mother's trailer, took off his hat, and buried his face in it, the only shade he could find. He hid his shame in it, screamed all his rage into it, begged for God's help in it, and then he cried. For what she'd done to him and for the shit he'd done that had put her in a position to hurt him again in this lifetime. He'd lied and abused the power of his badge — for noble reasons, sure, but reasons that might now send him to prison. He thought of his uncle William in his hat and badge riding high in the cab of his old Ford truck, how when Darren was even a little too old for it, he'd let the boy sit right next to him in the cab, close enough that Darren could lay his head on the man's shoulder, could feel safe against the impenetrable wall of his goodness. Mack had been William's friend too. Maybe his uncle would understand what Darren had tried to do. Or maybe he'd call him the worst kind of fool.

He would have to tell Mack but still try not to scare him. Darren had convinced himself on the drive over to the McMillans' cabin at the northwest edge of San Jacinto County that there was no reason to panic. The best thing they could do now was stick with the story they'd always told, continue to keep secret the night at Mack's house when the old man had pointed a gun at Ronnie "Redrum" Malvo's head, furious with him for coming onto the property, for scaring his granddaughter Breanna, for all the ways he'd been harassing her for weeks.

There was a fire going inside the A-frame cabin. Darren could see a curl of smoke coming through the chimney, could smell a mix of chestnut and pine in the fireplace. He parked his Silverado behind Mack's ancient Ford truck. There was another car in the driveway, a little Chevy Spark, red as an apple.

Darren glanced inside the compact car on his way to the cabin's front porch. He saw a few college textbooks and a dream catcher hanging from the rearview mirror. He guessed Mack had scraped together some money to get Breanna a car so she wouldn't have to walk around town anymore or catch a bus up to Polk County, where she was in school, so she would never have to come face to face with the likes of a Ronnie Malvo and his kind ever again.

Mack opened the door before Darren even

knocked.

Inside, the TV was on, and Mack was drinking a beer and eating a ham sandwich off a TV tray, watching a game show. He didn't bother to offer Darren a beer or even a glass of water, and that's when Darren sensed something was seriously wrong. He took a closer look at the undershirt Mack was wearing, saw it covered in stains of a variation in color and placement that suggested he'd been in it for days. His hair was knotted in places, like he hadn't run a comb through it in a while, and his eyes glazed over as he looked at the TV.

Darren sat down next to Mack. "Vaughn come by here again?" he said, wondering if this was the cause of what appeared to be a psychological decline of some sort. This was the most undone Darren had seen him since this all went down, and that included the night he'd cried with Darren when he realized how close he had come to killing a man. Maybe the actual doing of it was slowly starting to tear him apart.

"Listen, Darren, we got to talk."

"I know about the gun. I know they have it."

"What?" Mack stood suddenly, knocking the TV tray so that his beer bottle fell on its side. It soaked the plate and his sandwich and spilled onto the woven carpet at his feet, which Darren saw were both bare and ashy.

"Now, look, it don't immediately change anything," Darren said. "I've been working on an angle that will protect you in this thing, I promise you."

Mack sank back onto a couch that was the color of marigolds gone brown with age. He let out a grunt that sounded almost like a macabre chuckle, a private marveling at some dark joke. "Bre, honey, get on in here. It's Darren, honey."

She came from the other room wearing black leggings and an oversize sweater that came down to her knees. She must have been in the middle of braiding her hair, because half of her head was puffed out, as cottony as quilt stuffing, only black and shining with coconut oil. "Yeah, Paw-Paw?"

Her grandfather gave her a stern look and said, "Sit down."

She did as she was told, taking a seat as far away from her grandfather and Darren as she possibly could while still being in the same room, on that same couch. She wasn't looking at Darren but down at the comb in her hand. She pulled strands of hair from it and watched as they floated to the carpet below.

"It's time, child," Mack said. "Tell the man what you told me."

Darren looked from one to the other, sensing that the moment had been choreographed, something that they'd been meaning to stage for some time. The clang of bells from the game show filled the air, and then Mack reached for the remote from a side table and turned off the television so that the cabin fell into silence and also grew darker by several degrees. It was only then that Darren realized the curtains were drawn, the rest of the world shut out.

Breanna looked up at Darren and said, "I shot Ronnie Malvo."

Mack let that hang in the air for a few minutes, let Darren roll the words backward and forward until he felt he'd finally gotten him to grasp what he'd been saying for so long, that there was more to this that Darren didn't understand. "So you see," he said, "I'm not the one here who needs protecting."

Apparently, there was a lot more. Ronnie and the girl actually knew each other, if not socially, then in the way of a trading partnership. Personal beliefs and politics aside, Ronnie would sell drugs to anyone, and despite the nearly corporate-level organization of the Aryan Brotherhood's meth busi-

416

ness — which Darren knew from his work on the task force actually overlapped with the Mexican gangs' in South Texas — he peddled weed and pills to college kids on the side. Breanna had bought from him a few times and turned around and sold it to some drill-team girls she knew. "It was just weed," she said, eyes on the floor.

"But why?" Darren said, almost singing the words like a hymn, a plaintive plea for understanding a situation he'd been reading wrong for months. "Why did you kill him, Breanna? Why did you shoot the man in cold blood?"

Ronnie didn't like her turning a profit off him and threatened to cut her off, and they may or may not have started hooking up so she could keep making side money selling to her friends. But then Ronnie quickly tired of worrying about his Aryan brothers discovering the lack of purity in his sexual appetite, the black girls — plural — he'd fucked. He wanted all his money back, came up with a number Breanna owed him for the drugs and gave her forty-eight hours to deliver an amount of money she'd never seen in her lifetime. That was the real reason Ronnie had come by Mack's house all those nights ago. Sure, he was harassing Breanna — but money was at the root of it. "He said he would hurt Paw-Paw if I didn't get him all of it. But I didn't have it, Mr. Mathews."

By now, Darren had stopped listening. He felt like his head wasn't on right; it was too heavy for his neck, like his hat was the only thing actually holding his head in place. That if he lifted the Stetson, his skull might roll right off his body and onto the floor at Mack's feet. "I shouldn't be here," he said, standing.

He didn't want anything to do with this.

This whole time, he'd thought he was saving an elderly black man who had seventy years' worth of justification for shooting a white supremacist threatening his granddaughter on his property, but in fact, he was protecting a millennial black girl who was putting out to get weed from a man who called her a nigger.

Yes, Pop, I am some kind of fool.

He thought he owed Mack everything, owed his elder what the world couldn't and wouldn't give him for most of his life: protection. But what did he owe Breanna McMillan, a girl who had ignored history and gotten in bed with the enemy? "They just talk like that, not all of 'em really hate black people. It's like any other gang. They just showing out, you know."

"They kill people, Breanna," Darren said.

"Not Ronnie." She said it with a note of tenderness that made Darren want to vomit. He was done. He was getting the hell out of this mess he'd made, getting the hell out of Dodge. He heard Mack calling his name from the porch as he walked to his truck. But he didn't look back; he might not *ever* look back.

He drove to the house in Camilla in a blind rage.

He saw Clayton had called twice since he'd left Mack's place, and he could only imagine that perhaps word was spreading — among the family, at least — that Mack's girl was in trouble. But he turned his back on all of it, felt a hole in his chest where his heart ought to be when it came to saving Breanna from a plight that was so different from the one he'd imagined Mack had been in this whole time. Mack had been a victim; Breanna was a child divorced from history and therefore lost. Actually, she was nineteen, he remembered, hardly a child, so there was no excuse for the choices she'd made. He was too angry to feel sorry for her. And if finding out that Breanna was the killer had with lightning speed changed the way he felt about the righteousness of the crime, had he ever really been right about any of it? Was he right to have gotten a false

419

confession from Bill King to save a nineteen-year-old girl from a twisted relationship she *chose* with Ronnie Malvo?

He walked into the house in Camilla carrying a bottle of Jim Beam he'd picked up at Frank's Liquor on Route 150 in Coldspring and set the first record he could find on the turntable of his uncles' hi-fi, felt fate's hand when Little Milton's "I Can't Quit You, Baby" came through the speakers a few seconds later.

I can't quit you, baby . . . so I'm gon' have to put you down for a while. The words melted inside guitar licks weepy with self-loathing. He turned the volume way up, loud enough that he could hear it on the back porch where he went to sit, boots on the wooden railing, with the bourbon and the view of the pines surrounding the property, the old pond that had dried some over the years but was still wet and deep enough to attract bluebirds. Two of them — twins, Darren thought — flew from the woods behind the house and landed in the uncut grass at the edge of the pond. It nearly covered their bodies as they pecked their beaks in the water, looking up every few seconds to see what the other was doing, and then, by some quiet communication that existed between only the two of them, they decided to fly off the property at the same time, one dipping below the other as they cut across the sky, then reversing the formation so the other took the lead, and before he knew it, Darren was thinking of his uncles William and Clayton. Clayton had never forgiven William while he was still alive for taking Naomi from him, for becoming an officer on the wrong side of the law, for getting himself killed. And the split between them had broken something in Darren too, had cleaved his soul in two, made him unsure of who he was half the time or what he believed. He drank and watched the trees sway, watched bluebirds and warblers fly, saw a red-tailed hawk seem to dust the pine tops with his wings, and he waited for the dull comfort of ceasing to care, knew his tipping point was within reach.

He didn't know how long he'd been sitting there when he heard a car pull up around the front of the house, but it was long enough that the A side of Little Milton's *Grits Ain't Groceries* album had finished playing, which was the only reason he heard the car in the first place. He sat up suddenly, boots clacking on the floorboards of the back porch, having a panicked thought that it was Frank Vaughn come to arrest him. He left the bourbon on the porch railing and walked back into the farmhouse, through the living room, and into the parlor, feeling as he stood before the front door a sting of sweat breaking out under his shirt. He paused there for a moment, long enough to see if he could remember all the words to a favorite Freddie King song as a way to work up some courage. *Let me down easy, baby, tell it to me slow.* He was just lit up enough from the liquor to hum the tune softly as he opened the door.

Randie Winston was standing on the porch.

And then he was sure he was drunk.

She was wearing a crisp white shirt and black jeans and offered a tiny shrug that told him she knew as well as he did how improbable this moment was, how potentially insane it was that she was standing on the doorstep of the home in which he was raised. She gave him a faint smile. "You told me I should see it."

He didn't invite her inside because he still didn't trust what he was seeing. Despite his home training, he simply leaned against the doorjamb and marveled at the woman standing in front of him. She looked the same. But better. Because she was here. Because she'd come as far as she had to in order to see him again.

"How did you even —"

"You say the name Mathews around here and about five people will pop out of nowhere and point the way. It was surprisingly easy to find you, Darren." Her smile faded then, slid right off her face. "Look, if this is too weird —"

His answer was a kiss, a hand on her back.

She opened herself to him, parting her lips so that he got a taste of her, bittersweet in a way that made him think of anise and honey. She reached a hand around the back of his neck and kissed him deeper, pulling away only to train her eyes on his, to sigh gently. Then she laid her head on his shoulder, and he rested his chin on her hair, his arms still wrapped around her. They stood like that for a long while, leaned up against each other, warm despite a December breeze blowing through the open doors of his family home, bringing the scent of Texas pines.

ACKNOWLEDGMENTS

First thanks go to my publishing family: Reagan Arthur and Joshua Kendall, who have not only created a publishing house that I am deeply proud to be a part of but also treated me and my work with the utmost respect and enthusiasm (and patience). I am deeply appreciative of you both. Big thanks to Sabrina Callahan, Lena Little, and Pamela Brown for letting the world know about Darren Mathews and sending this series off with a bang. Likewise, I'd like to thank my UK publishing family at Serpent's Tail: Rebecca Gray, Hannah Westland, Drew Jerrison, Anna-Marie Fitzgerald, and Valentina Zanca. I so respect the care and intelligence with which you have published all of my books. And finally, Richard Abate, to whom I owe the world. Thank you for your faith in me, your sharp insight, and your friendship.

To my East Texas family: Thank you to

my dad, Gene Locke, for staying with me in a cabin on Caddo Lake when I was too scared to stay by myself. And thanks to my grandmother Jean Birmingham for letting us borrow your pistol. To my mom, Sherra, thank you for keeping me anchored in where I come from and for your bluesy sense of humor. Thank you, Tembi, my sister and sharer of my earliest memories in Coldspring and Lufkin and Marshall. You're my road dog till the end. Thanks also to my stepmother, Aubrey, for laying out the welcome mat all the times I've come to stay at the country house in San Jacinto County to get a little East Texas dirt under my feet. And to all of my Texas family, thank you for your stories and your love and support.

To the folks in Jefferson and Caddo Lake, who helped me write this book: Thanks to Randie and Sam Canup, owners of the Hoot 'n Holler guest cottage in Uncertain, Texas, for a gorgeous stay on the lake (and if you're the ones who paid for my lunch anonymously at the Big Pines Lodge on my last day in town, thank you for that too). Thanks to Captain Ron and his lovely companion Jean, from Manchester, England, who run Captain Ron's Swamp Tours in Karnack, Texas. You helped me see the interior of one of the most majestic places on earth, and I thank you for that. To Tammy and David Griot, owners of the White Manor Oak B&B in Jefferson, thanks for your hospitality. The amazing guitar collection in your hotel was worth the trip.

To Dr. Cheryl Arutt, thanks for the psychological care you provide, for which I am forever grateful. There would be no book(s) without our Thursday mornings.

And finally, to my two greatest loves: Clara, in your eyes, I am reminded why storytelling matters so much. I have seen the way books have grown your heart and mind, and it's my greatest privilege to share a love of books with you. And to Karl, my best friend, my patient partner, I am so thankful I have a husband who supports my creative life. Thanks for making space for me to write books. I love you dearly.

ABOUT THE AUTHOR

Attica Locke is the author of the 2018 Edgar Award winner *Bluebird, Bluebird*; *Pleasantville*, which won the 2016 Harper Lee Prize for Legal Fiction and was long-listed for the Baileys Women's Prize for Fiction; *Black Water Rising*, which was nominated for an Edgar Award; and *The Cutting Season*, a national bestseller and winner of the Ernest J. Gaines Award for Literary Excellence. She was a writer and producer on the Fox drama *Empire* and the upcoming Hulu adaptation of *Little Fires Everywhere*. A native of Houston, Locke lives in Los Angeles with her husband and daughter.